THE GREAT BOOK OF DREAM CARS

BY JAMES FLAMMANG AND THE AUTO EDITORS OF CONSUMER GUIDE®

PUBLICATIONS INTERNATIONAL, LTD.

Louis Weber, C.E.O.
Publications International, Ltd.
7373 North Cicero Avenue
Lincolnwood, Illinois 60646

Manufactured in Yugoslavia.
h g f e d c b a

ISBN: 0-88176-685-2

Library of Congress Catalog Card Number: 89-63615

Photography

Sam Griffith- 14, 15, 26, 27, 28, 29, 30, 136, 192, 193, 194, 195, 196, 197. **Auto Car & Motor Publications**- 16, 17, 144. **David Gooley**- 38, 39. **John L. Matras**- 37, 38. **Nickey Wright**- 130, 131, 132, 133, 134, 135, 166, 167, 170, 171, 210. **Mitch Frumkin**- 141. **Mirco Decet**- 145. **Roland Flessner**- 158, 159. **Daniel Lyons**- 198, 199, 200, 201, 202, 203. **Chuck Giametta**- 205, 206, 207, 208, 209, 210, 211.

Owners

Harold Van Brocken- 20. **Violette and Bruce Jacobs, M.D.**- 78, 79. **Bill and Pat Locke**- 80. **Wayne Nelson**- 132, 133, 134, 135. **Richard Foster**- 166, 167, 170, 171. **Jack Bart**- 198, 199, 200, 201, 202, 203. **Phillie and Sandy Lopiccolo**- 76. **John Weinberger**- 136. **Ed McCoughlin**- 130, 131.

Credit List

Dave Hederich, Chevrolet Public Relations; Mike Spencer, Acura PR; John Aycoth/Edward Aycoth & Co., Aston Martin PR; Avanti PR; Reg Abbiss, Rolls-Royce PR; Rob Mitchell, Susan Williams, BMW PR; Larry Gustin, Gary Smith, Buick PR;

Bill O'Neil, Chris Wallace, Cadillac PR; Nancy Talarico/Hank Forssberg, Inc., Ferrari; T. Ohkusa, Mitsubishi PR, Japan; Tom Jakobowski, Antonio B. Cervone, Chrysler PR; Mary Maxwell, Ford PR; John Chuhran, Mercedes Benz PR; Colin N. Cook, Jaguar PR, England; Mike Cook, Jaguar PR, USA; Patricia Schuetz, Excalibur PR; Ken McKay, Ferrari Tech Center; Ferrari PR, Italy; Ross H. Ruehle, Oldsmobile PR; Poller & Jordan Ad Agency, MVS Venturi; Ed Lechtzin, Sheila Main, Pontiac PR; Kim Derderian, Peugeot PR, USA; M. Alloiteau, Peugeot PR, France; Daniie J. Perez-Vitoria, Renault PR, France; Fredi Valentini, Pininfarina PR, Italy; Klaus Reichert, Porsche PR, Germany; Klaus Parr, Porsche PR-Archives, Germany; Martha A. McKinley, Porsche PR, USA.

Special Thanks To

Chuck Jordan, V.P., GM Design; Floyd C. Joliet, GM Design Staff; Tom Land, Ford Design Staff; Vernon G. Smith, Steve Foley Rolls-Royce, Northbrook, IL.; George Stauffer, Stauffer Classics Ltd. (DeTomaso Pantera), Blue Mounds, WI; John Weinberger, Tom Majchrzak, J. Scott Rothermel, Continental Rolls-Royce, Maserati, Ferrari, Hinsdale, IL.

TABLE OF CONTENTS:

Jaguar XJ220

INTRODUCTION

Those who never dream are destined to lead lives of tedium. Fantasies help enrich our waking lives. Five-star restaurants tickle our fancies, even if our normal lunches emerge from the nearest fast-food emporium. We pay homage to ultra-posh hotels that boast sunken tubs and gold fixtures, even if our own out-of-town nights are spent at spartan chain motels along the highway.

Stately homes and elegant public buildings add art and beauty to our lives. We don't have to live in a mansion to enjoy its architectural character. Its best face, in fact, is often the one presented to the outside world, not the one reserved for its inhabitants.

And so it is with automobiles. Even if the car that carries us to the job every day isn't likely to stir anyone's imagination, we need to know that somewhere out there are motorcars that ignite our passions. Luxury cars, exoticars, supercars, dream cars—by whatever name, each fires our imaginations, even if we never have an opportunity to own one, or even to drive one.

Dreams take many forms, and automotive fantasies are no exception. While many dream cars offer a futuristic shape, breathtaking acceleration, and gadgetry out of the pages of science-fiction stories, such attributes are not the only

prerequisites for dream car status. A dream can be flamboyant or subtle. Space-age or traditional. Extravagantly high tech or elegantly simple. Open-topped or tightly sealed, spacious or intimate, spartan or gadget-laden.

What dream cars have in common is the ability to turn heads and send minds into happy orbit. They inspire awe, amazement, longing—and yes, perhaps a twinge of envy. The promise of dizzying speeds may be the most common lure, even when the dream car is an undrivable concept vehicle— perhaps even one wholly devoid of a powertrain.

Certain dream cars suggest that the "impossible dream" sung of in *Man of La Mancha* is the only kind worth dreaming. At the very least, a dream car must be difficult to attain. If everyone could own one, or if a new example idled at every corner, such a vehicle wouldn't be worth dreaming about, no matter how fetching its qualities.

You'll find two kinds of dream cars: those built for sale, and those for show. Many exist today in dealers' showrooms, or will arrive soon. Others are one-of-a-kind concept vehicles, created mainly to travel the auto-show circuit each year, and unlikely to see production in the foreseeable future. A few,

such as Peugeot's Oxia and Renault's Megane, have seen auto-show duty in Europe rather than in America.

Production vehicles that are regarded as dream cars combine rarity and special characteristics in a way that places the car well above all the others. To begin with, dream cars seldom emerge from an assembly line—certainly not the kind that has flourished since 1913, when Henry Ford applied the mass-production principle to his Model T. Many of the cars in this book are built wholly, or in large part, by hand. Aston Martin and Rolls-Royce engines, for example, are assembled by a single individual. Styling, too, is of vital importance. Although most production dream cars offer fresh designs that are contemporary if not futuristic, several (Excalibur, Porsche 911) carry on with classic, timeless styling.

Nearly all production dream cars are limited-production models or one-off exotics. No more than a few thousand, and more likely just a few hundred, are built each year. Outputs may even be counted in dozens, or less. Even if your pocketbook should allow such a purchase, you face the prospect of a waiting list.

Dreams don't come cheap. Astons, Ferraris, and Lamborghinis, among others,

Chevrolet dreams about the future with its Corvette Indy (above).

command prices well into the six-figure bracket. No one knows for sure how much a Ferrari F40 or Porsche 959 supercar might fetch—if either were permitted to enter the United States, that is. Estimates of the Jaguar XJ220 price, if the car is ever produced, have topped half a million dollars and could leap higher.

Not-for-sale concept cars are typically created by an automaker to display test ideas for the future. Even when they're bizarre, futuristic designs, traces of current models from that company normally lurk somewhere in the profile or detail work. The goal is to deliver an alternate vision of the corporate identity, not to defy it.

Not all concept cars are fabricated from thin air by major studio design teams. Oldsmobile's Aerotechs, for instance, evolved from a racing-car design, built to showcase the new Quad 4 engine. Ford's Splash was penned by four young design students. Other cars, such as the Zender Fact 4, were created not by a major automaker but by small suppliers to the industry.

For several reasons, manufacturers devote great effort to these vehicles that probably will never see production. At the auto shows, for one thing, concept cars lure visitors to look over the company's practical wares. The cars also encourage designers and engineers to stretch their imaginations and create three-dimensional forms. Ideas, plans, and drawings are great as far as they go, but nothing is quite so rewarding as

creating a real steel or fiberglass body atop a full-size chassis, perhaps with a real engine under the hood (even if it doesn't run). Designers can let their minds soar, and can initiate and accept challenges. Always, these talented men and women attempt to answer the perennial question: "What if ....?"

Concept cars also educate customers. They reveal not merely what is, but what could be. Rather than plunging headlong into new technology, a manufacturer can release a little taste of it, gauge customer reaction, and use this input to shape the next generation of an existing car. Such examples as Plymouth's Speedster and Pontiac's Stinger are built to evaluate a new marketing notion—in this case, whether a strictly "fun" car might prove salable. Many concept vehicles don't disappear when the show is over but hang around as "works in progress," available as test beds for the next generation of ideas.

The trickle-down theory also applies to dream cars. Features that first appear on a concept car, or a costly production model, often emerge on mid-priced automobiles a year or two later. Anti-lock braking, for instance, started out in the mid-1980s on a handful of European luxury cars. Soon afterward, American luxury models offered anti-lock, either as standard equipment or an option. Little by little, the number of automobiles that can be ordered with ABS continues to grow.

Mercedes has introduced an automatically-rising roll bar on the 500SL

roadster. Will this innovation follow a similar evolutionary path to other open-topped automobiles? Possibly. Video rear-view "mirrors" and radar-enhanced vision, as seen on several concept vehicles, may take longer to arrive. Although the technology exists, navigational systems can't appear in real-world vehicles until satellite networks could provide the necessary signals for their operation.

Crowds gather around the latest concept vehicle—and even the production dream car on the street—to gape and point nearly as one, sharing in the excitement. It's a circus for adults, a representation of brash color and freshness in what is sometimes a lackluster, cookie-cutter culture. If the stamped-out sedans and hatchbacks are what we actually buy, the inspired dream cars are the special treats for our eyes and imaginations.

We need those unattainable cars, the ones that no one can have, at any price. We also need the kind that exist, yet remain just out of reach. Then, we can always say to ourselves, well, maybe next year ....

Now and then, each of us benefits from viewing the world with childlike wonder. Let's live. Let's dream. Let's savor all the cars dreamers have created, as seen in photographs or gleaming beneath the sun or auto show lights. Whether you're fortunate enough to own one of the dream cars portrayed in these pages, or if they remain confined to your imagination, you're sure to enjoy them all.

ACURA NS-X

Even more than sumptuous luxury sedans and limos, sports cars inspire fantasies. Few enthusiasts have never imagined themselves at the wheel of a sleek, low, road-hugging machine—the kind that can whip through a tight turn, sure-footed and steady, with the flick of an expert wrist. Fascination with sports cars surged as the Nineties approached, and several surprising automakers prepared to take advantage of their revived appeal.

Acura, the luxury divison of American Honda, is one such automaker. Success in the marketplace doesn't always bring full rewards to a company. Although successful indeed on the sales floor and in customer satisfaction, the twin Acura models that debuted in 1986 suffered from a twinge of an image problem, at least in the performance department.

Well before the first Honda automobiles hit American shores, the company had become widely known for technologically advanced motorcycles. But Honda also has a car-racing history, having built a Formula One racer in 1964 with a then-unusual transverse V-12 engine. Still, Honda's cars are known more for efficiency than pizzazz, for reliability rather than power. Even the luxury-oriented Acura Integra and Legend, though sprightly performers, retain a slightly sedate aura. In short, they lack all-out excitement.

What the company needed was a shocker, a dream car that would lure potential customers into the showroom. It came in the form of a prototype for a high-performance sports car. Better yet, a "pure" two-seater that, eventually, would go into actual production.

You could almost feel the tension in the air as a room packed full of journalists and automotive writers awaited the unveiling of the new sports car in February 1989, at the Chicago Auto Show. Not until a month earlier had Honda even admitted the existence of an in-progress sports machine. American Honda's public relations people stretched that tension to its limit, prolonging the agony until the cover finally slipped off the shapely red form of the NS-X, to a chorus of "aahs." Following a question-and-answer period, the journalists crowded the stage, leaving little space for anyone else to get a good look at the car.

Dramatic is the only word that could describe this black-over-red beauty. Short of a Lamborghini Countach, the NS-X's design is as striking as you're likely to find. And this one looks more like an auto-mobile—rakish, yet real—than some of the radical creations in the low-production marketplace.

Viewed from the side, the Acura sportster appears dominated by an expanse of glass up top, with its steeply sloped windshield and backlight. Yet there's plenty of metal up there as well, in the form of a sizable B-pillar to support the roof. Since that pillar blends nicely into the overall form, it isn't so noticeable. Visibility

promises to be excellent, since the canopy sits about as far forward as it can go.

Smoothly rounded doors continue the car's aerodynamic theme, yet the bodystyle is an engaging blend of approaches: Squint your eyes a little and the side profile of that tall, integrated back spoiler looks almost like a tail fin left over from the 1950s.

The car's aggressive impulses are most evident from the front, with the headlamps safely ensconced beneath twin covers. Thin parking-light strips look like fangs being bared for battle, while the wide air intake seems so low as to practically drag on the ground.

For special cars, the little touches count most. Touches like the NS-X's shapely oval outlets for the twin exhaust pipes, and aluminum suspension components that look as sharp as they perform. Quite a few cars in this league carry air scoops along their bodysides. Acura's sculptured scoop appears eager not merely to draw in the air, but to gobble it up in voracious gulps as the car leaps forward in a rage.

As Honda president Tadashi Kume explained, the car "was designed to provide

This is one dream car destined for many driveways. A tempting balance of power and practicality, Honda's mid-engine NS-X sports car (both pages) threatens to alter the supercar balance of power.

Honda's aim was a supercar that drivers of even average ability could use with confidence. Their NS-X attacks flaws usually associated with the breed: An expansive greenhouse (above) enhances visibility, while the cabin (opposite page) is luxurious and driver-friendly.

true world-class, sports car performance [with] the optimum balance between high-performance technology and human-fitting design." That technology included plenty of lightweight materials, led by an aluminum monocoque unibody, for a tempting power-to-weight ratio that approaches 10:1 lbs./hp. The car tips the scales at a feathery (for this league) 2,860

pounds. In fact, the entire body/chassis structure weighs well under 500 pounds. Not much chance for rust with that aluminum physique, either.

Ready to deliver an estimated 270 horsepower, the 3.0-liter, 24-valve V-6 engine is mounted transversely, amidships. Its four-cam design evolved from the powerplant found in Acura's Legend. Each

wheel is sprung independently, with each corner featuring a beautifully crafted, almost fragile, double wishbone setup. Four-wheel disc brakes might be good enough for some, but Honda added an anti-lock system to ensure quick stops on slippery surfaces. Tied in with the smooth shifting 5-speed manual—or 4-speed automatic— transmission is an electronic Traction Control System that should tame the drive wheels during quick starts off the line.

Will the NS-X perform as admirably as its looks and components suggest? A projected acceleration time of less than 6 seconds to reach 60 miles an hour, with the potential to hit a whopping 155, suggests the Acura will rarely be left behind. Lack of a turbocharger also means there's no

annoying turbo lag to delay the rush of forward acceleration.

What Acura wanted was to create "true driver's cars" that are "fun to own." This one is claimed to be the most costly and strongest performing automobile ever offered in America by a Japanese concern.

Acura's sports car differs from many rivals in one important respect: it's easy to drive. Honda's goal was to create a car that serves as "an extension of the driver's body." You need not be an expert to coax the full package of performance out of NS-X's sleek form. Research & Development chief Nobuhiko Kawamoto explained to *Car* magazine that a Ferrari, for instance, "demands too much of the driver" who craves its full capability, and can become

"frightening." Acura's version has been created to give "sensible" drivers of ordinary skill the "pure pleasure of driving." Why, the NS-X even rides nicely, in contrast to the rough-and-tumble motion of many exotic sports cars.

Inside the spacious, leather-lined cockpit, the driver faces a large tachometer and speedometer. Behind the twin seats, a glass partition keeps noise inside the engine bay, away from driver and passenger ears. Looking beyond the instrument panel, the cowl line is far lower than normal, with little to impair the view forward, to the sides, and to the rear, which is surprising for a mid-engine vehicle.

The code name NS-X (which stands for "New Sports Car X") will disappear by the time the car goes on sale. The real thing won't be cheap either, with an expected price tag between $50,000 and $60,000. Nor will it be plentiful. Only 3,000 per year are expected for U.S. sale, each assembled at a new plant next door to Honda's research and development center in Japan.

Just about every company calls its latest creation the "next generation." With the NS-X, Acura has earned a pretty strong claim to that title. The production version won't be identical to the prototype, of course. There's been speculation, for instance, that features such as variable valve timing, which boosts economy at low speeds and quickens response farther up the scale, might find their way into the V-6 engine.

Within months of its Chicago debut, more than a dozen additional NS-X prototypes were built, some of which have been driven on road courses in Japan and Germany to provide data for further development. By the time the car arrives at dealer showrooms, the elusive dream should translate into an alluring reality for those who can squeeze enough dollars out of their pocketbooks to enjoy the privilege.

ACURA NS-X

SPECIFICATIONS

Manufacturer:	Acura Automobile Division, Honda Motor Co. Ltd., Tokyo, Japan
Body design:	2-passenger, 2-door coupe; unitized aluminum body/chassis
Powertrain layout:	mid-engine, rear-wheel drive
Wheelbase (in.):	98.4
Overall length (in.):	169.9
Overall width (in.):	70.9
Overall height (in.):	46.1
Track, front (in.):	59.5
Track, rear (in.):	60.0
Weight (lbs.):	(est.) 2860
Approximate price:	$50,000-$60,000
Engine type:	transverse dohc V-6 (24-valve)
Displacement (liters/cu. in.):	3.0/183
Horsepower @ rpm:	(est.) 270 @ 7300
Torque (lbs./ft.) @ rpm:	(est.) 209 @ 5500
Fuel delivery:	port fuel injection
Transmission:	5-speed manual or 4-speed automatic
Suspension, front:	independent, double wishbones
Suspension, rear:	independent, double wishbones
Brakes:	front/rear vented discs, anti-lock

PERFORMANCE

Top speed (mph):	155+
0-60 mph (seconds):	(est.) under 6.0
Quarter-mile (seconds):	(est.) under 14.0
mph @ quarter-mile:	NA

ASTON MARTIN
LAGONDA

True quality in design, as in all of life, is timeless. An automotive shape that mesmerizes at one moment should attract similar attention a year, even a decade, later. In the low-production luxury-car rivalry, fads simply will not do.

True quality is also expensive. And exclusive. On all counts, Aston Martin's luscious Lagonda saloon qualifies handily. (How lightly *saloon*—the British term for sedan—rolls off one's tongue!) Its timeless design looks as inspired today as it did more than a decade ago, when the Lagonda first appeared in the hands of a favored European few. Not until 1984 did it arrive in America, albeit—as with all Astons—in tiny numbers.

With a 1989 price tag approaching $200,000, this is about as far from a bargain-basement motorcar for the masses as one can get. Some say a Lagonda is well worth the megadollar entry fee, of course; while critics insist you can get just as posh four-door, five-seat comfort for a lot less money.

No less than with thoroughbred horses or show dogs, cars that matter must possess a pedigree. Mercedes-Benz does—naturally. So do Rolls-Royce, Ferrari, and a handful of others. Yet few exceed the majestic lineage of the Aston line, heralded for its capacity to mix opulence with capability, tradition with finesse, in motorcars made the old-fashioned way:

by hand. Who'd ever guess that the Aston company is currently three-quarters owned by Ford, the foremost originator of assembly-line production?

In this modern age of swoop-sided sports cars, the Lagonda's admittedly squarish lines may appear a tad antiquated. Actually, the latest edition is a bit more rounded and contemporary than its forerunner, which first appeared at the London Motor Show in 1976. No matter. This masterpiece of posh shows off those angular lines proudly, with a distinction all its own. A side-by-side trio of rectangular lamps on either side of the simple vertical-bar grille makes the car look even wider than it is. In profile, the clearly-defined wedge shape

Aston Martin's angular Lagonda is bigger than the Lincoln Continental. The Aston's hand-made quality, powerful 4-cam V-8 engine, and noble bearing, however, help it shrink high speed dashes across the continent. This is 140-mph motoring at its plushest.

ASTON MARTIN LAGONDA

SPECIFICATIONS

Manufacturer:	Aston Martin Lagonda Ltd., Newport Pagnell, England
Body design:	4/5-passenger, 4-door sedan; steel/aluminum body, steel frame
Powertrain layout:	front-engine, rear-wheel drive
Wheelbase (in.):	114.6
Overall length (in.):	208.0
Overall width (in.):	71.5
Overall height (in.):	52.0
Track, front (in.):	60.2
Track, rear (in.):	61.6
Weight (lbs.):	4622
Approximate price:	$197,000
Engine type:	ohc V-8
Displacement (liters/cu. in.):	5.3/326
Horsepower @ rpm:	(U.S.) 263 @ 5000
Torque (lbs./ft.) @ rpm:	(U.S.) 292 @ 4500
Fuel delivery:	4 Weber carburetors
Transmission:	3-speed automatic
Suspension, front:	unequal-length wishbones, coil springs, anti-roll bar
Suspension, rear:	de Dion axle, coil springs; self-leveling
Brakes:	front/rear ventilated discs

PERFORMANCE

Top speed (mph):	(est.) 140
0-60 mph (seconds):	(UK) 8.4
Quarter-mile (seconds):	(UK) 16.6
mph @ quarter-mile:	NA

conveys a startling impression in a sedan so low and so long, suggesting that a Lagonda is, if anything, even weightier than its actual (and ample) tonnage indicates.

Step inside for a moment. Here you have the richness of Wilton carpeting, the elegance of fine Connolly leather (which emits just the sort of luscious aroma you'd longed for), the expanses of expertly-polished burled walnut. No crass vinyl or plastic to invade upon the fashionable apparel of the fastidious Aston owner. All-electronic instruments, arranged in what some early observers derided (and others praised) as a display worthy of science-fiction novels, include a vacuum-fluorescent speedometer. The automatic transmission's shift lever is down on the console. In all, the cockpit has the look of a far more sporty creation, rather than an ultra-civilized luxury sedan.

Take hold of the seat adjuster. That's right, there's all the room you need for legs and arms; though as in every modern car, those in back could always use a bit more. This is a car of size—over 17 feet in length. A car of presence. Of potential. A car that exclaims not brashly, but in a subdued and dignified manner, that you've made it.

Equipped from the start with everything deemed suitable for its clientele, the Lagonda has nearly no option choices. A set of fitted leather luggage and special paint or trim is just about all you can order. Naturally, there's air conditioning, power seats, and the expected luxury accoutrement lineup.

Lagonda's heritage stretches back several years before the turn of the century, when Lagonda founder Wilbur Gunn traveled from Ohio to England and, later, turned toward the youthful automobile trade. He named his creation after an Ohio creek. While producing Lagondas for decades, the company was sold in 1947 to Sir David Brown, who'd recently bought the Aston Martin firm. Forty years later, Ford purchased its 75 percent share. Fortunately for Aston lovers, the Ford empire has steered clear of day-to-day operations, and business continues as before. In addition to the big saloon, Aston in the 1980s has produced a trio of Vantage and Volante two-door models, all powered by a similar V-8 engine.

William Towns gets credit for the Lagonda's design, and the rebirth of this famous old nameplate. Like all Aston Martins, this body is built by hand from ordinary sheets of steel and aluminum, at a modest factory in the small town of Newport Pagnell. About 2,200 man-hours are required to turn out each car. All that handwork—metal pressing, bending, welding, hammering followed by coat after coat of paint, trim, polishing, and testing—

takes time. Some four months of time. A single employee assembles the car's four-cam, 5.3-liter V-8 engine, trading his expert efforts for the right to autograph an engine plaque.

In Europe, the Lagonda's V-8 churns out 289 horsepower and 321 pounds/feet of torque. With that kind of power, passing through a Chrysler TorqueFlite 3-speed automatic transmission, the car can hit 60 mph in a trifle over 8 seconds. To meet U.S. emissions requirements, the engine must be detuned, losing 26 of those horses. Even so, it qualifies as one of the fastest luxury, four-door sedans sold in the world.

Gas mileage? As they used to say about yacht prices, if you have to ask about either the car's cost or its EPA mileage ratings, you can't afford one.

Some critics have branded the Lagonda as a trifle noisy, at least when compared to a Rolls or Jaguar. They claim the company brochure goes a bit far in claiming "supreme tranquility" for the car's inhabitants; that unwanted sounds from the wind and tires penetrate vividly into the cabin. Another complaint is that things get rather raucous when speeds approach triple digits because of the high-revving engine. Since few roads in the world permit such speeds, that's perhaps not such a formidable obstacle. In any case, the Lagonda reminds its driver that he or she is at the helm of a powerful machine.

Like any luxury conveyance, the heavy Lagonda isn't built for wild rides around hairy curves. Instead, it's most at home on long stretches of straight road, carrying civilized folk from here to there in superlative comfort. A self-leveling rear suspension compensates for passengers and luggage, and brings the car up to proper riding height. Still, the suspension is derived from that used in the more brutish and sporty Astons, and tires are ruffian-sized Avon Turbospeeds; so a Lagonda handles more precisely than many big-car owners might expect. Vented disc brakes on all four wheels halt the big sedan handily, though anti-lock brakes are not available.

In an era when so many cars have barely had a hand laid upon them at *any* stage of manufacture, the allure of a truly hand-built motorcar is irresistible. Astons, sad to say, are among the few survivors of that breed.

Enveloped in aromatic Connolly hides and rich Wilton carpeting, the Lagonda's accommodations are strictly first-cabin (right). No autocrosser, the big Aston acquits itself well in curves and gobbles huge stretches of straightaway without effort.

ASTON MARTIN VIRAGE

James Bond, as portrayed by Sean Connery in the 1960s action films, loved his Aston Martin. So did many real-life sports car fans who had an opportunity to drive or simply view the lovely DB series coupes of that era. Aston's V-8 continued the familiar sporting tradition into the 1970s, followed by a Vantage and Volante later in that decade. But as the 1990s approached, it was time for something new.

What's new is the shimmering silver Virage, which debuted at the Birmingham (England) Motor Show in late 1988, scheduled for U.S. sale sometime in 1990. Popular? Before anyone even got a peek at the show car, the company had more than 50 orders on the books—all from current Aston owners—with substantial deposits paid in advance. Several hundred more poured in during the months following the auto show. For a car that's expected to sell for the equivalent of at least $160,000 in England, that's popular.

Not that the car is completely new. Not at all. As co-designer John Heffernan has stated, the replacement coupe was created as an "evolutionary successor" to the renowned DB4/5/6 and V-8. Aston chairman Victor Gauntlett adds that it cannot be revolutionary, but must instead "stand in line with every postwar Aston

Martin and be the self-evident successor to that tradition."

Therefore, the newest Aston is again a rather large, heavy (nearly two tons), front-engine coupe with rear-wheel drive. If that description seems to fit an older American muscle car more than a traditional Britisher, it suggests how much performance can be expected from Virage. Not suggested is the rare level of handcrafted workmanship that goes into this bold high-speed traveler from Newport Pagnell, the traditional cockpit "teardrop" profile that carries on in this latest edition, or the increased attention to modern aerodynamics.

Far more than most, in this age when curvaceousness is thought synonymous with aerodynamic efficiency, the prototype Virage—viewed from the front—is a car with corners. Virtual right angles, even. Rich curves are reserved for its profile. Even so, the Virage looks definitely rounder than its predecessor V-8 coupes, with an undeniable wedge form, low cockpit, and precise detailing. Ample, flush-mounted glass promises unfettered visibility.

Flush rectangular headlamps are new for Aston, allowing the front end to drop for an overall wider look. Chrome is nonexistent, and the car displays only a handful of small identifying insignias.

Even underneath, the attention to detail persists. No crude exhaust pipes or mufflers protrude downward. Instead, they fit into niches on the chassis. The added smoothness helps aerodynamics, of course, along with the underbody tray that stretches rearward from the front spoiler; but also lends the car a cleaner look, with no unsightly pieces visible.

Similar care and expert workmanship go on under the hood, which opens to reveal an engine that looks as stunning as it performs. Neat plates hide the valleys between sparkplugs, whose cables flow gently into their electrical source. Cam covers atop each bank of cylinders are beautifully detailed. Fuel-injector lines aren't left exposed either, but sport their own attractive covers. Makes one wonder why the engine compartments of so many other cars are tangled mazes of components. In the Aston tradition, a brass plate atop the powerplant identifies the one person who actually put it together.

While the show prototype displayed an incomplete mock-up interior, production versions will blend the traditional with the contemporary—just as the car itself manages to do. Nobody is likely to complain about either ambience or comfort. Rich, crimson-color Connolly leather (*de rigueur* for this

league) trims the seats, doors, and console. Pale gray suede fabric covers the roof interior and the door pillars. Wilton carpets show a similar hue. Along both the instrument panel and the doors, burled walnut veneer delivers the final touch of European real-wood elegance.

A full complement of gauges can be found in the instrument panel; however, they're not separate units. Instead, a solid black panel surrounding the top of the steering column contains markings for each gauge, and serves as a background for their orange needles.

Memory adjustments return each front seat to its preselected position and send outside mirrors to proper viewing angles. No need to get your fingers chilled wiping away winter's snow from the mirrors, either—they're electrically heated. So are both the windshield, back window and the seats.

The excitement doesn't stop with Virage's body and interior. Acceleration to 60 miles per hour arrives in 6 seconds or so, and one hundred in about 15; this puts the

car on a par with the world's fastest. Not to mention top speed, which runs in the neighborhood of 150 mph.

Virage's engine, though based on its predecessors, got its start on the western side of the pond, at the Callaway Engineering facility in Old Lyme, Connecticut. That's where some of the hottest Corvette, Formula One, and Indy car engines have been created.

American editions of the prior V-8 coupe had been detuned to meet stringent U.S. emissions standards, causing horsepower and torque numbers to fall off. However, Victor Gauntlett now insisted Americans should "know how a *real* Aston Martin feels." For that reason, the engine had to develop into a single configuration that could be sold worldwide, meeting each nation's requirements.

Callaway accepted the assignment in 1985. Experiments began in 1987 with the conversion of an existing two-valve-per-cylinder V-8 to a four-valve-per-cylinder design. Although the Callaway team, headed by Tim Good, manufactured prototype parts; the final development

Virage's cabin (opposite page) blends elegance and sportiness—a suitable venue for 130-mph cruising. Aston's exterior styling (above) celebrates the Virage's masculine nature.

work took place at the Aston plant. In a year and a half, the job was done. Retained was the original aluminum block, along with the crankshaft and connecting rods; all new, the two 16-valve cylinder heads. End result: an all-alloy, double-overhead-cam, 36-valve beauty that displaces 5,340 cubic centimeters and produces 330 horsepower.

Although a 5-speed ZF manual shifter will be available, most Virages are expected to carry a Chrysler-built 3-speed automatic. Later on, a 4-speed ZF automatic might be introduced.

While the front suspension evolved from the standard Lagonda's, the rear design, still using the de Dion axle, is new and made of aluminum to cut down on weight. Avon Turbospeed tires are as big as one would expect for a car that can travel comfortably at triple-digit speeds, mounted on tough-looking alloy wheels. Bilstein gas shock absorbers help hold cornering lean down to near-zero.

In the traditional Aston manner, Virage's body is hand-formed from aluminum panels. Unlike earlier Astons that hung their body panels onto structural tubing, Virage confines its tubing complement to the roof area. Composite-type materials are used for bumpers and spoiler, as well as for the undertray beneath the car. Their weight-reduction attributes were also tempting for hood and deck panels, but that idea was rejected in favor of customary bumped-metal construction.

Virage, in French, means "corner." Specifically, it may call to mind the well-known corners that make up the LeMans road race, which Aston won some three decades ago.

If the new Virage helps propel the old-line Aston Martin firm into the present, the future looks even better. Still to come are a Virage convertible, and possibly a turbocharged Vantage model. None will appear on U.S. shores in significant number, though. After all, part of the Aston tradition is that only five or six cars emerge from the factory gate each week. In fact, only about 11,000 Aston Martins have been produced in the company's entire existence, since 1914. Yet, if the prototype foreshadows the future at Aston Martin, the superb Virage will carry the great Aston tradition into the 90s.

ASTON MARTIN VIRAGE

SPECIFICATIONS

Manufacturer:	Aston Martin Lagonda Ltd., Newport Pagnell, England
Body design:	2+2-passenger, 2-door coupe; aluminum body, box-section steel frame
Powertrain layout:	front-engine, rear-wheel drive
Wheelbase (in.):	102.8
Overall length (in.):	186.5
Overall width (in.):	73.0
Overall height (in.):	52.3
Track, front (in.):	59.4
Track, rear (in.):	59.9
Weight (lbs.):	3947
Approximate price:	$160,000+
Engine type:	dohc V-8 (32-valve); design by Callaway Engineering, Old Lyme, CT
Displacement (liters/cu. in.):	5.3/326
Horsepower @ rpm:	330 @ 6000
Torque (lbs./ft.) @ rpm:	350 @ 4000
Fuel delivery:	Weber-Marelli fuel injection
Transmissions:	5-speed manual or 3-speed automatic
Suspension, front:	unequal-length wishbones, anti-roll bar, coil springs
Suspension, rear:	de Dion axle, trailing arms, Watts linkage, coil springs
Brakes:	front/rear discs (rear outboard)

PERFORMANCE

Top speed (mph):	155
0-60 mph (seconds):	approx. 6.0
Quarter-mile (seconds):	NA
mph @ quarter-mile:	NA

*Virage's take-no-prisoners bodywork
celebrates the Aston Martin tradition of
a powerful V-8 loaded beneath a long hood,
the most rakish of rooflines, and flanks that
bulge with no-nonsense wheels and rubber.*

AVANTI

Breathtaking was a fitting word to describe the Avanti when it first appeared, way back in 1962. It was a futuristic, even alien-seeming automobile. Those who spied one on the street had to do a double-take to make sure it was real. Seldom had such a clean, advanced design emerged from an American manufacturer. That this manufacturer happened to be Studebaker, a company struggling through what were to be the final gasps of its long existence, came as a shock to the general public and enthusiasts alike.

Yet even more astounding, the Avanti lives on today, nearly three decades later. And even though the car's basic shape has changed little over the years, it's luring a new crop of customers and even bigger numbers of awed onlookers—proof that classic styling never grows obsolete.

Think back, for a moment. Kennedy was President. Vietnam's civil war was noted only by a handful of American advisers, and the "beat" generation had not yet begun to evolve into the Sixties counterculture. In American automobile design, this was still the age of excess. The tail fins that exploded onto back ends through the 1950s had only recently slimmed down or disappeared. Chrome was still in; clean, unadorned lines were out. Bodies were bulbous; grilles massive and garish, if not grotesque.

Then came the Avanti, wearing a slim, rakish body, no grille at all, and the barest minimum of brightwork. How could it possibly succeed? Yet it did—at least well enough to survive the demise of Studebaker and take on a life of its own, under the leadership of four subsequent owners. The

present company hopes to take the still-striking fiberglass-bodied sports car farther forward than any predecessor. Which, since Avanti *means* "forward" in Italian, is the only logical direction.

Famed industrial designer Raymond Loewy, who created a long list of American icons including the Coca-Cola bottle and Lucky Strike cigarette package, as well as a selection of memorable Studebakers, was commissioned in 1961 to come up with a "Gran Turismo" (GT) vehicle. Studebaker was already preparing its GT Hawk for the marketplace—a handsome evolution of the award-winning 1953 Studebaker Starlight coupe, perhaps Loewy's most lauded design. Loewy and his team took only a week to deliver the initial sketch, which eventually found its way to the Smithsonian Institute as a prime example of modern sculpture, and on the road as the Avanti.

Loewy later claimed he had "decided on a design concept almost immediately," which evolved from three earlier European experimental cars. One of them, the Lancia Loraymo, displayed the sort of tapered "Coke-bottle" shape that would become Avanti's trademark. Other elements

Industrial designer Raymond Loewy, creator of the Coca-Cola bottle, penned the original 1962 Avanti for Studebaker. The automaker went under in 1966, but the classic Avanti (both pages) lives on.

included a wedge-type profile and the missing grille. Instead of traditional grillework, the Avanti's front end was a smooth, sloped plane, with an air intake located below the bumper.

The stubby rear end was no less unique, described as an "upswept ducktail" that carried wraparound tail lamps and a thin bumper. Wheel-arch curves were said to resemble trajectories of objects re-entering the earth's atmosphere, a result of Loewy's experience as a NASA consultant.

The Avanti was unveiled in April 1962, emerging from an ancient Studebaker plant in South Bend, Indiana, that had once produced covered wagons for westward-bound settlers. Customers had a choice of an R1 Jet Thrust engine (a modification of the standard Studebaker V-8) or a supercharged R2 edition. A handful of R3 and R4 models, with more powerful V-8s, also were built.

After Studebaker moved to Ontario, Canada, early in 1964 (only to expire completely two years later), Nate Altman and Leo Newman, partners in a South Bend Studebaker dealership, bought the rights and tooling for the Avanti. A year later, the hand-built Avanti II was born. Stephen Blake took over in 1982, and Michael Kelly purchased the foundering (actually bankrupt) firm four years later. In 1988 his partner in the venture, J.J. Cafaro, bought 95 percent of the assets. Meanwhile, the operation had moved from South Bend to Youngstown, Ohio.

Only in 1986 was there no Avanti produced. Although today's Avanti coupe looks surprisingly similar to the original, a vast number of mechanical alterations have taken place. The original sat on a Studebaker Lark Convertible frame. Obviously those couldn't last forever. So there was a switch to a General Motors chassis in the 1980s. The current Avanti uses a chassis and powertrain from a Chevrolet Caprice. Koni shock absorbers help to produce a firm—occasionally harsh—ride, with more precise handling than the ponderous Caprice.

Ever since severing the Studebaker connection, Avanti has used General Motors engines. A 5.0-liter (305 cid) V-8 that delivers 170 horsepower is standard fare today, with a 350 cid IROC version optional by special order. Vice-president of product and dealer development Gary

Fielding says the standard powerplant satisfies nearly all of today's customers, even if it can't approach a Corvette's performance; few buyers have asked for the bigger engine. A dual exhaust delivers a gracefully resonant tone, reminiscent of the exhaust bark from the original Studebaker Avanti.

Not that everything in the car's appearance has remained untouched for twenty-plus years. Among other subtle adjustments, today's version carries ground-effects body panels, heavier bumpers, and deep-set, rectangular headlamps.

Inside the modern Avanti's fiberglass body, molded at the Youngstown factory, is a proliferation of lustrous Carpathian burl elm wood—including an optional thick wood steering wheel, ready to remind the enthusiast of classic cars of the 1930s. The hides of at least eight cows are needed to create each car's leather upholstery. Hand stitching alone takes some 16 man-hours, hand sanding 110 more. In all, no less than 900 man-hours of handcrafting are required before each Avanti is ready to roll out the door. Signatures of those employees who worked on the car appear in its owner's manual.

More significant than any chassis/engine modifications was the decision to reach beyond the original coupe design to offer an Avanti convertible; and later, a touring sedan. The first ragtop Avanti appeared in 1987 and, except for the absence of a top, looks identical to the coupe. Only the most adamant purists may take offense.

The Avanti name has been held by a succession of owners, but the grille-less nose, wasp-waist profile, and tapered tail have endured. Studebaker mechanicals have given way to Chevrolet power and underpinnings, however, and a convertible verson (below) bowed in 1987.

The sedan, mounted on a stretched wheelbase, was shown at the Greater New York International Automobile Show in spring 1989. Up front, and at the back, it's pure Avanti. In between, the transition from coupe to sedan has definitely altered the feeling of the form, raising the roofline a bit. Yet a surprising number of the original lines have survived—notably the familiar curve of the rear (side) window, now part of the back door. Cafaro expects that the sedan will "open up a whole new world to Avanti," making it more attractive as a family's primary car, as well as a distinctive business vehicle. Even a limousine is in the planning stage. Sedan

extras include an optional back-seat TV, fold-down picnic tables (borrowed from British luxury sedans), and a compartment for a cellular phone. The revived company is trying hard to develop name recognition for the long-lived Avanti. Offering a bright red convertible as a prize on TV's *Wheel of Fortune* didn't hurt a bit. Neither did a lavish 1989 debut at the National Automobile Dealers Association convention in New Orleans.

A stated goal of producing 1,000 cars a year reaches far beyond any former owner's achievement. Like many other luxury makes, Avanti hopes to attract people who want to drive a "personal statement," but

don't want to see a duplicate on the road every day. An ongoing attempt has also been made to enhance quality control, to avoid the defects (especially cracked fiberglass bodies) that plagued Avantis earlier in the 1980s. "We've brought in true car builders," Cafaro insists, not just enthusiasts; and Avanti is now "built by professionals." While admitting that typical buyers aren't necessarily lured by the car's Studebaker origin, Cafaro believes the coupe serves as the Avanti "heritage" and vows to keep it in the lineup. Judging by the stares both two-doors attracted at their New Orleans reception, the aging Avanti may thrive well into the next century.

AVANTI
SPECIFICATIONS

Manufacturer:	Avanti Automotive Corp., Youngstown, OH
Models available:	coupe, convertible, sedan
Body design:	4-passenger, 2-door coupe or convertible; 4-passenger, 4-door sedan; fiberglass body, steel frame
Powertrain layout:	front-engine, rear-wheel drive
Wheelbase (in.):	109.0 (cpe/conv), 116.0 (sdn)
Overall length (in.):	193.0 (cpe/conv), 200.0 (sdn)
Overall width (in.):	70.5 (cpe/conv), 73.5 (sdn)
Overall height (in.):	55.0 (cpe/conv), 53.0 (sdn)
Track, front (in.):	59.7 (cpe/conv), 60.7 (sdn)
Track, rear (in.):	58.7 (cpe/conv), 59.7 (sdn)
Weight (lbs.):	3550 (cpe/conv), 3700 (sdn)
Approximate price:	$37,982 (coupe); $47,982 (convertible); $47,000 (sedan)
Engine type:	General Motors ohv V-8
Displacement (liters/cu. in.):	5.0/305
Horsepower @ rpm:	170 @ 4400
Torque (lbs./ft.) @ rpm:	250 @ 2800
Fuel delivery:	fuel injection
Transmission:	4-speed overdrive automatic
Suspension, front:	double wishbones, coil springs
Suspension, rear:	4-link live axle, coil springs
Brakes:	front discs, rear drums

PERFORMANCE

Top speed (mph):	approx. 125-130
0-60 mph (seconds):	approx. 8.0
Quarter-mile (seconds):	NA
mph @ quarter-mile:	NA

Avanti means "forward" in Italian, but today's translation also includes a luxury-touring sedan (above). Hides from no fewer than eight cows slather the gadget-ladened cabin in hand-stitched leather (left).

25

BENTLEY
TURBO R

Bentley badge (above) stands for dignity, tradition, pedigree—all the stately virtues of Britain's leading luxury-car firm. When mounted at the leading edge of the sizzling Turbo R, the graceful wings also stand for performance rivaling that of a Corvette rather than the related Rolls-Royce.

Some limited-production cars emit an aura of brute force. Others emphasize radical shaping, or high-tech gadgetry. A few choose to display bubble-top futurism, or flaunt their racing-car origins.

Like its parent company, Rolls-Royce, what the thoroughbred Bentley conveys is a sense of restrained elegance and strength. The Turbo R is the most powerful Bentley ever, but it's power that is groomed and refined. Civilized power. Power that doesn't care if it gets an opportunity to be tested or not. This is a car that knows what it has on tap, ready for the sudden heavy lurch of its gentlemanly driver's right foot. The Turbo R's driver cares not a whit who else knows what it can deliver.

As the British say, a Bentley is "pricey." To say the least. Its $149,500 price tag on this side of the Atlantic actually tops that of most Rolls-Royces, though Bentley has long been thought the less expensive of the pair.

Some cynics insist you can purchase just as much luxury for half the price—and comparable performance for even less. But what you cannot obtain elsewhere is the priceless Rolls/Bentley heritage. Slide across the Turbo R's sumptuous leather seat and you feel as though you're ready to drive not just another motorcar, but a part of history.

For those who can afford it, piloting a Turbo R into the company parking lot is the perfect way to demonstrate quiet wealth—the kind that need not call attention to itself. Like the related Bentley Mulsanne, a Turbo R appeals to professional types in their late 30s and early 40s—a decade or so younger than the typical Rolls buyer. The buyer of the Turbo R may be seen as more than a gentleman. He's also a sporting fellow, able (when necessity dictates) to unleash the potential of what the car's manufacturer

Thoroughbreds like the Bentley Turbo R (both pages) need no gauche nameplates— not with that classically simple grille. Huge headlamps and foglamps offer just a hint of this muscular Bentley's sporting character.

describes as the "fastest four-door production car on earth."

By fast, we're speaking of acceleration to 60 miles an hour in 6.7 seconds, and one hundred in less than 20. For purposes of passing, a leap from 50 to 70 mph takes only 4 seconds. That's Corvette time. Although the Bentley is turbocharged, the engine exhibits little turbo lag and is large enough to give it that low end grunt a 5200-pound car requires. Step on the gas and the Bentley moves out in a hurry, without delay. After all, a gentleman hasn't the time to wait around.

In typically conservative British manner, the company elects not to disclose horsepower and torque figures, and claims "only" a 135 mph top speed. Most observers place the actual limit rather higher up the scale. In fact, a Turbo R traveled 140 miles in a single hour to set a British National Endurance Record, actually beating a Lamborghini Countach. Breeding beats the beast, one might say.

The Bentley's power comes from a 6.75-liter (412 cid) aluminum V-8; an intercooled Garrett AiResearch turbocharger stuffs in the air/fuel mixture when it's needed most. American observers have estimated horsepower at a hair under 300, though German documents (where power must be disclosed for legal reasons)

have revealed a figure of 325. Rather than sheer horsepower, explained chief engineer Phil Harding to *Motor Trend*, Bentley strived for "low-speed torque, to give you that aircraft-at-the-end-of-the-runway sensation." Many drivers would expect a 4-speed automatic, but the Bentley uses a 3-speed. With all that torque at hand, the extra gearing isn't quite so vital. And at highway speeds, the big V-8 is just lazing along.

It's not easy to think of a useful convenience that's missing from the Turbo R's list of standard equipment. Dual-level air conditioning, for instance, automatically compensates for the sun's warmth, so inhabitants need never suffer a sudden wave of heat or tinge of chill. Seats have a 4-position memory. A light warns of icy road conditions, translating traction information supplied by a sensor system. Fold-down tables in back allow picnicking at any moment in one's travels. On the option list are such entertaining essentials as a cocktail cabinet that fits into the console, and a trunk-mounted refrigerator to chill the glasses.

Rather than climbing into the customary luxury car's driver's space, the Bentley owner slips into a cockpit created by a downward-swept central console. Whereas a Rolls owner is likely to be found in the back seat, Bentley people normally wear the driver's cap themselves. The traditional dashboard incorporates full analog instrumentation, including a tachometer—no digital gadgetry clutters a Bentley's panel, though its precision speedometer is silently electronic.

Connolly leather is the only possible choice for a car of this caliber. Anything less—well, that would be like choosing a burger and fries over a five-star meal. Thus, eleven flawless hides make up the Turbo R's upholstery, hand cut and stitched by craftspersons who know their leather. Driver and passenger feet are cushioned by thick Wilton wool carpets. Luscious hand-rubbed burled walnut veneer lines the dashboard, which could at a glance be mistaken for a Rolls/Bentley panel of decades past.

Motorists who smoke never have to face the prospect of confronting leftover ashes. The Bentley's ashtrays empty themselves automatically. All that unpleasant residue disappears into a hidden bin, eventually extracted by—if one is so fortunate—someone else.

Neither Bentley nor Rolls strays from its familiar radiator shell design of simple vertical strips. The Turbo R is no exception, carrying the traditionally elegant grille into the final decade of this century. Massive 7-inch round headlamps are complemented by matching foglamps. A few of the touches found on the Bentley are less commonly found in a luxury motorcar, but apropos because of the Bentley's sporting character. Those include a deep front air dam, flared sill panels, and rear wheel skirts.

Needless to say, this is a big and heavy car, tipping the scales at more than 2½ tons. Without the use of aluminum for doors, hood and truck lid, it would be weightier yet. To keep the car on an even keel, the four-wheel independent suspension is augmented by automatic hydraulic leveling at the rear, which adjusts body height in response to the load carried. Power assistance to the steering mechanism has been halved from earlier models, to give a semblance of the sort of road "feel" that's found on other sporting motorcars. Unlike many luxury automobiles, the Bentley's cushiony ride isn't accompanied by a frightful feeling that control might be lost at any moment if the road gets rough.

Traditional craftsmanship by hand transcends time. Each Bentley takes more than three months to build, which accounts for the limited supply. Only four or five per week are ready for U.S. dealerships, and most of those are typically spoken for well in advance. Among the many tasks involved, the body is cleaned five times and brushed with special metal wool. Each hand-assembled engine is tested on the road for a hundred miles or so, and the final paint coat doesn't leave the spray gun until road evaluation is completed.

Since the early 1950s, when the Bentley Continental ranked as the world's fastest production sedan, Bentleys have been criticized as being little more than siblings to Rolls-Royce: basically, a Rolls without the familiar RR insignia. The marque rose taller with the introduction of the Mulsanne Turbo in 1982. An evolution of the Mulsanne, the Turbo R found an ample supply of customers in Europe for three years after its British debut, before heading for America late in 1988.

The Turbo R brings back memories of the Roaring Twenties, when Bentley raced at LeMans, bringing home five victories. Originally an independent firm, founded by W.O. Bentley, it merged with Rolls in 1931, continuing to turn out sportier machines than its luxury-oriented mate.

As L.J.K. Setright wrote in *Car* magazine, Bentley "occupies with effortless superiority and unforbidding remoteness a pinnacle entirely its own." Is it decadent? Excessive? Perhaps. In any event, this "flagship of the Bentley marque" is hardly a car for everyone; yet it's one whose virtues are evident to every person who chances to gaze upon its graceful and old-fashioned beauty. To feel the surge of its mighty turbo V-8 is a mere bonus. Since only a couple of hundred reach the U.S. yearly, few of us even get a chance to gawk.

Few would suspect that beneath the Bentley's gentlemanly bonnet lies a 6.75-liter V-8 engine, fed its fuel courtesy of an intercooled Garrett turbocharger. The manufacturer never deigns to divulge horsepower ratings of its motorcars. Still, the V-8 can propel 5,200 pounds of sedan to 100 mph in under 20 seconds—reminiscent of a jet plane streaking down the runway.

TURBO R

BENTLEY TURBO R

SPECIFICATIONS

Manufacturer:	Rolls-Royce Motors Ltd., Crewe, England
Body design:	5-passenger, 4-door sedan; monocoque steel body and frame; aluminum doors/hood/deck
Powertrain layout:	front-engine, rear-wheel drive
Wheelbase (in.):	120.5
Overall length (in.):	207.4
Overall width (in.):	79.0
Overall height (in.):	58.7
Track, front (in.):	61.0
Track, rear (in.):	61.0
Weight (lbs.):	5270
Approximate price:	$149,500
Engine type:	turbocharged, intercooled ohv V-8
Displacement (liters/cu. in.):	6.7/412
Horsepower @ rpm:	(est.) 297 @ 3800
Torque (lbs./ft.) @ rpm:	(est.) 487 @ 2400
Fuel delivery:	Bosch MK-Motronic port fuel injection
Transmission:	3-speed automatic
Suspension, front:	unequal-length control arms, coil springs, anti-roll bar
Suspension, rear:	independent coil springs, semi-trailing arms, struts, gas springs, anti-roll bar, panhard rod
Brakes:	front/rear discs (front vented); anti-lock

PERFORMANCE

Top speed (mph):	135+
0-60 mph (seconds):	6.7
Quarter-mile (seconds):	15.7
mph @ quarter-mile:	NA

All-wheel independent suspension and snug steering help the Turbo R maneuver past its luxury mates. Down-swept console (above) adds a sporting flair, while exquisite wood harks back to Bentleys of a bygone day. Connolly leather, pleated to perfection, engulfs occupants as they stretch their legs on woolly Wilton carpets.

B M W   M 1

Some cars don't get the chance they deserve. The 1978-81 M1, BMW's first, and so far only, mid-engine production car, is a case in point. Though conceived as a "homologation special" for production-class sports-car competition, the M1 never actually ran under official BMW auspices because the firm's motorsport policy veered toward building Formula 1 engines soon after the M1 was finalized. As a result, only 450 examples were built, all but about 50 of them fully equipped road cars. Needless to say, they've all become prized collector's items.

Depending on the source one consults, M1 denotes either "mid-engine car, first type" or "Motorsport One." The latter seems more probable, referring as it does to BMW Motorsport AG, the subsidiary of the Bavarian automaker that builds and develops racing BMWs as well as production-based, high-performance limited editions, of which M1 was the first.

The car was born in 1972 with the founding of BMW Motorsport by one-time race driver Jochen Neerpasch. BMW's racing 3.0 CSL coupes were beginning to lose ground to Porsche's 911s in the European Touring Car Championship, and a new production-based World Championship of Makes for Group 5 cars was in the offing. Neerpasch wanted a machine that would not only give BMW supremacy in both arenas but that could be evolved to remain competitive through the mid-Eighties. That BMW would bother with a roadgoing version was only to satisfy

sanctioning bodies with the fact that the M1 was, in fact, an "assembly-line" model.

For the familiar reasons of inherently good mass balance and race-bred charisma, Neerpasch decreed a midships engine layout for his new racetrack hopeful. He didn't have far to go for inspiration, for 1972 also saw the unveiling of a glamorous mid-engine BMW experimental, called simply the Turbo and shaped by the talented Paul Brache, then BMW design chief. The Turbo was low, sleek, and purposeful, with gullwing doors *a la* the Mercedes 300SL and a mid-mounted turbocharged version of the lusty four-cylinder engine from BMW's compact 2002 sports sedan. Neerpasch knew a good thing when he saw it, so the Turbo became the starting point for Project E26, which would culminate in the M1.

From the first, it was realized that the small numbers involved, initially only 400 cars, would make E26 too costly for a firm of BMW's size to pursue alone. Accordingly, design, development, production, and overall coordination were farmed out to

If they knew what was behind that familiar front-end, collectors would clamor for a chance to own BMW's race-oriented M1 road car (both pages). Sleek mid-engine design, stemming from the design firm headed by Giorgio Giugiaro, lacked the gullwing doors of the Turbo from which the M1 evolved.

exoticar maker Lamborghini in Italy, which was not only more experienced with low-volume projects but anxious to do the work in order to help extricate itself from a dire financial situation.

BMW's regard for Italian expertise, as well as the growing renown of Italian designer Giorgio Giugiaro, led BMW to contract with his Ital Design (then also involved with the ill-starred DeLorean) for body styling and construction. Ital was told to retain some "BMW identity," which partly explains the Turbo-style version of BMW's trademark "twin-kidney" grille motif. Still, the overall package was somewhat heavy-handed next to Brache's effort (especially around the rear quarters), lacking not only the Turbo's gullwing doors but its grace and excitement, as well.

Given BMW's illustrious powerplant history, the one part the German company contributed to the M1 was, to no one's surprise, the engine: a much-modified version of BMW's smooth, potent "big-block" straight six. Designated M-88, it featured a cast-iron 3.5-liter block, as on the production unit, topped by a new aluminum head running a pair of chain-driven overhead camshafts to operate four valves per cylinder instead of the usual two. Bosch-Kugelfischer mechanical injection fed fuel to the individual ports.

The combination of Teutonic thinking and Italian specialist know-how should have worked beautifully, but it didn't. The trouble started when a sizeable Italian government loan earmarked for M1 production materials was apparently diverted to other purposes by an increasingly desperate Lamborghini management. Even with that, Lamborghini slipped over the financial brink soon after the M1 was locked up. The results were a lot of finger-pointing in Munich and, as one British journalist recounted, "tales of BMW staff swooping on the Sant'Agata works to liberate designs and tooling."

There was no choice but to regroup, and BMW hastily contracted with two other Italian firms: Marchesi, for the multi-tube chassis, and Trasformazione Italiana Resina (TIR), for the fiberglass body. Final assembly was shifted to Baur, the German coach builder long associated with BMW.

But by the time it was all sorted out, the calendar read 1979 (the M1 had debuted at the Paris Salon in October '78) and BMW was wearying of a project that wasn't likely to generate either the victories or the attendant publicity that had been expected. The M1's sole moment in the competition spotlight came with the 1979-80 "Procar" series, a sort of European International Race of Champions staged before major Grand Prix in which top F1 drivers competed against each other (and a few non-GP

pilots) in identically prepared M1s. But this was little more than a side show that hardly did justice to what BMW had wrought.

And more's the pity, because the M1 remains a superbly executed modern supercar by any standard. As in Lamborghini's Countach (the production version of which was actually engineered alongside the M1), the engine rides longitudinally behind a two-seat cockpit to drive the rear wheels via a 5-speed transaxle (by ZF). Suspension is all-independent, with coil springs and twin A-arms at each corner. Brakes are big discs all around. Wheels and tires are massive 16-inchers, with the rears wider than the fronts—as is common with tail-heavy high-performers. All this adds up to vice-free handling, very high cornering grip, and excellent stopping power—in short, real racetrack ability.

That attribute was hardly unexpected when you consider that the M1 was developed in three versions: a 277-horsepower road car, built to satisfy the 400-unit homologation minimum; a Group 4 Touring Championship racer with 470 bhp and suitable body and chassis modifications; and a Group 5 rocket with an alleged 850 bhp or so from a downsized 3.2-liter turbo engine. The Group 4 version was the one used in Procar.

For all that, roadgoing M1s are quite plush and unusually practical for an exoticar; their comprehensive equipment runs from air conditioning to full carpeting. They were—and are—as nice on the road as any midships Ferrari, and probably better built. The highly reliable 24-valve M-88 engine is another plus for would-be owners. One might criticize the M1 for its limited luggage space and rear vision, but this car is hardly the first "middie" so afflicted.

The tragedy of the M1 is that it was a great car abandoned before it could prove itself. One British writer, looking back on it all, aptly termed the M1 a "glorious disaster. It may have cost the BMW board sleepless nights and one of the biggest bills in their history, it may have cost Neerpasch his job, it may have cost the private [owners] of the 400 road versions DM 100,000 apiece, but yet such beauty and magnificence never comes cheap."

Will BMW again attempt something this specialized? Perhaps, but it likely won't be mid-engined and certainly won't be built in cooperation with a company on shaky financial ground. Meantime, we can revel in the latest iteration of the rapid M5 supersedan, the sophisticated new V-12-powered 850i coupe, and the charming Motorsports-built Z1 two-seat convertible with its unique drop-down doors. The last has so far been reserved for Europe only, but they're all dream machines and they all started with the M1. Not a bad legacy for a "disaster."

Slatted back window (right) doesn't let the driver see much to the rear, but few owners were likely to complain. Of the 450 M1s built, a full 400 were fitted for the road rather than the race course. Even the competition versions never raced under the official BMW banner, heeding the starter's flag only in a minor series of "Procar" events. A tiny squarish variant of the traditional "twin-kidney" is little more than a suggestion of a grille—but enough to let fans know that this is a BMW to watch. Later, in modified form, the 6-cylinder engine burst into renewed life beneath the hood of M5 sedans from BMW Motorsport.

Racing-car origin of the M1 can barely be detected in the functional, but far from stark cockpit (opposite page). Creature comforts more appropriate to a tamer vehicle include air conditioning and plush carpeting. The 6-cylinder engine, tucked into a neat compartment, whipped out 277 horsepower in road form.

BMW M1

SPECIFICATIONS

Manufacturer:	BMW Motorsport, AG Munich, West Germany
Body design:	2-passenger, 2-door fastback coupe; fiberglass body over multi-tube inner structure and chassis
Powertrain layout:	longitudinal rear/mid-engine, rear-wheel drive
Wheelbase (in.):	100.8
Overall length (in):	171.7
Overall width (in.):	71.8
Overall height (in.):	44.9
Track, front (in.):	61.0
Track, rear (in.):	62.0
Weight (lbs):	3000
Approximate price:	$53,000 (1979)
Engine type:	dohc I-6, 4 valves/cylinder
Displacement (liters/cu.in.):	3.5/211
Horsepower @ rpm:	277 DIN/266 SAE net @ 6500
Torque (lbs./ft.) @ rpm:	243 DIN/229 SAE net @ 5000
Fuel delivery:	Kugelfischer-Bosch mechanical port fuel injection
Transmissions:	ZF 5-speed manual transaxle
Suspension, front:	independent; upper and lower unequal-length control arms, coil springs, tubular hydraulic shock absorbers, anti-roll bar
Suspension, rear:	independent; upper and lower unequal-length control arms, coil springs, tubular hydraulic shock absorbers, anti-roll bar
Brakes:	front/rear discs

PERFORMANCE

Top speed (mph):	162
0-60 mph (seconds):	5.5
Quarter-mile (seconds):	13.7
mph @ quarter-mile:	102

NOTE: all data for production model

BMW 850i

Smooth is the only word that adequately describes the newest BMW coupe, designed as a replacement for the two-door 6-series. So smooth are its body lines that the car looks almost as though it were carved in one piece, from a massive block of steel. Few pieces of rolling sculpture actually enter the marketplace ever looking this tempting—or could even hope to offer the luxury and performance of the 850i coupe.

Anyone who's driven the big BMW 750i or 750il sedans that appeared in 1987 knows the meaning of restrained elegance. It would be difficult to conjure up any conveniences and comforts that are missing from the 750's sumptuous interior. Neither would that lucky driver be likely to express even the slightest hint of disappointment over the blazing performance—and satisfying sound—of the mighty V-12 engine under its beautifully crafted, forward-lift hood.

The 750 is a big car that makes big promises. Even better, it's one that can, and does, deliver on each and every one of them. So, will this two-door edition on the same platform, carrying the same engine, prove to be any less an example of near-perfection in its league? Not likely. The 850i is a magnificent mix of styling cues from each of the mid-size and larger BMWs in the current lineup, and is expected to create quite a stir when the first examples head toward American dealerships.

Stay away unless you like your cars to be noticed and admired for their graceful silhouettes. Tall rocker panels are the size of ground-effects moldings, but don't protrude outward at all to spoil the clean bodyside surface. Flush glass all around and the high-visibility greenhouse blend beautifully into each adjoining metal surface. The long hood meets the steeply raked windshield with barely a joint. A bodyside crease in both front and rear fenders melts ever-so-gently into the door skin.

There's no clumsy B-pillar to detract from the flowing side view, either. No pillar at all, in fact; just a rubber seal between the side windows—in true hardtop style. Up top is a modest metal sunroof; at the rear, a stubby little deck. Hugging the ground are hefty tires on an elegant set of wheels with heavy "spokes." High-intensity pop-up ellipsoid headlamps sit above the energy-absorbing plastic nose, far ahead of the driver's eager eyes.

More than mere beauty flows through the 850i's body. A powerful poise radiates from the car's modern aerodynamic lines. Nothing radical or spaceship-like, of course. Nothing garish or gaudy. Yet even before the engine is fired up, the car looks prepared, confident, girded for gentlemanly and civilized rivalry. Standing taut at a stoplight, it tugs only gently at the leash—just enough to keep its driver aware of its performance potential. Even if it's never to be tested on the rolling battlefield of the highway, this is a car that knows its capabilities and need not shout them to the uninformed crowd. Secure in that knowledge, the 850's occupants may simply relax and enjoy the bounty of comforts within the car's rich, leather-lined interior.

While the 850's predecessor in the 6-series BMW line carried a 6-cylinder engine under its hood, the 850i doubles that amount. Carrying on the contemporary penchant for bigger and more exotic powerplants, the coupe borrows the potent and silky all-alloy V-12 from its 750 sedan brother.

Heavy-footed Bimmer buyers can expect acceleration from a standing start to 60 miles an hour in less than 7 seconds; possibly leaning toward 6. But no one will ever know what the car could do on a no-limit open road (probably about 174 mph), because an electronically-controlled governor holds speed down to a mere 155 miles per hour.

Later on, a 3.5-liter 6-cylinder engine (currently used in the M5) may power an 835 version. BMW may even enlarge the V-12 to 5.4 liters and 400 horsepower, to power a future 8-series coupe. The horsepower race of the Fifties seems to have returned, but flaunting far bigger numbers than before. For now, though, 300 should be enough to satisfy anyone whose driving chores take place on a real road instead of a race course.

Not everything offered by the 850i is borrowed from other BMWs. A new five-link rear suspension, for instance, replaces the trailing-arm design that's been used in both the 5 and 7 series. The reworked suspension is said to deliver a noticeable boost to control and stability during both cornering and lane-changes. BMW is even experimenting with steerable back wheels, an innovation that may arrive in the future.

Ride qualities are electronically controlled, too. The system adjusts shock-absorber rates according to the car's speed and load, as well as to the type of road surface. Anti-lock braking is standard. So is traction control, activated by a button inside the car.

Those who like to shift for themselves don't have to accept the 4-speed automatic transmission, or be satisfied with a mere five forward speeds in the manual gearbox. No, the optional transmission in the 850i has a total of *six* speeds. That's another first for the BMW lineup, guaranteed to please anyone with a fondness for the gearshift lever.

Not until the latter half of 1990 will American buyers be able to put an 850i coupe in the garage, though Europeans can enjoy that pleasure perhaps half a year earlier. Near-perfection in a roadable performance coupe doesn't come cheap, of course, and the 850's price tag is almost certain to top the $70,000 cost of a 750 sedan. That's a pricey neighborhood, but few observers predict a shortage of eager customers when the 850 makes its long-awaited entrance into American show-rooms. For those who crave the feel of wind in the face when motoring down the highway, 1991 should bring BMW's convertible version of the 8-series coupe, eager to rival the latest Mercedes SL ragtop.

To call the 850i the BMW equivalent of a Porsche 959, as some have done, might be stretching a bit. Without a doubt, though, the pretty and potent coupe propels BMW into the supercar league.

If BMW's 750il sedan feels like energy incarnate, its 850i offshoot (opposite page) also looks the part. Manual-shift fans are likely to grow rapturous, faced with the prospect of six forward speeds to choose from. Rear view might be the only one seen, if an 850i driver chose to respond with like crassness to a challenge from a boorish inferior. A governor reins in speed to a "respectable" 155 mph, just in case temptation turns momentarily irresistible.

BMW 850i

SPECIFICATIONS

Manufacturer:	Baverische Motoren Werke AG, Munich, West Germany
Body design:	2+2-passenger, 2-door coupe; steel unibody
Powertrain layout:	front-engine, rear-wheel drive
Wheelbase (in.):	(est.) 106.3
Overall length (in.):	191.2
Overall width (in.):	74.2
Overall height (in.):	53.6
Track, front (in.):	60.2
Track, rear (in.):	61.3
Weight (lbs.):	(est.) 4000
Approximate price:	$71,400 (in Germany)
Engine type:	ohc V-12 (32-valve)
Displacement (liters/cu. in.):	5.0/304
Horsepower @ rpm:	300 @ 5200
Torque (lbs./ft.) @ rpm:	332 @ 4100
Fuel delivery:	LH-Jetronic fuel injection
Transmissions:	6-speed manual or 4-speed automatic
Suspension, front:	MacPherson struts, lower A-arms, anti-roll bar
Suspension, rear:	5-link, coil springs
Brakes:	front/rear discs, anti-lock

PERFORMANCE

Top speed (mph):	155 (governed)
0-60 mph (seconds):	6.8
Quarter-mile (seconds):	NA
mph @ quarter-mile:	NA

No nasty B-pillar, garish brightwork, or foolishly flared rocker panel mars the fine lines of the 850i's shapely form. Inside (left), the businesslike dashboard is joined by a sporty console that's packed with choices. One of them flicks on traction control, to keep an 850i from spinning its wheels. BMW's supercoupe isn't meant to stand still technically, with such 21st century ideas as vision enhancement and distance warning possibly on the way one day.

BUICK WILDCAT

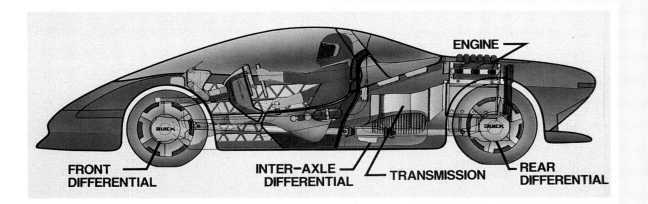

FRONT
DIFFERENTIAL

ENGINE

INTER-AXLE
DIFFERENTIAL

TRANSMISSION

REAR
DIFFERENTIAL

Conventioneers who spotted the Wildcat in its first public appearance, at the 1985 Specialty Equipment Manufacturers Association extravaganza in Las Vegas, might be forgiven for asking, "Could this be a Buick? Tomorrow's Buick?" One observer was heard to exclaim that "it looked like it would go better backwards than it would forwards."

Even though Buick has a long history of involvement with performance cars, and even racing cars, it's never quite been able to shed its stodgy image. People who weren't even *born* when Buicks had portholes somehow "remember" that the products from Flint, Michigan, are cars your father would drive.

Active participation in motorsports was one way to alter that image and attract younger customers. So Buick delved into IMSA GTP vehicles, the Trans-Am sports

Could a front end like this really be worn by a Buick (left)? Not in any dealer's showroom, but it carried Buick's badge onto auto show floors. Mid-mounted V-6 engine (above) of the latest Wildcat drives all four wheels. Early viewers of the experimental design wondered which way it was headed (below).

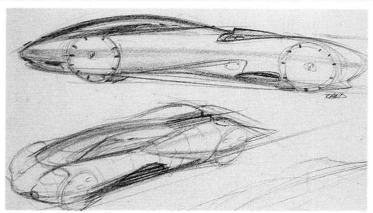

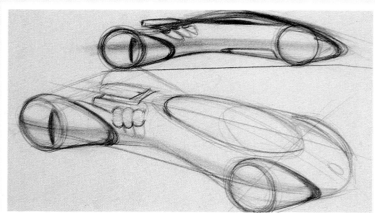

car circuit—even dragsters and Indy cars. For the broader public, Buick created a series of striking auto show concept cars, designed to broaden the marque's appeal and invigorate its staid image. One of the most memorable of these attempts has to have been the *first* Wildcat, which hit the auto show circuit in 1953.

In the 1960s, this non-stodgy name went on a series of production Buicks, known for big engines and big proportions. Later yet, this far different Wildcat, low and bubble-topped, emerged from the Buick design studio. Initially billed as "a look at the future," the most recent Wildcat is one show car that hasn't shown its age.

Buick called the latest Wildcat "an expression of muscular sculptural forms and exciting new mechanicals." Though not all of the mechanicals proved quite so thrilling, few could forget the car's dramatic glass-roofed, curvaceous form; not to mention its awesome bodyside air scoops and aggressively feline road stance. Depending on your perspective, you might see in its lines a teardrop, a shark, a rocketship—even a mushroom. Hardly a sharp edge could be found in its flowing, organic body structure.

Onlookers were advised that if a car like this were to go into production, they would virtually wear it and use it "like a pair of form-fitting driving gloves." Sounds like overblown automaker hype, but the claim isn't far from the truth. Even a glance at the low-riding creation makes one want to climb inside and take a fast spin around the block, if not the race track.

To do so, you couldn't just open a door and plop in. No, you'd push on a solenoid in the left rocker panel, which raised the canopy. At the same time, the steering wheel would tilt upward to let your physique slide gently downward to the driver's seat. Not as easy as it sounds, since both driver and passenger must endure a tight squeeze before the canopy was ready to drop down again into the drive-away position.

Though the original show car wasn't capable of driving anywhere, a functional version was already under development, to be used for engineering tests as well as touring the nation alongside a CART Indy racer. A handful of lucky outsiders even got a chance for a limited test drive.

Though not a pace car, both examples were built with support from the PPG company, which funds the authentic pace vehicles. Wildcat was created not only as a show attraction, but to serve as a test platform for Buick ideas and as a tool to gather data.

Projected on the windshield ahead of the driver, near the normal line of vision, a "head-up" display showed speed and odometer readings, in either English or metric measures. Even the shift quadrant showed up there, so eyes rarely would have to leave the road ahead. An upgraded head-up display appeared later on selected examples of the new Oldsmobile Cutlass Supreme, and is likely to show up in various cars of the 1990s. Not every high-tech feature of a concept car eventually makes it to production, but this one will—and ranks among the better ideas of its day.

Mounted in the center of the instrument panel was a flat video screen, similar to the Graphic Control Center that appeared on the 1986 Buick Riviera. Wildcat's version showed a broader range of data: everything from oil temperature, engine torque, and compass points, to the engine's spark curve and tire slippage. It even displayed the "g" forces that emerged when the driver cornered, stomped the gas, or braked hard.

Essential gauges, including the tachometer, resided in the steering wheel hub. No need to twist your head to watch a gauge as the car turned a corner, of course—the instruments sit still while the wheel rotates.

While most cars, whether production or show models, hide their engines under an opaque hood of some sort, Wildcat flaunts its mid-engine powerplant. Everyone could take a peek at the 3.8-liter V-6, with its 24-valve, double-overhead-cam configuration, which protruded upward from the rear deck. Ahead of the 230-plus horsepower engine sat a 4-speed automatic transmission, sending power into a chain-

Huge bodyside scoops are only part of Wildcat's startling design. Squint a bit and its smoothly flowing lines might take on the hazy form of a teardrop, a mushroom, a rocketship. What looks like a science-fiction creation came to embryonic life as a student exercise, then started to take serious form in Design Studio Number One. Rough in-house sketches (left) eventually evolved into a final design by Dave Rand and Bill Porter. No metal structure lurks beneath this bundle of curves. Instead, it's all a blend of fiberglass and carbon fiber.

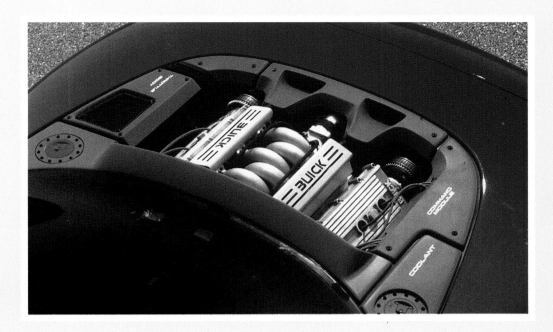

Dimensions of the Wildcat 3.8-liter V-6 (above) are familiar to many a Buick fan; 24-valve design is not. Easy-to-find engine protrudes upward from the rear deck. The glass-roofed canopy is raised (below) by pushing a solenoid control in the left rocker panel.

driven transfer case and central differential. Yes, that's right, a transfer case means the Wildcat has full-time four-wheel-drive. About two-thirds of the output torque is delivered to the back wheels, one-third to the fronts.

Manual shifting was possible, overriding the automatic transmission via a motorcycle-type selector. A computer prevented over-revving of the engine. More important to drivers who evaluated the car was a governor that limited speeds to 70 mph. No telling how much an unfettered Wildcat might be able to deliver.

Powertrains and gadgetry aside, the Wildcat's body obviously proved to be its main attraction, just as its creators had intended. Crafted from a composite of high-strength fiberglass resins and carbon fiber, it required no metal structure. Even the suspension carriers bolted directly to the nonmetallic body, via steel sub-frames. The front-hinged canopy was made of cast gray acrylic and carbon fiber with glass-reinforced polyester resin.

Assigned first to Buick's performance group, the project began as an assignment for junior students at the Center for Creative Studies. Working for a year, the students were given free rein and turned in hundreds of sketches. Half of them worked on the body, the others on interior designs. Two students even spent a summer in the Buick studio. Eventually, the Wildcat took shape in Design Studio Number One, which normally delivers renderings for mid- and full-size Buicks. William L. Porter served as studio head, while David P. Rand was senior designer.

Eventually, a particular set of sketches looked just right, so Rand prepared a full-size drawing. Clay modeling came from the expert hand of Steve Jordan. The basic concept was described as "a pod pushing a pod." That meant an interlocking pair of pods, one for the driver and the other carrying the engine. Those massive side air intakes weren't just for show, but were necessities dictated by the placement of the car's radiator. From the start, the Wildcat was intended to be drivable, not just a showstopper—though it also showcased the paint and plastics of the PPG organization, which footed some of the bill.

Final development took place at Studio Two, with the actual body prototypes crafted by the Triad company. The car's sculptured-look interior, no less radical than its body, was styled by Nellie Toledo.

Wildcat's project manager, Ed Roselle, told *Car and Driver* at the time of the car's early appearance that "this is the type of car that a guy would take down to [Detroit's] Woodward Avenue in the 1990s." Hasn't happened yet, but now that the Nineties are here, what enthusiast or dreamer would turn down an opportunity to do exactly that?

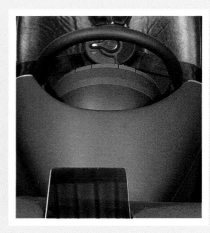

Wildcat's futuristic driving conveniences (opposite page) include a "head-up" instrument display that puts the speedometer reading and a shift quadrant diagram into the driver's line of vision. A Graphic Control Center reveals such esoterica as the engine's spark map display and the car's "g" forces. Major instruments reside in a stationary hub within the tiny steering wheel (left). A modified version of the Wildcat video display saw service in Buick's Riviera.

BUICK WILDCAT

SPECIFICATIONS

Manufacturer:	Buick Divison, General Motors, Flint, MI; body by Triad
Body design:	2-passenger, 1-door coupe; composite fiberglass/carbon-fiber body; front/rear subframes
Powertrain layout:	mid-engine, 4-wheel drive
Wheelbase (in.):	102.0
Overall length (in.):	172.7
Overall width (in.):	72.3
Overall height (in.):	43.7
Track, front (in.):	59.5
Track, rear (in.):	59.5
Weight (lbs.):	2910-3450
Approximate price:	NA
Engine type:	dohc V-6 (24-valve)
Displacement (liters/cu. in.):	3.8/231
Horsepower @ rpm:	230-250 @ 6000
Torque (lbs./ft.) @ rpm:	245 @ 4000
Fuel delivery:	sequential port fuel injection
Transmission:	4-speed automatic (GM THM700-R4)
Suspension, front:	unequal-length control arms, inboard horizontal coil-over shock absorbers
Suspension, rear:	unequal-length control arms, coil-over shock absorbers
Brakes:	front/rear vented discs, anti-lock

PERFORMANCE

Top speed (mph):	70 (governed)
0-60 mph (seconds):	8.4
Quarter-mile (seconds):	NA
mph @ quarter-mile:	NA

CADILLAC ALLANTÉ

Mixing Italian style with Detroit technology can deliver an unbeatable combination. Nobody produces bodies quite like the Italians, and Cadillac has earned a worldwide reputation for technical prowess as well as for creature comforts. Although Cadillac's image and market share have been nibbled at in recent years by Mercedes-Benz and other luxury imports, the subtly elegant Italian/American Allanté stands as a proud reminder of Cadillac style.

An organization that had long promoted itself as the "standard of the world" would appear to have a powerful image built into its very name. Even so, Cadillac pinned high hopes on the two-seat Allanté when the car debuted as a late 1987 model, hoping to enter the market held almost completely by the Mercedes-Benz roadster. Presented properly, the Italian-style roadster could earn Cadillac an edge in the personal performance category, to match its long-standing prominence in the big luxury-car field. Early publicity reached for new highs in consumer hype. So did the hoopla surrounding the car's first appearances.

In the fall of 1986, months before it would be seen in the U.S., the Allanté was unveiled at the Paris Auto Salon. Its first American showing wasn't even "in the flesh," but on TV—at the hands of fictional tycoon

J.R. Ewing, of the popular *Dallas* series. Then, in the spring, the real thing emerged to dazzle the eyes of potential customers. The debut didn't occur in a common arena or convention center, but at a series of black-tie concerts held in upper-crust American homes.

"The new spirit of Cadillac," it was called. Coachwork was designed (and handcrafted) in Italy by the fabled Pininfarina design and coachwork firm. Pininfarina had formerly laid creative hands on such masterworks as the Ferrari Testarossa and Rolls-Royce Camargue, and now declared that working with Cadillac was "the realization of a lifelong dream." The master's signature appeared in script on each Allanté cowl. Cadillac could hardly have asked for a more fitting accolade from an automotive legend.

No one was likely to call the Allanté shape far-out or futuristic. Instead, it proved to be a subtle blend of the traditional and the modern—contemporary and refined.

Striking, but not numbing, with tasteful, flowing lines; nothing harsh or disturbing. Not everyone who saw one from a distance might mark it as a Cadillac, but the design was sure to catch the eye. Allanté aimed toward the well-to-do motorist with a sporting nature—the man or woman who liked to be seen driving in style, but not necessarily stared at in shock. It had to be special and unique, yet remain unmistakably Cadillac.

In Italy, the body was carefully crafted from premium German steel and Swiss aluminum alloy. Carefully painted and fitted, it then flew to Detroit on a specially fitted Lufthansa 747, in what came to be known as the "Allanté Airbridge." John O. Grettenberger, Cadillac's General Manager, explained that the Airbridge "represents a joining of technology and artistry from two nations, each with a long automotive history." Final assembly at the Detroit-Hamtramck plant was followed by a 25-mile test drive.

Cadillac identity is most evident on the front end of the Italian-bodied Allanté (both pages), designed and built by the renowned Pininfarina firm. The luscious steel/aluminum body travels to America for assembly.

Cadillac's influence was most evident up front. From the side, Allanté displayed a contemporary wedge profile and steep windshield, along with a modest forward rake. A tiny dip along the door reached toward the tall rear deck.

Beneath Allanté's sculptured hood resided a high-output 4.1-liter V-8 engine with sequential port fuel injection, mounted transversely (crosswise). Bosch III anti-locking brakes provided safe and sure stopping power. Driver and passenger would of course be swathed in restrained luxury. Both sat firmly yet comfortably within Recaro seats, hand-fitted with Italian leather and capable of adjustment in 10 directions. The driver's seat found its spot with the ability to remember positions for two different drivers. A combination of modern digital and traditional analog instruments filled the dash in front of the driver. Musical entertainment was furnished by a "second generation" Delco-GM/Bose Symphony Sound system.

No loud, harsh sport machine, the Allanté was designed to allow its pair of occupants to carry on a civilized conversation at normal highway speed, without raising one's voice—even with the convertible top down. Even so, the exhaust supplied a subtly alluring note. Special touches included a trio of glass windows at the rear of the soft top. No crass plastic window in this luxury roadster! Those who were less thrilled by the prospect of everyday open-top motoring could install a removable hardtop.

Like any luxury automobile worthy of the name, Allanté carried a massive list of standard equipment and only one extra-cost option: a cellular telephone, already becoming a virtual necessity for the sort of client who might be most interested in the roadster from Detroit and Italy. In addition, all Allantés had a headlamp washer, illuminated entry, and theft-deterrent system.

Sadly for Cadillac, sales fell short of expectations. An early call for 6,000 to be built was quickly halved, and barely more than half that reduced number actually found buyers. The initial price of $54,700 may have been too much even for Cadillac fans (though in fact, many early models sold for thousands less than the sticker amount). Second-year sales rose to 3,065, despite a modest price hike.

Although the 4.1-liter V-8 had been deemed wholly adequate, customers seemed to want a bit more power. Cadillac responded for the 1990 model year by upgrading to a 4.5-liter version, which produces 200 horsepower rather than the original 170. Unfortunately, it also produced a federal gas guzzler tax of $650. Being realistic, though, a few hundred dollars' penalty is hardly likely to dissuade many customers, at least in this league.

Cadillac's Grettenberger explained that while nobody was overjoyed about the guzzler status (a "first" for Cadillac), Allanté's customers "wanted higher performance and quicker acceleration." Now they had it. Besides, the Allanté could now be advertised as offering the highest torque (270 pounds/feet) of any front-wheel-drive car in the world. Even the exhaust tone hit a new, pleasing note. The revised Allanté can accelerate to 60 miles an hour in 8.3 seconds and reach a top speed of 135 mph. Not exactly supercar figures, but respectable

Allanté is ready for any kind of weather, wearing either a removable hardtop (below) or a soft top (opposite page). In response to complaints of inadequate power, the original 4.1- liter V-8 grew to 4.5 liters for 1990.

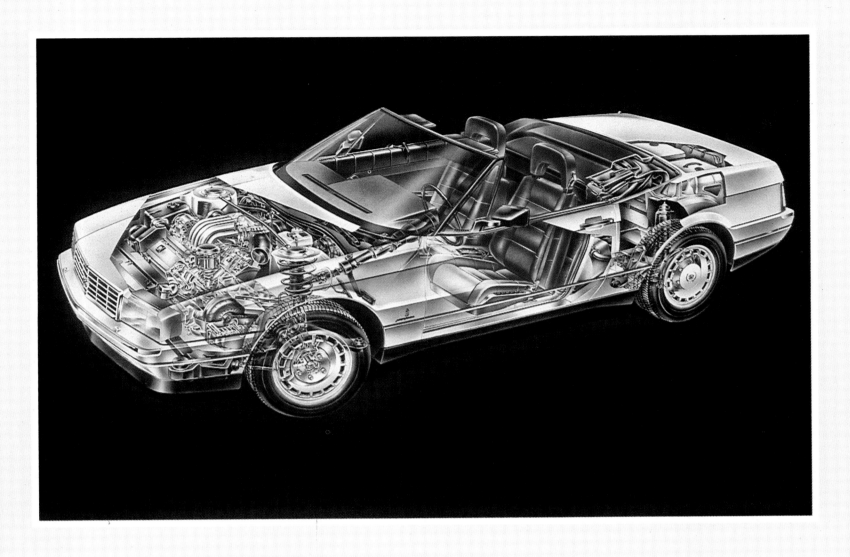

*Allanté in 1990 became the first front-drive
car in the U.S. offered with traction control.
It also got a driver's-side airbag and was
offered for the first time without the
removable hardtop.*

Allanté's graceful aerodynamic body is designed to allow both occupants to talk normally, even with the top down (opposite page), while rolling down the highway. Recaro leather seats (left) cradle the driver and passenger in firm comfort, ready to enjoy the roadster's tempting conveniences. Tri-Mode Damping in recent Allantés manages to mix sports-car feel with a traditional luxury ride. Traction control, another late addition, helps keep eager front-driven wheels from slipping.

CADILLAC ALLANTÉ

SPECIFICATIONS (1989)

Manufacturer:	Cadillac Motor Car, Detroit, MI; body by Industrie Pininfarina, Turin, Italy
Body design:	2-passenger, 2-door coupe; unitized steel construction
Powertrain layout:	front-engine, front-wheel drive
Wheelbase (in.):	99.4
Overall length (in.):	178.6
Overall width (in.):	73.5
Overall height (in.):	52.2
Track, front (in.):	60.4
Track, rear (in.):	60.4
Weight (lbs.):	3492
Approximate price:	$57,183
Engine type:	ohv V-8
Displacement (liters/cu. in.):	4.5/273
Horsepower @ rpm:	200 @ 4400
Torque (lbs./ft.) @ rpm:	270 @ 3200
Fuel delivery:	sequential multi-port fuel injection
Transmission:	4-speed overdrive automatic
Suspension, front:	MacPherson struts, coil springs
Suspension, rear:	fully independent, coil springs
Brakes:	front/rear discs, anti-lock

PERFORMANCE

Top speed (mph):	135
0-60 mph (seconds):	8.3
Quarter-mile (seconds):	16.6
mph @ quarter-mile:	83

enough for its target audience.

Handling got a boost, as well, with the Cadillac/Delco tri-mode Speed Dependent Damping system, designed to blend the soft ride of a luxury car with the firm, controlled road feel of a sports car. How can that be? Under 25 mph, the car is in comfort mode to produce a "boulevard" ride, familiar to Cadillac owners going way back. As the car speeds up, the suspension struts automatically adjust to a firmer setting. Over 55 mph, it's in sport mode. In addition, "dive control" shifts the struts into firmest (sport) mode as the brakes are applied. It also prevents the front end from listing during hard acceleration, remaining firm until the car is underway. Each "shift" occurs without delivering an abrupt shock to the car's occupants.

Adjustable suspension wasn't the only improvement. Traction control, a first for American production automobiles, is now standard on the Allanté. Also, new variable-ratio power steering gives the greatest boost at low speeds, when it's most needed, as well as a better "feel" of the road. Wheels and tires grew, too. P225/55VR16 Goodyear Eagle VL size tires now give the Allanté a stauncher stance. For Allanté to achieve performance-car status that rivals such roadsters as the Mercedes-Benz SL, extras of that sort are essential.

The pepped-up Allanté, then, delivers an even more tempting combination of European road manners and Cadillac creature comforts than the first edition. The company goes a step further, claiming that an Allanté "represents grace, power, and all things worth having." Well, maybe not *all* things; but this luxury roadster parked in your driveway might well be *one* of the things worth having in this life.

CADILLAC SOLITAIRE AND VOYAGE

Of all the automakers that exhibit concept cars at shows worldwide, few have a history approaching that of Cadillac. As far back as 1905, the tall and stubby experimental Osceola, designed by Cadillac founder Henry Leland, emerged to test the burgeoning company's ability to create a closed coupe. This at a time when all automobiles went topless. So Cadillac's history as an innovator can be traced to the marque's origins.

Late in the Eighties, the Cadillac tradition of displaying show cars that make one's eyes glaze over in awe and delight continued, this time with a pair of dramatic renditions of "21st century" motoring. First came the four-door Voyage, in time for the 1988 auto show circuit. A year later, Cadillac sent off a two-door Solitaire that retained many of the Voyage's mechanical and design elements, yet managed to convey a personality all its own. Both express ideas for the kind of car that might be required a decade or two from now, when superhighways allow unimpeded coast-to-coast travel at speeds in the 200 mile-per-hour realm.

Anyone stuck in rush-hour traffic or suffering reckless lane-changes on today's "superhighways" might be permitted a moment of scoffing at the thought of speeds far into the triple-digit range. Still, the era of controlled highway travel at velocities rivaling those of airplanes has been a science-fiction staple for decades, and only

now are dream cars beginning to make this fiction a reality. Should it become reality, Cadillac stands readier than most to provide suitable vehicles.

Raves greeted the Voyage's debut in January 1988 at the GM "Teamwork and Technology" show, held in New York's Waldorf Astoria hotel. Measuring two feet longer than a production Seville, the massive four-door "bullet style" Voyage carried a V-8 engine under its elongated hood—but had plenty of space available for the V-12 that would arrive later. Although identical in size to the 4.5-liter V-8 introduced on regular Cadillacs for 1988, the Voyage edition delivered nearly twice the horsepower, capable of cruising at an estimated 180 miles an hour.

As futuristic as the Voyage was, with aerodynamic lines that would have been unimaginable in years past, fans of Fifties cars could detect more than one design element in the Voyage skin that harked back to that era. The tightly-knit tapered-side grille, for one, could have been mounted on a Caddy of earlier vintage without creating a stir. The black exterior paint and the

sheer size of the Voyage majestically conveyed Cadillac's reputation for bulk and strength.

Matching (removable) front and rear fender skirts had never been seen on regulation Caddies, of course, but almost looked like they might have been. Taking advantage of today's technology, the front skirts were designed to move outward automatically when the car had to turn abruptly. They weren't stuck on just for show, but to help create an amazingly low drag coefficient (only 0.28) for such a large vehicle.

Voyage's upper greenhouse, from the base of the windshield all the way to the bottom of the tail lamps, was a single, continuous sheet of tinted glass—that's visibility! High-intensity tail lamps and turn signal indicators weren't plain old bulbs, but modern-day Light Emitting Diodes. Forming a continuous strip, the rear lamps were hidden under glass; only the rear-vision video camera was visible, sending views from the back to a screen in the driver's compartment. High-visibility automatic flashers replaced customary

A mere glance at the grille (above) of the twin 21st century Cadillacs brings back memories of Caddies past. Basic design and mechanicals differ little between the Solitaire 2-door (opposite page, top) and Voyage 4-door (bottom).

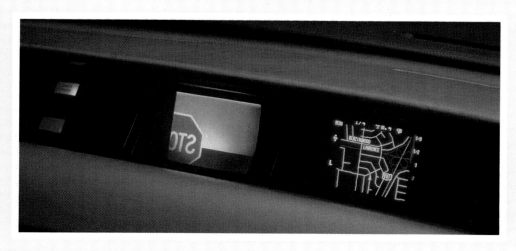

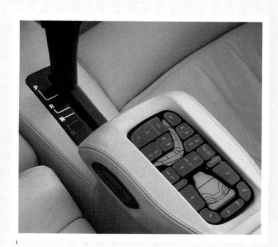

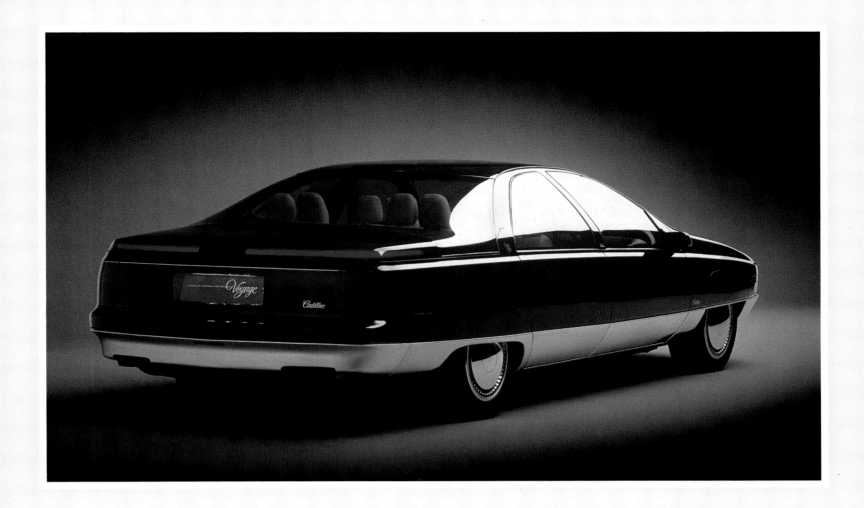

Cadillac's Voyage sedan (both pages) starred at auto shows in 1988. Removable fender skirts are part show, part aero, helping the bullet-shaped vehicle to slice through the wind. Although the dual headrests look ready to crush the front occupants' heads, the seats themselves offer a reassuring selection of more than 20 adjustments. Getting lost will be a phenomenon of the primitive past with the ETAK navigational system (far left), which shows where you are, where you're going, and how to get there.

reflectors, to be sure oncoming traffic would see the Voyage if it were parked at roadside during the night. After all, even a 200-mph electronically-controlled machine might break down now and then.

Windshield wipers are tucked away beneath a cover at the windshield base, rising on an elevator when needed. Both inside and outside mirrors were created to dim automatically to protect the driver from glare as bright lights approached.

Getting into the car required no keys or locks; only the knowledge of a code for the keyless entry system. Pick the right one and the doors would open, front windows slide down a couple of inches, and seat and steering column move aside to allow graceful entry. Back windows also tilted outward. Shut the door and the seat would shift into correct position for the driver who happened to be filling its cushion—having memorized three different settings. And if that position wasn't quite right, more than 20 pneumatic and mechanical adjustments allowed all the refinements anyone could possibly want. Mirrors adjusted themselves, too, for each driver who'd requested a setting.

Once inside, cold wintry mornings could quickly be forgotten as the pre-heated seats emitted their warmth to back and backside. And if that weren't enough, a little massage was available to get the blood going before the day got underway; or get rid of those

annoying "pins and needles" feelings during a long drive. Business calls could be handled without even touching the built-in phone, since it recognized the driver's voice and dialed numbers automatically.

Don't know where you're going? Not a problem. The ETAK navigation system would be ready to display your present location and destination within a map on a color video screen, even picking out the best route to follow.

Created under the direction of Vice President Charles M. Jordan, the Voyage is more than a mere styling exercise from the General Motors Design Staff. It was created as a working prototype that could hold four passengers. Cadillac chief John O. Grettenberger called it "a rolling laboratory designed to evaluate future Cadillac vehicle concepts." An electronic 4-speed transmission delivered power to all four wheels.

If a four-door concept car for the 21st century attracted so many enthusiastic gapers, why not a similarly stimulating two-door coupe? Thus arrived the Solitaire, which toured the 1989 show circuit. Both its electronic/mechanical features and form evolved from the prior Voyage. Shifting to a deep maroon color scheme helped disguise the fact that the grille, the front and rear movable skirts, and a host of other details were little more than carryovers.

An expansive dome of tinted, safety net

glass stretches from the Solitaire's windshield base to the rear passenger area, intended to provide not only superior visibility but the feeling of a convertible. The windshield darkens automatically as soon as the bright sun comes out, while the dome may be controlled by the driver to block out a portion of the sun's rays. That way, the interior can stay cooler on hot, sunny days, and use the sun's warmth to keep the interior warm on cold days.

Electrically-powered doors, some of the longest in GM's history, demanded the use of an articulated hinge. The Solitaire's doors move slightly forward as they open. The keyless entry system can also be used to release the hood or trunk lid. Seats travel all the way forward to permit easy entry into the back (unless they happen to be occupied, that is) then return to the pre-selected position as the door shuts; and while the Voyage had 20 seat adjustments, the Solitaire added four more. Some comfort-minded folks are never quite satisfied, it seems. Once again, both heat and massage are available to soothe chilled or tired muscles. Air bags mounted in the steering wheel, instrument panel, and rear seatbacks were installed for each occupant.

Mirrors disappeared completely, with only a set of video cameras providing a view of oncoming traffic from the back, seen on a liquid-crystal color video screen inside the car. Lack of stick-out mirrors makes a slight difference in aerodynamics, and a bigger improvement in the car's flush appearance. Body-colored louvers, front and rear, create the illusion that the car carries neither headlamps nor tail lamps.

Under the hood this time, replacing the Voyage's V-8, lurks a dual-overhead-cam, 48-valve V-12 engine with port fuel injection. Developed in conjunction with Lotus, the 6.6-liter powerplant produces 430

Success of the Voyage concept car led Cadillac to develop a 2-door version, the Solitaire (both pages), to tour the following season's auto shows. Surrounded by so much glass, riders could be excused for thinking they were in a convertible. As the sun emerges, though, the windshield darkens automatically. Cockpit (above) looks even more familiar and friendly when high-tech gadgetry is shut off. No old-fashioned mirrors need apply, either; video delivers the view from the rear. Cadillac developed Solitaire's 48-valve V-12 engine (center), prepared to whip out 430 horsepower, in conjunction with the Lotus company. Huge doors (left) ride on articulated hinges, moving forward a bit as they open for entry.

horsepower, along with 470 pounds/feet of torque. Computer-designed tires ride special 20-inch cast aluminum wheels.

Prepared to carry four passengers in unheard-of swiftness and ease, the Solitaire was called "Cadillac's vision of the ultimate in road-car performance, comfort, convenience and style." Like its predecessor, it was created to serve as a test vehicle, not just a showpiece. Whether highways capable of ultra-fast speeds—and humans capable of handling them—ever emerge is an open question, of course. But a look at either of Cadillac's visions evokes a hope that such a day will arrive soon, and that cars like these will be available for our enjoyment.

CADILLAC SOLITAIRE AND VOYAGE

SPECIFICATIONS

Manufacturer:	Cadillac Motor Car Division; Detroit, MI
Body design:	4-passenger, 2-door coupe (Solitaire) and 4-passenger, 4-door sedan (Voyage); metal body and frame
Powertrain layout:	front-engine, rear-wheel drive
Wheelbase (in.):	119.6
Overall length (in.):	214.2 (cpe), 212.6 (sdn)
Overall width (in.):	78.2 (cpe), 77.8 (sdn)
Overall height (in.):	54.3 (cpe), 53.4 (sdn)
Track, front (in.):	NA
Track, rear (in.):	NA
Weight (lbs.):	4100 (cpe), 3800 (sdn)
Approximate price:	NA
Engine type:	dohc V-12 (Solitaire), ohv V-8 (Voyage); V-12 developed by Cadillac and Lotus
Displacement (liters/cu. in.):	6.6/403 (cpe) 4.5/273 (sdn)
Horsepower:	430 (cpe), 275 (sdn)
Torque (lbs./ft.):	470 (cpe), 330 (sdn)
Fuel delivery:	port fuel injection
Transmission:	4-speed automatic (electronic shift)
Suspension, front:	independent MacPherson struts, coil springs
Suspension, rear:	independent; transverse fiberglass spring
Brakes:	front/rear discs, anti-lock

PERFORMANCE

Top speed (mph):	(est.) 180-200
0-60 mph (seconds):	NA
Quarter-mile (seconds):	NA
mph @ quarter-mile:	NA

If American highways ever develop to the point of permitting speeds past 180 miles an hour, designers in the coming century need look no further than Cadillac. Either Voyage or Solitaire could send tomorrow's travelers coast to coast in blissful comfort and sophisticated style. Air bags for each occupant would help to provide the level of safety that will be demanded. And who can imagine what other technical delights a real-life Cadillac might hold in the next century?

CHEVROLET CALIFORNIA IROC CAMARO

While most concept cars never reach real-life proportions, every once in a while, a concept car with real-life possibilities tours the auto-show circuit. Chevrolet's Concept IROC Camaro, built for the 1989 show audience, ranks as one of the most promising concept cars. During its debut at the Los Angeles Auto Show in January of that year, it attracted plenty of attention from Californians and visitors alike.

And why not? It's a curvaceously fluid vision of tomorrow, bound to excite both long-standing Camaro fans and people who have never experienced the rush of exhilaration a sporty 2+2 coupe can deliver.

Just a glance at the amount of glass reveals the car's California influence and the attempt to lure the eyes of western-state motorists, in particular. No surprise, then, that the design emerged from the General Motors Advanced Design Concept Center at Newbury Park, California. Center director John Schinella describes the Camaro's form as "smooth, rounded—yet aggressive" and ready to "take in the California sunshine." You have to look pretty hard to find any angles or sharp edges in the shapely profile, which rides a wheelbase some 3 inches longer than the current Camaro, though it's almost half a foot shorter from stem to stern.

Most striking of the design features—beyond the dramatically flamboyant glass, which wraps around most of the roof—is the aggressively pointy (if rounded) dip-down nose. Viewed in conjunction with the elongated headlight housings, the wide air intake slot above the integrated bumper makes Camaro's front end look like the grin of a hungry, yet patient, fish. The sloping hood swoops into a sharply raked windshield, creating a streamlined look that almost makes the attractive current Camaro seem stodgy by comparison.

Tall, rounded wheel wells surround the front and rear tires, while the inwardly-curved, lower bodysides ride close to the ground. Flush-mounted side glass and mirrors hovering at the end of elongated, integrated nacelles complete the startling aero appearance. Even though the side pillars aren't exactly tiny, they're barely noticed because of the fluidity of the Camaro's packaging.

Sunshine appears almost to radiate from the California Camaro's rakish physique (both pages). Created as a paean to West Coast lifestyles, the flamboyant design relies on glass and flowing curves to hint at the direction of near-future Camaro coupes. The gaping, fishlike grin formed by the air intake suggests the pleasure that awaits.

While the car displays a distinct forward rake, the back end isn't as tall as some—it doesn't look like it's about to dive head first into the ground. Slimly tapered tail lamps and a sliver of spoiler blend neatly into the rear flanks. The glass hatchback opens fully, all the way down to the bulky, integrated bumper, revealing a sizable luggage compartment.

The concept Camaro was given quasi-gull-wing doors that pull upward, and haul part of the glass roofline along with them. They also shift forward at a 45-degree angle, so you don't have to be a contortionist to slip into the driver or passenger seat. Seating is 2+2, just like today's Camaro; and more than likely is just as cramped in the back, though the 3-inch stretch in wheelbase should help some.

Once inside, you'll be facing a full set of analog instruments (and a digital speedometer) in a cockpit that feels more like that of an airplane than an automobile. In fact, the layout was inspired by Formula One racers. Just in case you forget where to sit, the swiveling driver's seat is red upholstery while the passengers rest on black. The red seat can even be custom-fitted to a single driver—which might cause a bit of discomfort and irritation when the spouse or youngsters take the car out for an evening. Maybe not, though, because the interior is designed to offer a precise relationship between arms, legs, steering wheel, and pedals—handling a broad variety of (human) body types and sizes. So maybe everybody will be relatively comfy.

That same precise relationship extends to the nearby, high-mounted gearshift lever, which travels from one ratio to the next with a mercifully short throw. No need to reach halfway across the front passenger to snick into top gear. Performance fans should love it.

Nobody likes to settle their designer jeans onto dusty upholstery, so Chevrolet has thoughtfully included a little vacuum cleaner in the console. Better wait until you're at a standstill, for safety's sake, before switching on the suction.

With both Camaro and IROC monikers

Glass and more glass, amid a ceaseless collection of curves. That's one way to describe the dramatic concept IROC Camaro that emerged from GM's California-based design center. Slipping into the tomorrow Camaro isn't as difficult as it looks, since the doors pull upward (left) and drag along a sizable chunk of adjoining glass. Inside, budding fighter pilots and LeMans racers should feel at ease—no surprise, since racing's Formula One circuit served as inspiration.

attached to the car, it's a sure bet that performance won't be ignored, though the folks at GM won't be ready for some time to name a specific powertrain for any production version. However, the prototype carries a dual over-head cam V-6. If a roadable version of the California Camaro were to appear, horsepower might run in the neighborhood of 250. All Camaros in the past have come with a choice of engines, so at least one smaller powerplant is sure to be offered. Not every customer demands the sensation of being rudely shoved back when tromping hard on the gas pedal. Hefty 17-inch tires (P235/50R17 at the prototype's rear) should handle the top end of the engine spectrum without flinching.

There's not much chance, either, that the future Camaro will give up its traditional rear-wheel drive. Anti-lock braking, evident in the show car, would likely appear on a production Camaro as well, since it's fast gaining popularity with motorists, and insurance companies alike, as a "must have" safety feature.

Following early directions from GM's design chief, Charles Jordan, a 50-person team handled the creative duties in California to make this "tomorrow" Camaro a potential reality. Amazingly, they went from a scale model to a full-size metal prototype in just six months. Yes, that's a metal body, not fiberglass or composite—quite a surprise for such a shapely form, created in so little time. Even if it had no other virtues, the car would demonstrate what can be accomplished using ordinary rather than exotic construction materials. Out of a half-dozen reduced-size, clay models, the California design team chose one body style and sent it to a California prototype builder to be turned into sheet metal.

Could this roundish, nearly roly-poly shape actually be the next F-body Camaro? A lot of experts, inside and outside of Chevrolet, think so. Or more likely, they believe that certain parts of the overall design could find themselves on the production Camaro of 1992 or '93. That could put an all-new Camaro for the Nineties onto the market just in time for the marque's 25th anniversary.

Few doubt that the California Camaro will, at the very least, influence the ultimate design, even if most of the individual elements disappear in the process—giving way to conventionality and practicality. Details such as the pointy nose, for instance, or the non-traditional doors, might fade away sometime during the race toward the marketplace. Nevertheless, neither the California nor the related Pontiac Banshee (also described in this book) are likely to be consigned to the dustbin when the time comes for a final rendering of tomorrow's 2+2 coupe.

A super-slim spoiler at the back (opposite page) displays the only razor edge on the California Camaro's body. Luggage for 2 travelers stows into a roomy cargo area, covered by a glass hatchback. A sizable helping of flush side glass and faired-in rear-view mirrors help to enhance the curvaceous Chevrolet coupe's fluid form, while the expanse of back glass delivers plenty of rearward visibility. Amenities inside go so far as a hand vacuum cleaner to tidy up the upholstery. Ever since their debut in 1967, production Camaros have ranked with the most sought-after cars of our time. If this California edition should ever turn to reality, customers just might be banging down the dealers' doors.

CHEVROLET CALIFORNIA IROC CAMARO

SPECIFICATIONS

Manufacturer:	Chevrolet Motor Division, Warren, MI and GM Advanced Design Concept Center, Newbury Park, CA
Body design:	2+2-passenger, 2-door coupe; steel body, steel frame
Powertrain layout:	front-engine, rear-wheel drive
Wheelbase (in.):	104.0
Overall length (in.):	186.4
Overall width (in.):	73.0
Overall height (in.):	48.8
Track, front (in.):	60.5
Track, rear (in.):	60.5
Weight (lbs.):	NA
Approximate price:	NA
Engine type:	dohc V-6 (24-valve)
Displacement (liters/cu. in.):	NA
Horsepower @ rpm:	NA
Torque (lbs./ft.) @ rpm:	NA
Fuel delivery:	NA
Transmission:	5-speed manual
Suspension, front:	MacPherson struts
Suspension, rear:	independent
Brakes:	front/rear discs

PERFORMANCE

Top speed (mph):	NA
0-60 mph (seconds):	NA
Quarter-mile (seconds):	NA
mph @ quarter-mile:	NA

Charles Jordan, General Motors' design chief, started the California Camaro project rolling. Then, a 50-person team took over the styling and development duties, sending the idea from scale model to a full-size metal prototype in six months. In development terms, that's equivalent to zooming up to 60 mph in 4 or 5 seconds. Could this rounded rogue with the pointy snout metamorphose into the next real-life Camaro? Even if the car itself fades into memory, its forward-leaping front end is likely to find itself leading the next-generation Camaro.

CHEVROLET CORVETTE STING RAY

Who can forget the 1963-67 Sting Ray? Certainly not the army of enthusiasts who regard it as the most desirable Corvette ever built. It was, of course, very desirable when new: the first real revolution in the Corvette's 10-year evolution, a styling showpiece and an engineering masterpiece.

It originated in late 1959 with the XP-720 program that drew from at least three earlier experimental projects. The first was the so-called "Q-Corvette," begun in 1957 as a smaller, more radical sports car sharing a rear transaxle, independent rear suspension, and all-disc brakes with a line of large, rear-engine sedans that General Motors was planning for 1960. Only a fastback coupe was contemplated, and its styling was amazingly predictive of the future Sting Ray's.

The entire Q-program was soon shelved as too complicated and costly, but Corvette engineers led by Zora Arkus-Duntov continued to toy with rear-engine designs even as Chevy introduced one in its first compact, the new-for-'60 Corvair. The advent of that car, plus Duntov's work with the experimental open-wheel CERV I single-seater, prompted a rear-engine Corvette proposal designed around the Corvair's air-cooled, flat-six power package. Again, however, GM managers just couldn't see the expense.

Meanwhile, GM design chief William

L. Mitchell had spirited away the development "mule" from the abortive Sebring Super Sport project, the long-distance racing Corvette consigned to the corporate attic after the Automobile Manufacturers Association's 1957 "anti-racing" edict. Mitchell decided to refurbish the car and campaign it on his own. Assistant Larry Shinoda adapted Q-Corvette lines to create a new open body for what Mitchell called the Stingray Special, built in his secret "Studio X" area at the GM Tech Center in Warren, Michigan. Dr. Dick Thompson, one of the winningest Corvette pilots in Sports Car Club of America (SCCA) competition, was signed to drive it in C-Modified events, then dominated by prestigious European machines. "The flying dentist" promptly ran away with the class championship in 1959 and '60.

The Stingray Special never raced as a Corvette, but it had a show-car look about it and its styling was a big hit with the public. As a result, the car figured heavily in planning for the XP-720 project, which sought to deliver a new road-going Corvette with more passenger and luggage room, better ride and handling, and even higher performance. The result was quite unlike any other car of the day. Apart from four wheels and two seats, the only things the 1963 Corvette shared with the '62 edition were steering, front suspension, a quartet of

A symphony in fiberglass, as fresh today as it was back in 1963, Sting Ray was the first all-new Corvette since the original '53 model. The best-handling and fastest, too—especially when powered by a big-block V-8. Not since the 1942 DeSoto had an American car hidden its headlamps.

327 V-8s, and fiberglass bodywork. Most everything else was changed, and definitely for the better.

The revisions began with a slight reduction in overall length and a wheelbase pared four inches from that of previous Corvettes (to 98 inches). Curb weight was pared too, thanks to a new ladder-type frame (replacing a heavy old X-member affair) and despite a new steel-reinforced cage that made for a stronger, safer cockpit. Though brakes remained 11-inch-diameter drums, they were self-adjusting now and the fronts were wider.

But the big news was independent rear suspension, a first for a modern U.S. production car. Conceived by Corvette chief engineer Zora Arkus-Duntov, it comprised a frame-mounted differential with U-jointed half-shafts acting on a single transverse leaf spring; differential-mounted control arms extended laterally and slightly forward to the hub carriers to limit fore/aft movement, and a pair of trailing radius rods were fitted behind. The suspension was elegantly simple and highly effective.

As for the Sting Ray's styling, it still turns heads nearly 30 years later, so you can imagine its tremendous impact in long-ago 1963. Besides hidden headlamps (the first U.S. car so equipped since the 1942 DeSoto), the traditional Corvette convertible gained a dramatic fastback coupe companion, inspired by Q-Corvette work. The latter's vertically split rear window proved quite controversial. Duntov lobbied against it, saying it hampered outward vision, but Mitchell huffed that "if you take that off you might as well forget the whole thing." Duntov ultimately won, leaving the split-window coupe a one-year-only model—and the most prized Sting Ray because of it.

Inside, the Sting Ray introduced a new interpretation of the "twin-cowl" Corvette dash motif used since 1958. Not everyone liked it, but one designer defended it as "a very fresh approach to two-passenger styling." It was certainly more practical, with such first-time Corvette features as a roomy glovebox with a proper door, cowl-ventilation system, and a full set of easily read round gauges, including a huge

speedometer and tachometer, all dead ahead of the driver. Corvette's "control tower" center console was slimmer, but still mounted a clock and an unusual new vertically situated radio with suitably oriented dial. Cost considerations precluded an opening trunk lid on both body styles, which was somewhat less than practical. Cargo had to be wedged in behind the seats, and if the convertible's top was down, you also had to disconnect that from its flip-up cover to gain access.

But such problems seemed trivial, because the Sting Ray was the fastest and most roadable Corvette ever. Not surprisingly, it quickly became the most popular, too: 1963 production was nearly twice the record '62 total. Performance had less to do with this than the wider appeal stemming from more available creature comforts. For the first time, you could order a 'Vette with leather upholstery, power steering and brakes, AM/FM radio, even air conditioning. Even more than its precedessors, the Sting Ray could be a posh *gran turismo*, all-out screamer, or both.

The Sting Ray evolved over the next four years through progressively cleaner styling, more power, and greater mechanical sophistication. Appearance was tidied up by either removing what little nonsense there was or making it functional (as with the dummy front-fender vents after 1964). The top fuel-injected version of the 327 V-8 went from 360 to 375 horsepower for 1964, while '65 brought optional 4-wheel disc brakes (for stopping power to match steadily escalating performance) and Corvette's first big-block V-8, the 425-bhp 396-cid "Mark IV." The next year saw a bored-out 427 big-block that one magazine reported could do 0-60 mph in just 4.8 seconds and fly to 140 mph—not bad for a civilized, fully equipped machine selling at around $5,000.

Corvette set new sales records in all but one of the Sting Ray years, peaking in 1966 at nearly 28,000. Horsepower seemed to set yearly records too. That peak came with 1967's stupendous L88, an aluminum-head 427 with 12.5:1 compression, wild cam, and big four-barrel carb, rated at no less than 560 bhp. Only 20 cars were so equipped (of

which three are known to survive today), but they symbolized how potent and capable this Corvette was.

Of course, many of these high-power Sting Rays went racing, though they often bowed to Carroll Shelby's stark, super-quick Cobras. Still, there were bright spots. Don Yenko took his Sting Ray to the SCCA national B-Production champ in 1963, a Roger Penske car won its class at Nassau '65, and 1966 saw Sting Rays finish 12th in the Daytona Continental and 9th at Sebring.

Aside from year-old engines for 1963, the Sting Ray stands as the only all-new Corvette between the original 1953 Motorama show car and today's sixth-generation 1984 design. Testifying to the genius and foresight of its designers, especially Duntov's, the basic Sting Ray would endure with only minor changes up through the final 1982 "shark" model.

But in the hearts of car lovers everywhere, the Sting Ray itself will always endure. It was—and is—very special, the kind of dream-come-true that happens only once in a lifetime.

Not one, but two Corvettes made up the Sting Ray series as a fastback coupe (both pages) joined the traditional convertible.

Because the controversial split back window lasted only one season, the solid-top '63 turned into the most prized Sting Ray of them all. In addition to performance and handling boosts, the reworked Corvette boasted a new load of available equipment, including leather upholstery, power steering and brakes, an AM/FM radio, and air conditioning. As in Corvettes generally, stuffing more than a briefcase into the tiny cargo area behind the seats demands some ingenuity.

Fans took to the new Corvette design in droves, revealed by first-year sales that doubled the 1962 figure. Underneath both open and closed bodies, a ladder frame replaced the heavy old X-member design. Sting Rays also carried the first independent rear suspension in a modern American production car. All the big-block editions enjoy strong collector demand, but most fans would swoon if they had a chance to take one home with the 560-horsepower version of the 427-cid V-8.

CHEVROLET CORVETTE STING RAY

SPECIFICATIONS

Manufacturer:	Chevrolet Motor Division, General Motors Corporation St. Louis, MO
Body design:	2-passenger, 2-door convertible and fastback coupe; fiberglass outer body with steel inner skeleton over separate steel chassis
Powertrain layout:	longitudinal front engine, rear-wheel drive
Wheelbase (in.):	98.0
Overall length (in.):	175.3
Overall width (in.):	69.6
Overall height (in.):	49.8
Track, front (in.):	56.8
Track, rear (in.):	57.6
Weight (lbs):	2860-3130
Approximate price:	$4037-$4353
Engine type:	ohv V-8
Displacement (liters/cu. in.):	5.4/327 6.5/396 (1965 only) 7.0/427 (1966-67)
Horsepower @ rpm:	250-375 @ 4400-6200 (327) 425 @ 6400 (396) 390-560 @ 5000-6400 (427)

NOTE: original base list prices.

Torque (lbs./ft.) @ rpm:	344-360 @ 2800-4000 (327) 415 @ 4000 (396) 460 @ 3600-4000 (427)
Fuel delivery:	1-4 bl. carburetor; 3 × 2 bl. carburetor 1967 427; port fuel injection 1963-65 327
Transmissions:	3-speed manual; optional close- and wide-ratio 4-speed manuals, 2-speed Powerglide automatic
Suspension, front:	unequal-length upper and lower A-arms, coil springs, tubular hydraulic shock absorbers, anti-roll bar
Suspension, rear:	independent; frame-mounted differential, halfshafts as upper control arms, upper and lower lateral arms, radius rods, transverse leaf spring, tubular hydraulic shock absorbers (anti-roll bar with 396/427 engines)
Brakes:	front/rear cast-iron drums; front/rear discs optional 1965-67

PERFORMANCE

Top speed (mph):	105-150
0-60 mph (seconds):	5.4-8.0
Quarter-mile (seconds):	13.4-16.0
mph @ quarter-mile:	85-105

CHEVROLET CORVETTE INDY

Some concept vehicles are strictly for show; others one day are meant to go. The Corvette Indy is one that combines both duties. If the eagerly-awaited ZR-1 option is meant to be the ultimate street 'Vette, the mid-engine Indy stretches toward the boundaries of not only all previous Corvettes, but the sports car world. If this is the future, most 'Vette fans are sure to want to grab a sizable handful of it.

What's the first thing you're likely to notice about the Indy? Its stunning shape. Though it debuted at the Detroit Auto Show in 1986, it resembles the California Camaro (also described in this book) that hit the auto exhibitions three years later. The next thing you might notice is that this 'Vette looks a lot more like something belonging on a race track than an "ordinary" Corvette. Not exactly a surprise, considering the "Indy" part of the car's name.

Not that the Indy is a simple lead-in to the later Camaro. It's far from that. This is a mid-engine design, suggesting the cream of the exoticar crop. A longing look at that far-forward cockpit in the ultra-low body (43 in.) will immediately set a Corvette

enthusiast's eyes aglow. The forward slope of the front hood is so steep that the car appears to be ready to leap into a foxhole; while the protruding back end has an almost fin-like profile.

Displaying a huge amount of glass, the windshield and backlight are so steeply angled that they appear almost horizontal. A super-wide air intake up front looks like a gigantic, barely-open mouth with only a pair of teeth remaining. Toss in those exquisitely slanted and tapered headlamps, massive bodyside airscoops, and the huge glass dome that serves as cockpit, and who could resist a chance to climb behind the wheel for a future-world spin? A few lucky folks have done exactly that, and they report the Indy belongs right up in the automotive stratosphere, along with the likes of the fabled Porsche 959.

Good concept cars never seem to be composed of the right materials to make it to production levels of completion. Therefore, the Indy soon evolved from strictly a concept car to a full-scale running prototype. Phase Three, rumored to have begun, was to be a preproduction

Sheer poetry in swift motion—that's a mid-engine Corvette Indy roaring 'round the bend (left). The tip-top of Indy's expansive glass greenhouse (above) stands only 42 inches tall. Since the scissor-style doors pivot up and forward, it's not essential to be a contortionist to slip inside.

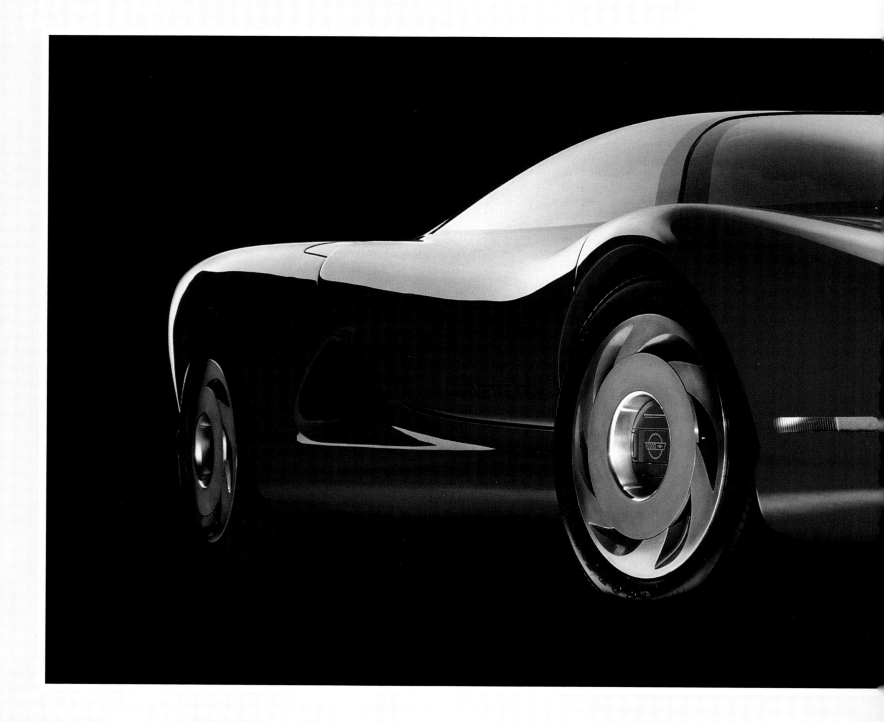

version—maybe the forerunner to a future 'Vette. So in addition to original duties as a show car, the Indy was created as a test bed to evaluate advanced technical systems. Chief engineer Fred Schaafsma called it a "work-in-progress vehicle." The 'Vette, while not only looking good at speed, appears to be a test mule for new Corvette technology.

The mid-engine layout was nothing new to Corvette engineers. Studies had begun as far back as 1959, with the single-seat CERV 1 (Chevrolet Engineering Research Vehicle), which eventually ran at speeds up to 200 mph. After that, the CERV 2 became the world's first mid-engine car with full-time four-wheel drive.

By the 1980s, Chevrolet was studying the technical developments of competitive exoticar manufacturers, such as the active suspension concept developed by Lotus.

Corvette head engineer Dave McLellan noted that the Indy was actually the result of a number of separate projects, including the desire to build a dramatic showcase for the Ilmor racing engine. Not to mention the fact that Chevrolet, like all automakers, could always stand one more image-booster to attract show audiences. Originally, it was a quickie project, directed by Jack Schwartz, which took just six weeks from the clay model stage to a complete (but inoperative) show car.

While the first Indy was strictly for show, two additional prototypes were to be fully roadworthy. One was meant for publicity purposes, the other for engineering research. Since it wouldn't be going anywhere, the show car carried the twin-turbo Ilmor engine mounted transversely behind the single seat. This motor was rated at a whopping 600 horsepower.

Technical features ran the gamut from soon-to-be-reality to sci-fi staples. Two of the Indy's features, anti-lock brakes and four-wheel steering, are now in production cars. Also, the car had a hydraulic active suspension, developed jointly with Lotus, which was controlled by microprocessor (like dozens of under-hood systems today). It needed no conventional springs, shock absorbers, or stabilizer bars. Indy's Kevlar monocoque chassis is also used in some top racing cars.

A relationship to real-world Corvettes is most evident in the Indy's pointed snout, with its barren slit of air intake. Teardrop headlamps never made it onto production models. Frightful air intakes look eager to gobble up pedestrians—or rival autos.

*Massive bodyside airscoops (above) and an
ever-so-gently swooping beltline help to deliver
the impression of never-ending length. So does the
Indy's stretched-out back end and the far-reaching,
bubble-like windshield and rear glass (right). Body
and chassis materials have race-car origins.*

Dave McLellan had some ideas that went a lot further, such as computer monitoring and control of the relationship between tire and road. A "drive-by-wire" system, similar to those used by fighter planes, would adjust the throttle electronically instead of by linkages and hydraulics, using a sensor to monitor the gas-pedal position. Also planned was a Cathode Ray Tube (CRT) information display on the dashboard, as well as the navigational system. A digitized map display could be programmed to show the car's current position, as well its destination. Electronic traction control would prevent wheel spin, responding to sensors that determined when one wheel was turning faster than the others.

The operative Indy, which emerged after the show car made its rounds, put some (though not all) of the technical ideas into practice. Hydraulic suspension, for one, which responds almost instantly to alter compliance in response to varying road and driving conditions. Also included were CRT displays. One atop the instrument panel displayed what was "seen" by the rear-view video camera that replaced mirrors. A driver's message screen showed operating data. An Etak navigation system was available for use, even if the satellite to provide the necessary signals wasn't yet ready to deliver.

Still under development were the drive-by-wire system, traction control, and four-wheel steering. But provision was made for retrofitting for all of these high-tech extras at a later date.

Indy's body was made of carbon fiber/Nomex composite, with a carbon fiber torque tube "backbone." Scissors-style doors, like those on the Lamborghini Countach, pivoted up and forward to allow drivers to enter without too much strain.

Under the ready-to-roll Indy's engine cover was an experimental all-aluminum 5.7-liter (350 cid) V-8 with 32 valves, code named 350/32, not dissimilar to what would later power the ZR-1. Since Lotus had been involved with the development of both, that's not exactly a surprise. The engine had double overhead camshafts, sequential fuel injection, and 16 exposed intake runners. Driving all four wheels was a modified 1974–85 Oldsmobile Toronado automatic transaxle.

Hitting the ground were 275/40ZR17 tires up front, and 315/35ZR17 in the rear. Seldom are you likely to see tires with a designation that starts with the number "3." That's *big*. In fact, each one looked more like a pair of tires side-by-side than a single gripper. Their wheels measured a full foot wide, machined from a chunk of solid aluminum. Ready to run, this Corvette was expected to manage a top speed of 180 miles an hour and reach 60

mph in less than 5 seconds.

If wishes were pennies, we'd take a jar-full and ask for a drive in this all-out example of Corvette capabilities—and then wish that the Bowling Green, Kentucky, plant would produce the real thing for real drivers. Since each prototype took a good half-million dollars to develop, that might be asking too much; but at least we can dream. Chevrolet called the car a "running vision of the future." As that future becomes reality for the Corvette, this Indy concept car gives us a glimpse of dreams to come.

CHEVROLET CORVETTE INDY

SPECIFICATIONS

Manufacturer:	Chevrolet Division, General Motors, Warren, MI
Body design:	2-passenger, 2-door coupe; plastic/carbon fiber/Nomex panels bonded to carbon fiber tub
Powertrain layout:	mid-engine, 4-wheel drive
Wheelbase (in.):	98.2
Overall length (in.):	189.0
Overall width (in.):	(est.) 79.0
Overall height (in.):	42.9
Track, front (in.):	63.9
Track, rear (in.):	66.1
Weight (lbs.):	3300
Approximate price:	(est.) $500,000
Engine type:	dohc V-8 (32-valve)
Displacement (liters/cu. in.):	5.7/350
Horsepower @ rpm:	380 @ 6000
Torque (lbs./ft.) @ rpm:	370 @ 3800
Fuel delivery:	port fuel injection
Transmission:	3-speed automatic
Suspension, front:	independent; unequal-length control arms, transverse-mounted (indirect active)
Suspension, rear:	independent; unequal-length control arms, transverse-mounted (indirect active)
Brakes:	front/rear vented discs, anti-lock

PERFORMANCE

Top speed (mph):	180+
0-60 mph (seconds):	under 5.0
Quarter-mile (seconds):	NA
mph @ quarter-mile:	NA

CHEVROLET
CORVETTE ZR-1

Few cars become legendary, and fewer yet become legends in their own time. Chevrolet's ZR-1 Corvette goes a step further, having become legendary long before anyone other than a handful of journalists sat behind the wheel.

What more can anyone ask than to have the "ultimate" of anything? That's how the ZR-1 Corvette has been described, and it's precisely what fans expected. If a plain old Corvette is superior to almost any sports car on the road, the ZR-1 can only be called *superlative*, offering more of everything that the 'Vette has been known for since it first emerged in 1953. Dave McLellan, Corvette's chief engineer, calls its all-new engine the "ultimate technological capability statement." During its public debut, former Chevrolet general manager Robert Burger described the ZR-1 as an "automotive work of art."

Casual observers probably won't notice anything unusual. At a glance, the ZR-1 looks pretty much like a standard-issue Corvette: sleek and low, like a cat waiting to strike, but no more radical than the thousands of two-seaters that have poured out of the Bowling Green, Kentucky, factory.

Enthusiasts spot those telltale square recessed taillights in an instant, along with the convex panel in which they sit. That's

the single most noticeable aesthetic difference between a ZR-1 and a standard 'Vette, which has for years displayed round taillights in a concave back panel. Farther down, a pair of rectangular exhaust outlets complement the tail lamp shape. A sure sign that there is more under the hood than just the standard 245 h.p. engine.

Viewing from the rear, the discerning eye notes the massive 315/35ZR17 Eagle Gatorback tires, over a foot wide, and the enlarged flares that had to be worked into the fenders to accommodate that much rubber. Only Ferrari's F40 supercar wears bigger road-grabbers. Measured at the rear wheels, the ZR-1 is 3 inches wider than other Corvettes. That change demanded new doors, rocker panels, rear fascia and upper panel; but it's the extra width, forming a graceful bulge, that catches the eye.

Those changes in form weren't what tempted the car's fans to reach for their checkbooks, of course. What caused their eyes to glaze over most were the early reports of the ZR-1's performance, and its brand-new powerplant. A reasonable person might presume that an ordinary Corvette traveled quickly enough to suit any logical purpose. Still, rumors of 180-mph top speed and acceleration to 60 miles an hour in about 4 seconds brought beads of perspiration to the brows of eager people who, in reality, spend most of their driving lives stuck in traffic. These enthusiasts even debated at length whether the new 'Vette would be able to travel 170 or 180 miles an hour; or if its new V-8 could deliver 370, 375, or 380 horsepower.

Early tests backed up the claims, producing 0-60 times around 4.3 seconds. A production ZR-1 will be able to zoom

Not so easy to tell from the front, but this is not your ordinary Corvette. Instead, it's the eagerly-awaited ZR-1 (both pages). Performance, not prettiness, was Chevrolet's Number One priority. With 380 horsepower, the fully-charged coupe needs little more than 4 seconds to hit 60 miles an hour.

up to a hundred and brake down to a halt in less time than a regular Corvette needs to reach 97 miles an hour. That kind of performance, says Dave McLellan, is "as fast as any manufactured car in the world."

Developed in conjunction with Lotus, the new LT-5 engine has almost nothing in common with the standard (L-98) V-8, even though their displacements are virtually identical. The all-aluminum design even has different bore and stroke measurements, along with unique four-valve-per-cylinder heads. Sixteen intake runners send in the air/fuel mixture to the eight cylinders. A primary and secondary intake port feeds each cylinder, controlled by a tri-valve throttle body. Electronics determines the fuel path, so power arrives in levels: just a little (through the primaries only) when the demand is slight, up to full-bore when requested by a foot all the way down to the firewall.

Since the early 1980s, Corvette people had been searching for an engine that could deliver a higher threshold of performance than the ordinary small-blocks of Corvettes past. They considered a turbo V-6, a twin-turbo V-8, and even a 600-horsepower non-turbo V-8, rejecting each on the grounds of excess noise and vibration, or overall inefficiency. What they needed was an engine that would be quiet, docile, smooth, economical, and undemanding— but able to change personalities in an instant, whipping out speed and response comparable to that of a race car. No less than prior 'Vettes, the ZR-1 had to be a car as much at home in rush-hour traffic as out on the open road.

After talking with various companies about possibilities, representatives of Chevrolet and Group Lotus met in the spring of 1985 (around the time GM purchased Lotus) to discuss the prospect of a four-valve-per-cylinder head for the existing V-8. This led Lotus's Managing Director Tony Rudd to suggest an all-new engine. A team was formed by 1986, and the design went from a concept to a running prototype in less than two years.

However, the Lotus-designed engine isn't built by an automobile company at all, but by Mercury Marine, at its Stillwater, Oklahoma, plant. Mercury was chosen largely for its reputation with precision

Mercury Marine, widely known for boat powerplants, took on the assignment of producing the all-new aluminum LT-5 engine (above), designed jointly with the Lotus firm in Britain. Though their displacements happen to be identical, the 32-valve ZR-1 engine, topped by 16 graceful intake runners, has little else in common with the standard V-8.

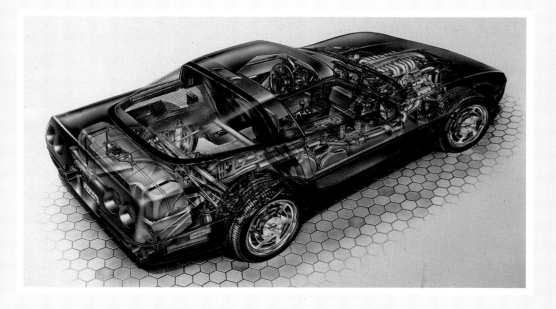

aluminum casting and machining. The block and crankcase are cast in Texas, with nearly all assembly done by hand. Click-type torque wrenches are even used for the final tightening of fasteners. This finally gives the Corvette that hand-built, exotic car reputation that it could never before offer.

Impressive as the new V-8 is, the standard 6-speed manual gearbox, which actually debuted as an option for regular 1989 Corvettes, is no less innovative. It replaces the aging Doug Nash 4+3 speed O.D. transmission that was chunky and difficult to use. The two extra gear ratios are only part of its appeal. To meet governmental gas-mileage requirements, Chevrolet took a bold approach, using what's described as a 1-4 "computer-aided shift schedule." In light-footed driving, the transmission skips second and third gear. Aim the lever from first toward second, and it locks out second gear and helps the driver shift directly into fourth. That's the economy mode. Tromp on the gas from the start, though, and each ratio plays its regular role. Cruising in sixth at legal highway speeds, with its leisurely 0.5:1 overdrive ratio, also boosts the gas-mileage potential.

Also new for '90 will be an upgraded interior that will include a new dashboard, new door panels, and new center console. The instrument panel will include analog displays as well revamped digital displays. Also included in the interior is a driver's-side air bag. This new interior along with the already sound Corvette body should go a long way in quieting squeaks and rattles that plagued previous 'Vettes.

Introduction of the ZR-1 wasn't so easy, following its public unveiling at Detroit's auto show in January 1989. Everybody seemed to want one, and quite a few fans were more than willing to pay the then-estimated $50,000 price. As it happened, ZR-1s didn't get to the dealers at all during the 1989 model year, even though 17 of them went to the Geneva Motor Show in Switzerland. After much deliberation and a host of rumors, the introduction was delayed until the 1990 model year.

Most surprising is the fact that the ZR-1 isn't a separate model at all, but an option

Aficionados require only a glance at the back end (above) to tell a ZR-1 from a plain old Corvette. Quartet of recessed rectangular taillamps in a gracefully bulging convex back panel, contrary to the usual round lamps, are a dead giveaway. Revised before the ZR-1's tardy debut, the dashboard (left) places analog gauges and digital speedometer on a field of black.

package. That package includes the LT-5 engine, 6-speed gearbox, a Z51 Performance Handling package, and new FX3 Delco-Bilstein Selective Ride Control that offers a console-selected choice of Touring, Sport, or Competition suspension settings. No choice at high speeds, though: The ZR-1 slips into firmer mode on its own as velocities zoom upward.

Other standard features include low air-pressure warning, signaled by a sensor and transmitter inside each tire. Also to help ease worry when turning over the truly exotic ZR-1 to a parking-lot attendant, or to the over-eager teenager at home, a "valet" key limits horsepower to about 200. Not that such a limit prevents abuse; a ZR-1 isn't exactly a slouch even when held back electronically.

Ranking in performance right up in the stratosphere with the likes of the costly Countach and Testarossa, and approaching the extremes of the yet-to-be-seen (in the U.S.) Ferrari F40 and Porsche 959

supercars, the ZR-1 is far more attainable. Also far less finicky, behaving like a down-to-business, real-world car rather than a petulant prima donna. Corvette has always offered world-class performance at a middle-class price, and ZR-1 is no exception. While the announced price of $58,995 is no pittance, an F40 or 959 could cost nearly five times that much—if you could get one at all, with total production barely into the hundreds.

About 3,000 lucky Corvette fans, on the other hand, will be able to get their hands on a ZR-1 during its first year. Even that limit isn't solely a matter of Chevrolet's choosing to hold production down, to keep demand high. Mercury Marine's inability to produce more than 4,000 engines a year, and the fact that Mercury Marine wants to adapt some of those for marine use is the limiting factor for production. For the rest of us, it's a pleasure just to know that such a supercar can emerge from Kentucky as well as from Italy or Germany.

CHEVROLET CORVETTE ZR-1
SPECIFICATIONS

Manufacturer:	Chevrolet Division, General Motors, Warren, MI
Body design:	2-passenger, 2-door coupe; fiberglass-reinforced plastic body, steel frame
Powertrain layout:	front-engine, rear-wheel drive
Wheelbase (in.):	96.2
Overall length (in.):	177.4
Overall width (in.):	74.0
Overall height (in.):	46.7
Track, front (in.):	59.6
Track, rear (in.):	61.9
Weight (lbs.):	3465
Approximate price:	$58,995
Engine Type:	dohc V-8 (32-valve); built by Mercury Marine, Stillwater, OK
Displacement (liters/cu. in.):	5.7/350
Horsepower @ rpm:	380 @ 6200
Torque (lbs./ft.) @ rpm:	370 @ 4500
Fuel delivery:	twin-port fuel injection
Transmission:	6-speed manual
Suspension, front:	independent; short/long arms, transverse monoleaf spring
Suspension, rear:	independent; 5-link transverse monoleaf spring
Brakes:	front/rear discs, anti-lock

PERFORMANCE

Top speed (mph):	180+
0-60 mph (seconds):	4.3
Quarter-mile (seconds):	13.3
mph @ quarter-mile:	110

Fender flares had to be modified to encircle the ZR-1's huge 17-inch Eagle Gatorback tires, which measure more than a foot across. The wider body also demanded a selection of new body parts, from doors to rocker panels. Corvette fans grew edgy as the ultimate two-seater was announced, then delayed—and finally turned into reality for the 1990 model year. Few automobiles have gained such legendary status and appeal as the ZR-1, even before hitting the market. But then, that's precisely what the ultimate of anything is supposed to do.

CHRYSLER'S TC
by MASERATI

Patience isn't always rewarded. When the Chrysler/Maserati joint-venture, two-seater luxury coupe was first announced in 1986, scheduled to appear as a 1987 model, both dreamers and cash-in-hand customers responded to its smooth, refined shape. A second announcement the next year still brought shivers of delight from those who envisioned themselves softly positioned in the driver's seat.

By the third pronouncement, even the TC's staunchest advocates were beginning to wonder if this dream car would ever make the transition to real life. The staff at *Automotive News*, a trade paper, even branded it "flop of the year" in late 1988. But sure enough, by early 1989 the first convertible/hardtop coupes slipped off the boat, ready for delivery into the hands of their California customers. A few months later, the rest of the country could also get its collective hands on one. The TC (which stands for Touring Convertible) had, at long last, arrived. Similar to the Cadillac Allanté, Chrysler's TC by Maserati is a joint venture between Detroit and Italy.

Was the long wait worth it? Chrysler's first luxury two-seater drew a few early razzes along with its raves, but much of the criticism seemed to result more from the business-related side of the equation than from the car's personal qualities. Unlike designer jeans that offer a well-known name tag but few other distinctive features, the TC is more than just a simple blend of Italian coachwork and American technology.

From a distance, in particular, it's picture perfect: neither dramatic nor futuristic, but a tasteful display of Italian style that suggests a little of yesterday as well as some of tomorrow. The "Coke bottle" shape, while far from new, is quite a bit more

evident in the TC than in most examples. The lower bodyside curves inward sharply, forming what Chrysler describes as "rakish sills." That they are. Body-color door handles and mirrors add to the smooth, flowing side view. So do the attractive, spoke-like cast aluminum wheels. Up front, a black-and-bright Maserati-style grille wears the familiar Chrysler insignia. In case anyone is unsure of the car's pedigree, the trunk labeling makes it clear: "Chrysler's TC by Maserati."

A "Chryslerati" (as it has become to be known) is the perfect choice for those who don't want to spend a lot of time deciding on options and accessories. Buy a TC and all you get to choose are the body color and

Mixing the romance of Italian styling with the reliability of American engineering has produced many a memorable vehicle. Chrysler's tasteful TC (both pages) pursues that tradition. A dash of the past, just a hint of the future. Result: ecstasy for two, today.

engine type. Even the transmission choice is decided for you: A TorqueFlite automatic comes with the Chrysler-built engine, a 5-speed manual with the 16-valve Chrysler based, Maserati powerplant. No extras, no add-ons; the single base price buys the whole package.

Inside is where this Italian/American really shines. Hand-crafted leather is formed into twin bucket seats that look so soft and comfy that they practically invite you inside. They feel (and smell) just about as pleasant, too. Leather also covers the instrument panel and door trim panels, as well as the center armrest. Lustrous wood

frames the window/mirror controls on the door panel and tops the gearshift lever. The driver's hands grip a natural wood steering wheel—in traditional Maserati style. Dashes of interior plastic showed up on some early versions, but have been banished for the sake of maintaining the TC's luxuriant aura.

Carpets display the Maserati trident insignia. A ten-speaker Infinity II stereo system stands ready to entertain you, though it's a wonder how they found spots for that many speakers in a two-seater. Traditional round analog gauges rest in a hooded pod on the wraparound instrument panel.

A convertible/hardtop body means you have three ways to travel: solid top, soft top, or no top at all. The car comes with both a soft (convertible) top and a removable hardtop. Leave the hardtop at home and you still have the convertible top to protect you from inclement weather, and the option of running the wind through your hair with the top down. Few will even realize the top is there, since it stores so neatly beneath a flush-look metal tonneau cover. A glass rear window is installed, which gives increased visibility as well as improved appearance. The removable one-piece molded hardtop contains a tinted fixed-glass back window,

along with circular, beveled-glass opera windows—another luxurious and traditional touch. A lockable compartment behind the seats holds the mini spare tire, tools—even a clipped-in-place umbrella, in case the weather suddenly takes a turn for the worse.

Nearly every reasonable convenience is waiting for the driver's command: power windows, door locks, antenna, seats. Mirrors are electrically heated and powered. Remote releases open the hood, trunk, gas filler door, and tonneau cover.

Performance enthusiasts probably won't be thrilled by the Chrysler-powered version, which carries a turbocharged, intercooled 2.2-liter engine with 3-speed automatic transmission. That's the same engine used in the LeBaron GTC (but with stick shift in that application). In addition to the lack of a manual shift, acceleration to 60 miles an hour is almost 3 seconds slower than with the alternate powerplant. Maserati's 16-valve engine maintains the same displacement as the Chrysler 2.2, but puts out 40 more horsepower (200 versus 160), and almost 50 extra pounds/feet of torque. That cuts 0-60 mph times down to a respectable 7.5 seconds using the 5-speed Getrag shifter. As well, top speed stretches toward 135 mph.

Mediterranean-based beauty might be enough for some. Chrysler's TC by Maserati (both pages) also antes up sprightly turbocharged performance—all the more so with an available 16-valve engine under the hood and 5-speed manual gearbox at hand. The TC's folding top tucks neatly beneath a flush-look metal tonneau, barely noticeable along the smooth beltline. Tiny round beveled-glass opera windows in the removable hardtop add nothing to visibility, but deliver one more distinctive touch.

99

Michelin tires are big enough to deliver taut handling. The TC's suspension, too, is fully adequate but hardly exotic: just gas-charged struts with front and rear anti-sway bars. Four-wheel disc brakes (front discs vented) incorporate a Teves anti-locking system that could come in handy on slippery roads. Twin chrome tips protrude from the stainless steel exhaust system.

Without a doubt, the TC would never have come about at all if Chrysler hadn't bought 15.6 percent of Maserati in the mid-1980s. The car emerged from an agreement with Chrysler's Lee Iacocca and the famed Alejandro DeTomaso, long-time head of Maserati.

The joint-venture coupe qualifies as a truly international vehicle. Large body stampings are produced in Turin, Italy, while body assembly is completed in the small town of Sparone. Then the whole thing goes back to the Innocenti plant, in Milan, for final production. Some 1,200 parts come from the U.S. and Canada, including the basic platform and Chrysler-version powertrain. The brake system, transaxle, and removable hardtop are of German origin. Tires French; wiring Spanish. While the Maserati engine uses the same block as Chrysler's, it adds a cross-flow aluminum head with twin overhead camshafts. Road-testing includes a drive around the L-shaped track at Milan.

TC Number One fetched a price of $120,000 when auctioned for charity, shortly after its arrival on U.S. shores. The original $30,000 price tag for regular folks jumped 10 percent after just a few months. Selected Chrysler-Plymouth dealers sell the car, and are hoping to move about 3,000 each year. Even though it took the car so long to arrive, it seems to have lived up to the expectations of its buyers.

But why did the TC take so long to arrive? Overenthusiastic promotion is one answer. The folks at Chrysler may have been just a tad overexcited, eager to preview the car a little too soon. Besides that, the melding of the Chrysler and Maserati companies, like many Euro-American joint ventures, didn't proceed quite as smoothly as the organizers might have hoped. After the car's debut, in fact, relations between the two sagged appreciably.

Beautiful if not bold, available (in relatively limited numbers) rather than strictly a dream, the TC is a car whose time finally arrived.

Chrysler/Maserati Touring Coupe comes equipped with soft and hard tops—able to deliver both wind-blown and snug-tight motoring for two, with the same sophisticated style and panache.

CHRYSLER'S TC by MASERATI
SPECIFICATIONS

Manufacturer:	Chrysler Motors Corp., Highland Park, MI.; Maserati S.p.A., Milan, Italy
Body design:	2-passenger, 2-door convertible/hardtop; steel unibody
Powertrain layout:	front-engine, front-wheel drive
Wheelbase (in.):	93.3
Overall length (in.):	175.8
Overall width (in.):	68.5
Overall height (in.):	51.9
Track, front (in.):	57.6
Track, rear (in.):	57.6
Weight (lbs.):	3200
Approximate price:	$33,000
Engine type:	Chrysler Turbo II turbocharged sohc 4-cylinder or Maserati 16-valve turbocharged dohc 4-cylinder
Displacement (liters/cu. in.):	2.2/135
Horsepower @ rpm:	(Chrysler) 160 @ 5200; (Maserati) 200 @ 5500
Torque (lbs./ft.) @ rpm:	(Chrysler) 171 @ 3600; (Maserati) 220 at 3400
Fuel delivery:	multi-point electronic fuel injection
Transmission:	5-speed Getrag manual or 3-speed automatic
Suspension, front:	dual path Iso-strut, anti-sway bar
Suspension, rear:	trailing arm beam axle, coil springs, anti-sway bar
Brakes:	front/rear discs, anti-lock

PERFORMANCE

Top speed (mph):	133-135
0-60 mph (seconds):	7.5 (Maserati), 10-11 (Chrysler)
Quarter-mile (seconds):	15.9
mph @ quarter-mile:	92

TC customers have few choices to make at purchase time other than body color, but may select from twin 2.2-liter turbocharged engines: either Chrysler's own or the peppier 16-valve Maserati (opposite page). Engine choice determines the type of transmission included. Touches of hand-crafted leather even show up on the dashboard (left), with its traditional round instruments, as well as door panels and armrest. Natural wood steering wheel is another Maserati tradition.

DeTOMASO
PANTERA GT5

Flamboyant lines of the original Pantera (top), marketed by Lincoln-Mercury dealers in the 1970s, persist in the recent GT5 edition—even with the addition of a tall (but graceful) spoiler.

"Aggressive" is a word that's tossed around a lot. Now and then, it's been used to describe vehicles that fail to deliver all, or even most, of what they promise. DeTomaso's Pantera, on the other hand, has the sports car breeding to back up almost any promise. Just a glance at its taunting lines tells you that it's itching for a fight. Even without the Group 5 spoiler and other extras that were tacked onto recent versions, it has the look of a race car.

What's most amazing is that the design is two decades old, and that it's changed surprisingly little over time, though the car disappeared from the U.S. marketplace for half a dozen years. The back-slanted, sloped angular body with its pointy nose and a roofline that continues all the way to the rear end might have passed for aerodynamic in the Seventies, but stands a world apart

from today's aero smoothies. Its shape is at once assertive and menacing. It's a throwback to a muscular, long-gone world, with a big American V-8 pushing a pair of occupants from behind.

Back in 1970, Ford joined forces with Alejandro DeTomaso to produce a mid-engine supercar that would shore up Ford's performance image in the U.S., and also serve as a replacement in Europe for the GT40. Styling evolved from the Mangusta, which was produced by DeTomaso starting in 1967. Pantera's clean lines flowed from the pen of American Tom Tjaarda, working at the Ghia Design studio. The Vignale organization in Turin, Italy, built the actual bodies, which proved to be roomier than Mangusta's.

Although the prototype that appeared at the New York Auto Show in 1970 used the Mangusta's chassis, the production

edition switched to pressed-steel unibody construction. But, the inability to master this new construction technique caused many early Panteras to become veritable buckets of rust.

Providing the power was a high-output, mid-mounted Ford 351-cid "Cleveland" V-8. At first, that engine delivered 310 horsepower in U.S. trim, and 20 more in European trim. That much power produced top speeds in excess of 160 miles an hour, at least in European trim. By 1973, though, tighter governmental controls took the U.S. rating down to 250 horsepower.

The engine fed a 5-speed manual gearbox mounted in the rear transaxle. Disc brakes halted all four wheels, and air conditioning helped lure American customers. So did the price tag, which was a mere $9,995. Anyone who bought a Pantera at the time could have wound up with a car

Raucous side scoops (left) in Pantera's most recent rendition suck cooling air through aggressive slats. Exquisitely crafted burled wood frames the round analog instruments in a handsomely fitted dashboard and downswept console (above). Driver and passenger are ensconced in leather, while the gear lever maneuvers within a shift gate.

that looks as startling today as it did then, in addition to having appreciated sharply in value. Provided it didn't rust away first, that is. And rusting wasn't its only malady. Both engine and occupants also had a tendency to boil over in hot weather.

On the favorable side, customers got the same kind of warranty that came with an ordinary Ford product, and could go to any Lincoln-Mercury dealer for servicing. Must have caused quite a stir in the service department when one of these beasts joined the Montereys and Comets waiting at the lube rack. "Panther" performance from the high-torque Ford powerplant, at least in upper-horsepower editions, approached that of the then-new Lamborghini Countach, or the Ferrari Testarossa that would arrive a decade later. Handling was similarly impressive.

Nothing lasts forever, they say, and

neither did the original Pantera—at least not in America. New bumper regulations and crash requirements helped take the car off the market. A rubber nose guard and enlarged bumpers weren't enough to meet the new standard, especially since Panteras failed miserably—indeed frightfully—when subjected to federal crash tests. And sales, while healthy enough, didn't warrant the sizable redesign that would put the cars into compliance with current requirements.

How many first editions were built? Lincoln-Mercury claims 6,091 total sales for the 1971-74 period, though other sources put the figure at a few hundred less.

In any case, while Europeans continued to buy Panteras through the remainder of the 1970s, Americans could only sit and dream. At least they were until an enterprising duo from Santa Monica, California formed a new company,

Panteramerica, to get the car re-certified and available once again. A few years later, distribution fell into the hands of a Wisconsin company, Stauffer Classics. Ford never resumed its connection with the car, and the new version is said to be a vast improvement over the original, at least mechanically.

After Ford's American-built cars dropped the 351 cid V-8, Panteras switched to an Australian version, also four-barrel carbureted, available with either 250, 300, or 350 horsepower. Prices, of course, rose sharply in the second time around, approaching the $60,000 mark by the end of the Eighties. Naturally, top speeds and acceleration times have varied through the years, depending on the type of engine installed. All could top 140 miles an hour, but sources differ on the ultimate peak speed, which might reach as high as 180. Acceleration from 0-60 mph

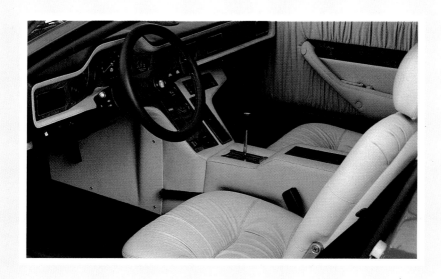

generally has run in the under-six-second neighborhood.

Inside the tight two-place cockpit is all-leather upholstery, with burled wood accents surrounding the instruments. Pantera's hand-built body is finished in hand-rubbed lacquer. Large disc brakes at each wheel feature vented rotors, fed by functional air scoops at front and rear. Huge Pirelli P7 tires (345/35VR15) take the engine's power at the rear, while slightly smaller Pirellis are mounted at the front.

A GT5 edition emerged in the mid-1980s, wearing a graceful but oh-so-tall rear wing spoiler high off its decklid, along with ground-effects flaring around the fenders and lower body, and a blunt air dam up front. Only a handful have been imported each year, mostly in the Group 5 trim, modified by the American distributor to meet federal emission and bumper standards. Well under 10,000 have been built through the car's 20-year history, for both the European and American market.

Few cars have had the pizzazz and potency to last so long, yet still look—and act—so tempting. A brand-new Pantera that will probably resemble the shape of the original is expected to appear early in the Nineties. So this elderly but spry-as-ever example of the muscular Italian/American sports car might even carry on into the 21st century.

Pantera's businesslike steering wheel (opposite page) looks ready for the race track, but the interior boasts a pleasing stock of comforts. Standard fittings include leather upholstery, power windows—even air conditioning. Without the tall spoiler, the muscular DeTomaso coupe looks almost subdued.

DeTOMASO PANTERA GT5

SPECIFICATIONS

Manufacturer:	DeTomaso Modena S.p.A., Modena, Italy
Body design:	2-passenger, 2-door coupe; steel unibody
Powertrain layout:	mid-engine, rear-wheel drive
Wheelbase (in.):	98.8
Overall length (in.):	168.1
Overall width (in.):	77.6
Overall height (in.):	43.3
Track, front (in.):	59.4
Track, rear (in.):	62.2
Weight (lbs.):	3268
Approximate price:	$55,000+
Engine type:	Ford ohv V-8
Displacement (liters/cu. in.):	5.8/351
Horsepower @ rpm:	350 @ 6000 (300 hp available)
Torque (lbs./ft.) @ rpm:	333 @ 3800
Fuel delivery:	Holley 4-barrel carburetor
Transmission:	5-speed ZF manual
Suspension, front:	unequal-length A-arms, coil springs, anti-roll bar
Suspension, rear:	unequal-length A-arms, coil springs, anti-roll bar
Brakes:	front/rear vented discs

PERFORMANCE

Top speed (mph):	140-180
0-60 mph (seconds):	(est.) 5.5
Quarter-mile (seconds):	(est.) 14.0
mph @ quarter-mile:	(est.) 99.5

Although Pantera's basic design harks back to 1970, a host of improvements accompanied its 1980s revival. After Ford halted production of the 351-cid V-8 for American vehicles, DeTomaso picked an Australian equivalent to slide behind the seats. Fewer than 10,000 Panteras have been produced over the years.

111

DODGE VIPER
R/T 10

While automakers in Detroit and around the world look perennially toward the future, a special few choose not to forget the past. Every once in a while, someone even introduces a car that resurrects favorite traditions of that past. Dodge's Viper, an unabashed throwback to the era of muscular sports cars, is the most exciting example in recent memory. All the more startling because it arrived in early 1989 as much more than a mere show car. Originally developed in conjunction with the legendary Carroll Shelby, the Viper came fully equipped with rumors and guarded statements that it just might one day roll off a real assembly line, and into a few dealerships. By the fall of '89, Dodge division general manager John Damoose had publicly stated that Chrysler planned to bring a production Viper to showrooms in 1991, for sale as a '92 model intended to rival the Corvette. Price, according to Damoose, would be $25,000-$30,000, and only 5,000 units would be built per year. These dramatic remarks perked up the ears of many an enthusiast who yearns to relive a memorable part of automotive history.

Viper is everything that the aero-look, gadget-laden modern-day sports car is not. It's tough. Assertive. Ferocious. Yes, even macho—a no-frills, back-to-basics example of what a handful of "classic" American

sports cars used to be, and might conceivably become once again. And in a reprise of the big-block era, the Viper even surpasses the old V-8s by embracing a *ten*-cylinder engine under its long, rakish hood. Dodge calls the Viper an "adventurous no-holds-barred approach to high performance." Even while standing still, they say, Viper "pulses with excitement." And once underway, its true roadster body "recaptures the thrill of open-air motoring."

Nothing other than curves seems to flow along the Viper body. From the teardrop headlamps and low, gaping grille to the stubby rear deck, the Viper's body is an exquisite blend of old and new sports car details. A wraparound front air dam barely clears the ground, while doors sweep back at a dramatic tilt to blend into the sculpted rear segment. The sharply curved air vents cut into the bodyside are there to help cool the massive V-10, as well as to thrill

onlookers. Huge, ground-grabbing tires are mounted on striking 17-inch Indy-style wheels. The car wears vented disc brakes at each wheel, and is fitted with independent suspension front and rear. Like most of the notable roadsters of history, the Viper design does not include windows—just the prospect of side curtains.

Viper's unique "floating" windshield appears barely attached to the car, held onto the body by a pair of thin outer pillars that blend into aerodynamic mirrors. A full-width sport bar over the cockpit provides rollover protection and holds head restraints as well as a high-mounted stop lamp. Inside is an almost stark, traditional, strictly driver-oriented instrument panel with big, round analog gauges and a shifter gate for the 5-speed manual gearbox.

What most observers see first, though, are the five gleaming chrome exhaust pipes that drift out of the bodyside scoop, feeding into a giant outside pipe that releases

Ready to roar full tilt out of the past comes
Chrysler's potential rival to GM's Corvette. Viper
(both pages) entered life as a show car, with
non-functioning V-10 engine. Rumors may soon
turn into reality, as Chrysler contemplates
production as a '92 model.

exhaust gases just ahead of the rear wheel. There's something about outside pipes that excites the imagination even of people who barely know what an exhaust system is supposed to do.

The very idea of a V-10 sends imaginations soaring, perhaps even more than a V-12 engine. Maybe it's because no such engine has ever powered a sports car—or *any* production car, and who doesn't fantasize about what's never been? Then too, any engine looks a little more potent when it's revealed by raising the whole front end rather than a dinky, prop-held hood.

Many observers assumed that the big new engine was little more than an old Chrysler V-8 with two cylinders tacked on, but company spokesmen insisted that wasn't the case at all. The 488 cid (8.0-liter) V-10 was developed as a likely workhorse for Dodge trucks in the 1990s. According to John Damoose, the production Viper will be offered with this engine, developing 400 horsepower; and with so many cubic inches displaced with every engine revolution, torque should be potent enough to deliver all the brute force anyone is likely to want, much less to need. This decision flies in the face of comments from critics, who wondered if a V-10 would be infeasible because of excess weight, and if the engine would have an inherent inability to meet stringent CAFE mileage requirements. Damoose said that Dodge also plans to offer the Viper with a 300-horsepower, 360 cid V-8.

Crowds practically applauded the Viper during its debut at Detroit's auto show in 1989. Everybody could tell it was something special. Enthusiasts knew it was essentially a latter-day edition of the fabled Shelby Cobra, a super-performance sports car produced in the early 1960s by race-driver-turned-entrepreneur Carroll Shelby. Between 1962 and 1966, Shelby modified a total of 1,011 AC sports cars, imported from Britain, adding a choice of four Ford V-8 engines. Hairiest of the lot was the 427-cid edition, which ranked among the fastest street-legal sports cars on record. It was also a car that looked like an escapee from the race course, and that sounded even tougher than its statistics suggest.

This isn't Shelby's first performance-oriented association with Chrysler; he also built the subcompact Shelby Charger in 1983. Dodge, too, has a long history of performance cars, including the legendary hemi-powered machines of the 1960s.

While the Cobra influence is strongest, it's easy to see elements of early Ferraris and E-type Jaguars in the Viper shape as well. Styling fell under the direction of Tom Gale, Chrysler's design chief. The actual

The very idea of 10-cylinder performance (opposite page) sets muscle car fanciers to trembling. A flamboyant quintet of snaky header pipes (above) bursts out of Viper's bodyside scoop (below) to feed spent gases to a huge—and hungry—main exhaust collector. While Dodge can mimic Cobra's look, its teeth-bared exhaust might have to be tamed in Viper form. A production version probably will switch to roll-up windows.

prototype was built in California, using hand-formed steel and fiberglass.

Nobody is more responsible for the Viper project than Chrysler president Robert Lutz. Along with a handful of other Chrysler executives, as well as Carroll Shelby, Lutz shepherded the project from idea to completed concept, and still wanted to see it on the road. One major reason for this isn't hard to understand. Lutz just happened to own an Autokraft Cobra, one of those big-block beauties left over from the muscle car era. As he told reporters, modern sports cars have become too "effete, effeminate, sophisticated." Viper, in contrast, signals a move "back to raw power." Dodge

ads featuring the Viper tout the company's "unrelenting passion for pure, unadulterated performance" and praise the reborn supercar's "classically seductive styling."

Enthusiasts wonder if a ready-for-the-road Viper will maintain its show car look and contain all of its tasty features. According to John Damoose, the production Viper will be almost identical to the show car. Still, it should be remembered that reality must succumb to the dictates of the workaday world. That means listening to the marketplace, to government regulators, to accountants, and on and on. Whether the Chrysler or Shelby folks can ever reproduce anything approaching the exhaust snarl of

Fans of muscular sports cars from the 1960s see the Viper as a familiar blast from the past—a throwback modernized only a little from its Shelby Cobra origins. Unlike so many modern vehicles, the Viper wasn't created by committee, but evolved from ideas tossed out by zealous top executives. The evolving design (below) shows hints not only of the early Sixties Cobra, but of Ferraris and E-Jaguars.

the original AC Cobra in this era of catalytic-converters is open to debate. The dramatic floating windshield will probably fade away, and side curtains seem unlikely. Regardless, Dodge vice-president Jerry York predicted soon after the car's debut that a street Viper would be "very close" to the current shape, but with a revised "windshield area to accommodate a folding roof." Not many modern-day customers, it's thought, would accept a real-world car lacking roll-up windows and a snug-fitting top. Even so, York added, a production Viper would still be a "no-nonsense ultimate-performance driving machine." Damoose sees it as "a real collector car, a move back to ultimate performance."

Not everyone, of course, takes a fancy to the Viper's retrograde notion of what a sports car of the Nineties should be. Fans love its sensuous lines, while critics are more likely to label its shape grotesque and excessive. Whatever the future has in store for the Viper, the car has clearly made its mark as an object of fierce attention. Striking and unusual, the Viper seems tailor-made for the more aggressive dreamers among us. It's nice to know that some of the higher-ups in Detroit are dreaming, too, and that they've apparently found a way to make one of their dreams come true.

DODGE VIPER R/T 10
SPECIFICATIONS

Manufacturer:	Dodge Division, Chrysler Corp., Highland Park, MI; prototype built in Newport Beach, CA
Body design:	2-passenger, 2-door roadster; fiberglass/steel body, steel frame
Powertrain layout:	front-engine, rear-wheel drive
Wheelbase (in.):	96.2
Overall length (in.):	172.0
Overall width (in.):	75.6
Overall height (in.):	46.2
Track, front (in.):	59.6
Track, rear (in.):	60.8
Weight (lbs.):	2400 (minimum)
Approximate price:	$25,000-$30,000 (if produced)
Engine type:	ohv V-10 (prototype car)
Displacement (liters/cu. in.):	8.0/488
Horsepower @ rpm:	400+ @ not announced
Torque (lbs./ft.) @ rpm:	450 @ not announced
Fuel delivery:	multi-point fuel injection
Transmission:	5-speed manual
Suspension, front:	independent; torsion bars
Suspension, rear:	independent; torsion bars
Brakes:	front/rear ventilated discs

PERFORMANCE

Top speed (mph):	(est.) 155
0-60 mph (seconds):	NA
Quarter-mile (seconds):	NA
mph @ quarter-mile:	NA

Viper's back-to-basics dashboard is designed to meet all of the driver's demands—but not a whole lot more. No flashy digital displays, video screens, or high-tech mini-keyboards are likely to distract the exuberant owner of a production model either, if that fortuitous event comes to pass. Just a set of big round gauges (above), like the brawny sports cars of past decades. Five-speed gearbox goes one big step beyond Viper's ancestors, which managed to survive with fewer ratios.

EXCALIBUR

Drivers who yearn to be noticed turn to the long and dramatic Excalibur sedan (above), named for the sword of heroic legend. Glistening exhaust pipes carry no gases but add to romantic appeal.

Many a dreamer gazes forward, imagining what might yet be. Others look backward, pondering what used to be. Excalibur, probably the best known of the neoclassic car makers, takes the latter approach, harking back to the classic car era of the 1920s and '30s with a quartet of massive vehicles that never quite existed on the roads of that day, but look as though they should have.

Hand crafted for well-to-do customers who like to flaunt their success, any Excalibur draws stares like a cow draws flies. Opulence is the car's hallmark; self-indulgence its *raison d'etre*. Larger than life, named for the mythical sword that could be wielded only by a rightful heir to the throne of ancient legends, the tough-to-ignore Excalibur blends nostalgia with romance. Whether gliding through Beverly Hills, rolling down the Las Vegas Strip, or just motoring up to the local supermarket, the Excalibur looks like it's carrying a carload of celebrities. And that observation just might prove accurate.

How ironic, then, that the current car stems from a Studebaker and is built in Wisconsin. Based loosely (though not rigorously) on the 1928 Mercedes SS, one of the most majestic classics of all time, the Excalibur conceals its Studebaker origins completely.

First of all, the Excalibur is big—and looks even bigger. Even the shorties, the open-topped Roadster and Phaeton, ride a 124-inch wheelbase and measure 17 feet overall. The Touring Sedan adds an extra 20 inches to both dimensions; and the Grand Limousine—well, its wheelbase is the size of the Roadster's full length! That's a limo 23 feet and 8 inches from stem to stern, weighing in at 5,700 pounds. If you want to be noticed, you couldn't ask for a more suitable conveyance.

Huge, sweeping front fenders taper into the running boards. Every Excalibur carries side-mounted, encased spare tires on each front fender. The traditional-look grille is set far back from the separate flex-style bumpers, allowing plenty of room for a full set of sweeping horns in between. Gleaming twin exhaust pipes poke out from the hood sides. They don't release any exhaust gases, but add to the look of power and majesty. Stainless steel spoked wheels carry modern-day tires rather than the old-fashioned wide whitewalls, and the stainless steel fittings are polished by hand.

Occupants relax on contoured, imported leather seats with 6-way power settings. The driver (or chauffeur) faces a detailed Zebrano wood instrument panel. Power windows and mirrors are standard. Only a handful of extra-cost options are available, including a vinyl-covered hardtop, two-tone or metallic paint, gold metal trim, stainless steel side spears, and a 12-speaker

stereo system for the sedan.

Under the immense hood sits not a huge old straight eight or a V-12 engine, but an ordinary, relatively modern General Motors V-8. The standard engine until 1989 was a carbureted 305-cid V-8, like the one used in Chevrolet's Caprice. A high-performance 350-cid version with tuned-port fuel injection, as used in the IROC Camaro, was formerly optional but now powers all current Excaliburs.

A 4-speed overdrive automatic transmission sends the power to the rear wheels, so today's driver need not contemplate the treachery of manipulating a balky manual-shift gearbox, as drivers of authentic vehicles that looked like this had to do half a century ago. A structural steel, square-tube ladder frame carries the car's fiberglass body.

This dream car's history reaches all the way back to 1951, when a Model J racing car was built in Milwaukee by the Beassie Engineering company. The coachwork

styled by young industrial designer Brooks Stevens rested upon a Henry J chassis. After racing for a while, the J faded into memory since no investors seemed interested in a production version.

A decade later, in 1963, the very same Brooks Stevens was hired as a design consultant at Studebaker. After doing some Lark show cars, he penned a "contemporary classic" inspired by the 1928 Mercedes SS, to be mounted on a modified Studebaker chassis, much like the previously mentioned

Loosely patterned on the design of the classic 1928 Mercedes SS, the Excalibur comes in two-door roadster (above) and phaeton (foreground) body styles, along with a four-door sedan and limo. Each example displays a set of handsome side-mounted spare tires on its sweeping front fenders. Flex-style bumpers, calling up memories of the classic era before World War II, stretch far beyond the traditional-style radiator grille. Few would guess that the Wisconsin-built "neoclassic" traces its ancestry back to Studebaker.

Avanti. Stevens's design had an open cockpit, cycle-style fenders, wire wheels, and external exhaust pipes. First called Mercebaker, the car soon took the name Studebaker SS. Displayed separately from the Studebaker models at the 1964 New York Auto Show, the SS was a big hit, and Stevens was prompted to start a business, SS Automobiles, to produce the car on a limited basis. Early examples used a Studebaker Lark convertible platform and that car's 289-cid V-8 engine.

Series I, built after Studebaker expired in 1966, carried a Chevrolet Corvette 327-cid V-8 that produced 300 horsepower—a whole lot of horses for that vintage. Fiberglass bodies replaced the original hand-formed aluminum, and sat on a Corvette-based chassis. Rated favorably by road-testers for performance and handling, partly as a result of its light weight, the Excalibur began to gain an impressive following among the celebrity crowd. The option list grew longer, so each car could be individualized.

Over the next two decades, a hundred or

so Excalibur Roadsters and Phaetons rolled out of the production facility at West Allis, Wisconsin each year. A four-seater Phaeton joined the original roadster in 1967, and the early cycle-fendered SSK model departed by 1970.

Late in 1986, the company was faltering badly, and underwent a financial reorganization under new management. The revived company introduced the Touring Sedan at a lavish reception in the Hotel Sofitel just outside Chicago, in 1987. Offering more room inside and a bigger trunk, as well as a solid top, it was intended to serve as a more practical neoclassic. A year later, the first Grand Limousine appeared, billed as "America's only true limousine" since it's not a stretch job or a conversion but built from the ground up. Several of the giant limos have even been shipped to Japan. The company also began to publish a lavish magazine touting the virtues of the car, and telling about some of the "successful" people who own one (or more).

Through the 1970s and '80s, dozens of

neoclassics and replicas appeared on the market. Nearly all faded away after a couple of years—some before selling even a single copy. Excalibur has managed to survive far longer than anyone might have dreamed; and plenty of people still dream of owning one whenever they spot its flamboyant profile rolling down the road. Part of the appeal lies in its reliable, standard-issue drivetrain, which Excalibur receives directly from General Motors. Mostly, though, it's those long sweeping fenders, the shapely side-mounted tires, and the dashing "exhaust" pipes. The Excalibur reminds us of a flamboyant bit of the past, available to us today.

Phaeton and roadster (right), the shorties of the Excalibur group, stretch 17 feet overall. Sedan (above) adds 20 inches. Beneath each aristocratic hood lies a conventional, modern General Motors V-8 engine. Celebrities took a fancy to the hand-crafted Excalibur in its early years.

As an expression of opulence, if not excess, Excalibur's immense Grand Limousine has few peers. Passengers stepping past the wide running board are bathed in luxury, sinking into precisely pleated upholstery (opposite page) to revel in such comforts as a full-feature stereo and mini-bar.

EXCALIBUR

SPECIFICATIONS

Manufacturer:	Excalibur Automobile Corp., Milwaukee, WI
Models available:	Roadster, Phaeton, Touring Sedan, Grand Limousine
Body design:	4-passenger, 2-door phaeton or roadster; 5-passenger, 4-door sedan; 7-passenger, 4-door limousine; fiberglass body on steel square-tube ladder frame
Powertrain layout:	front-engine, rear-wheel drive
Wheelbase (in.):	(2-dr) 124.0, (sdn) 144.0, (limo) 204.0
Overall length (in.):	(2-dr) 204.0, (sdn) 224.0, (limo) 284.0
Overall width (in.):	76.0
Overall height (in.):	(2-dr) 59.0, (sdn) 61.0, (limo) 64.0
Track, front (in.):	64.0
Track, rear (in.):	64.0
Weight (lbs.):	(2-dr/sdn) 4400, (limo) 5700
Approximate price:	(2-dr) $73,960, (sdn) $74,420, (limo) $115,000
Engine type:	General Motors L98 ohv V-8
Displacement (liters/cu. in.):	5.7/350
Horsepower @ rpm:	245 @ NA
Torque (lbs./ft.) @ rpm:	345 @ NA
Fuel delivery:	tuned-port fuel injection
Transmission:	GM 4-speed overdrive automatic
Suspension, front:	independent wishbones, coil springs, anti-roll bar
Suspension, rear:	solid axle, 4-link coil springs
Brakes:	(2-dr) front/rear discs; (sdn/limo) front discs, rear drums

PERFORMANCE

Top speed (mph):	NA
0-60 mph (seconds):	NA
Quarter-mile (seconds):	NA
mph @ quarter-mile:	NA

FERRARI
DAYTONA

Aside from his 250 GTO, Enzo Ferrari's 1968-74 365 GTB/4, popularly known as the "Daytona," ranks as perhaps the most coveted car ever to come from Maranello. It's certainly one of the most remarkable of roadgoing Ferraris. Unveiled in prototype form at the 1968 Paris Salon, it was not only the costliest car in Ferrari's 21-year history—just under $20,000—but the fastest. *Road & Track* magazine verified the factory's claimed 174-mph top speed and ran the standing quarter-mile in a blistering 13.8 seconds at 107.5 mph. What Ferrari had here was nothing less than an Italian-style "muscle car."

And what muscle. Replacing the 275 GTB/4, the Daytona rode a similar chassis with an identical 94.5-inch wheelbase but carried a double-overhead-cam V-12 bored and stroked to 4.4 liters. With no fewer than six twin-choke Weber carburetors and fairly high (for the day) 8.8:1 compression, output was 352 thoroughbred horses at 7500 rpm. As on the 275, a single dry-plate clutch

sent all this power to a torque-tube-encased propshaft and onto a rear-mounted ZF 5-speed manual transaxle with all-indirect ratios.

What styling, too. Ferrari fans and motoring press alike were initially divided on the Pininfarina design. But after more than 20 years, those who merely liked it when new simply love it now, while most of those who didn't care for it then have had a change of heart. "Aggressively elegant" describes the car's styling; so does "influential." In fact, many of the Daytona's features have since shown up on a number of lesser cars (including a few replicas, like the Corvette-based model seen on TV's *Miami Vice*). One Daytona feature that hasn't been seen elsewhere is the full-width plastic headlight cover used on early models. U.S. law prohibited such things, so hidden lamps were substituted for that market and, later, others as well, though not before several exposed-light arrangements were tried, all best forgotten.

As usual with Ferrari, Pininfarina designed and built the prototype Daytona, but Scaglietti handled production, which began about a year after the prototype. Incidentally, the press and not the factory was responsible for the Daytona name. It stuck, perhaps because it had long been legendary in auto-racing circles around the world. And really, what better handle for this speediest Ferrari ever than the name of the Florida beach city that bills itself as "The Birthplace of Speed"?

Journalists tacked the Daytona name onto Ferrari's 365 GTB/4, and the widely-known moniker stuck as the well-built muscle car became one of the hottest numbers ever to emerge from Maranello, Italy. Designer Pininfarina's signature (opposite page) appears prominently on the cowl, tied to the Ferrari crest.

The Daytona feels heavy behind the wheel—and it is, especially for a two-seater. Despite aluminum doors, hood, and trunklid (the remainder of the body was steel), curb weight ended up at near 3600 pounds. But the heft seemed to have little effect on handling, which was excellent, thanks to front/rear weight distribution near the 50/50 ideal. And, as the above performance numbers attest, horsepower and torque were more than abundant.

Equally abundant are drivers' vivid impressions of the Daytona, but then, it *is* that kind of car. In *Ferrari: The Man And His Machines*, author Pete Lyons quotes journalist and Ferrari expert Dean Batchelor, who was aboard the *Road & Track* Daytona for its top-speed runs and, at the right moment, had the prescience to take a snapshot of the main instruments. "The car was smooth as glass at that speed," he recalled. "It was easy." Even when grabbing fifth gear at 148 mph, Batchelor remembered that the Daytona picked up speed almost as fiercely as it had in second.

Lyons also quotes the book *Daytona*, where authors Pat Braden and Gerald Roush answered all the criticisms of the car's "trucky" nature: "The Daytona really only begins to come into its own at about 70 mph and hits its stride above 140 mph. At speeds below 80 mph the car is a bit bumpy, but the suspension begins to work smoothly as speed builds and steering becomes appropriate. Owners who complain of the heavy steering should remember their baby was designed for precise control at 174 mph. Parking lots were low on the priority list."

Most agreed that Enzo Ferrari still had his priorities straight. "On its big fat tyres, the [Daytona] could really be flung around the corners," reported racer-writer Paul Frere in Britain's *Motor*. "The general cornering attitude is that of a slightly understeering car, with a small tendency to tuck into the bend as the throttle is closed....There is practically no roll and the moderately light steering...is very precise." Frere frowned over the large turning circle—a clumsy 39 feet—and noise levels that rendered the radio useless at 100 mph. But, as with all Ferraris, "it's the engine that makes the music," he declared, "a music [the enthusiast] can enjoy...with such amenities as electric window lifters, air

American Daytonas wore concealed headlamps (opposite), while early Europeans got a full-width headlight panel. No-nonsense instrument panel (above) complements the three-spoke steering wheel. A simple stick gearshift beckons the Daytona's fortunate driver. Front-mounted V-12 engine (left) was the last of its kind in a Ferrari.

Only 127 of the 1300 Daytonas built were "spider" 365 GTS/4 convertibles (above). Latter-day conversion of closed coupes into open Daytonas could make the berlinetta coupes the rarer of the pair one day. Daytona's 4.4-liter engine (left) doesn't look so special at first glance, and raised a few eyebrows at the time since Lamborghini, for one, had turned to a mid-engine design. Half a dozen Weber carburetors helped the V-12 whip out 352 horsepower at a screaming 7500 rpm, to give any American ruffian of the day a run for its money—and leave it far behind. Authenticated 174-mph top speed is just one of its attractions.

conditioning (that could be improved) and a really capacious luggage locker—a Grand Touring car *par excellence*."

Ferrari made few alterations to the Daytona during its short run other than the aforementioned headlamp change and the addition of a companion convertible "spider," announced at the 1969 Frankfurt show as the 365 GTS/4. The convertible accounted for only 127 of the more than 1300 Daytonas completed altogether.

That low production together with high visceral and visual appeal explain why Daytona asking prices have lately soared into million-plus territory. Convertibles, of course, generally command bigger bucks than coupes—by a factor of 20 to 100 percent among Ferraris—which explains the advent of various firms that specialize in Daytona spider conversions. While some are done for enthusiasts who simply want an open car and really want it to be a Daytona, most customers are likely motivated by the spider's higher market value and the prospect of further appreciation. If this keeps up—though Ferrari keeps trying to stop it—berlinettas could be in shorter supply one day and thus, paradoxically, worth more than spiders, converted *and* original.

A few Daytona berlinettas raced with success, some with all-aluminum bodywork and engines tweaked to 405 bhp. They were formidable track performers, but the Daytona's chronically weak brakes were a problem. Even race-equipped cars tipped the scales near 3600 pounds (bigger wheels and tires and the increased load of larger fuel tanks offset weight savings in bodywork and some mechanical components); the brakes just weren't up to the cars' 200-mph top speed.

The Daytona's front-engine configuration raised a few eyebrows in the late Sixties because Lamborghini's V-12 Miura was a mid-engine design, as were Ferrari's own competition cars, and that layout was seen as the wave of the future. As events soon proved, it was, at least among two-seat Ferraris, making the Daytona the last such front V-12 in the classic Maranello mold.

Which also helps explain today's lofty asking prices—that and a macho character plus truly memorable design. But really, the styling was enough to assure this car the vast and loyal following it commanded almost from day one. In Lyons' view, the Daytona "was one of those uncanny leaps of aesthetic genius seen so often in Italian styling, and so seldom elsewhere. Somehow blending the raw-racer look of the previous competition *berlinettas* with the sweet, almost florid elegance of the 250 GT Lusso, the Daytona managed a fresh, modern statement all its own. Surely any roster of all-time great automobile bodies would be incomplete without the Ferrari 365GTB/4 Daytona."

FERRARI DAYTONA
(365 GTB/4 & GTS/4)

SPECIFICATIONS

Manufacturer:	Ferrari SEFAC S.p.A. Maranello, Italy
Body design:	2-passenger, 2-door fastback coupe (GTB/4) and convertible (GTS/4); steel body with aluminum opening panels over tubular-steel ladder-type chassis
Powertrain layout:	longitudinal front engine, rear-wheel drive
Wheelbase (in.):	94.5
Overall length (in):	174.2
Overall width (in.):	69.3
Overall height (in.):	49.0
Track, front (in.):	56.7
Track, rear (in.):	56.1
Weight (lbs)	3600
Approximate price:	$19,500 (1970)
Engine type:	dohc V-12
Displacement (liters/cu.in.):	4.4/268
Horsepower @ rpm:	352 @ 7500
Torque (lbs./ft.) @ rpm:	365 @ 5500
Fuel delivery:	6 Weber 40 DCN 20 carburetors
Transmissions:	5-speed manual (rear transaxle)
Suspension, front:	independent; upper and lower unequal-length A-arms, coil springs, tubular hydraulic shock absorbers, anti-roll bar
Suspension, rear:	independent; upper and lower unequal-length A-arms, coil springs, tubular hydraulic shock absorbers, anti-roll bar
Brakes:	front/rear discs

PERFORMANCE

Top speed (mph):	174
0-60 mph (seconds):	5.9
Quarter-mile (seconds):	13.8
mph @ quarter-mile:	107.5

Scaglietti built the Daytona's handsome body from a Pininfarina design—an elegant yet assertive shape that influenced later cars. A "heavy" feel led some critics to brand the Daytona trucklike. Even if true, this is one "truck" in which every enthusiast would love to hit the highway.

FERRARI GTO

Automobiles that can shift smoothly from a race course to the road have attracted enthusiasts since the early days of motoring. What could be sweeter than a sleek and low racer that can take off in a blaze of power, reach far into triple-digit speeds on the straightaways, grip the pavement like tentacles around the tightest curves, and then take to the highway without even pausing for a breather.

One of the top—maybe *the* top—examples of this schizophrenic breed is Ferrari's GTO of the mid-1980s, a sports car that performs at least as well as it looks—and that's high praise indeed. "GTO," incidentally, stands for *Gran Turismo Omologato*, which means a car that was built in sufficient quantity to be approved (homologated) for grand-touring class competition.

Ferrari had gone the GTO route before. Only 42 examples of this GTO's ancestor were built—the 250 GTO berlinetta of 1962. Nearly all carried a front-mounted 3.0-liter V-12 engine. That Scaglietti-built Ferrari was quick and lovely, and the limited quantity turned it into one of the vehicles in greatest demand by collectors. The design/engineering evolution continued into the Pininfarina-styled Dino 246GT of 1969-73, with its transverse V-6 engine behind the seats, rear-wheel drive, and rigid all-independent suspension.

In 1975, the 308 GTB arrived on the same chassis, but sporting a 2.9-liter, 4-cam V-8 engine. That one led to the 328 GTB and its 3.2-liter V-8, with four valves per cylinder, available in both coupe and open "Spider" editions. Both the 308 and 328 were road cars rather than racers (though no slouches when the gas pedal hit the floor), and were

Ferrari's GTO for the Eighties: a mid-engine screamer capable of catapulting itself from zero to 60 in 5 seconds. Aggressive spoilers and bulging fenders hint at the car's power.

available at regular Ferrari dealerships (if a Ferrari dealership can be called regular). Each sold in numbers that could be counted in thousands, rather than hundreds or dozens.

Ferrari then wanted a contender for FISA Group B competition, which required that 200 examples be built. Result: the GTO two-seater coupe, a car that was more powerful and technically advanced than its forerunners, ready and eager for racing and rallying. At the car's launch, Ferrari announced that precisely 200 would be built—the minimum number demanded by the rules. To meet another part of the racing requirement, the 328's engine had to undergo a slight reduction in size, to 174 cubic inches (2855cc).

Introduced at the Geneva Motor Show in March 1984, the GTO took a giant step beyond the 308/328 GTB design. Though similar in basic shape and mid-engine, rear-drive layout to those berlinetta coupes from which it evolved, the GTO lost much of the connection with its twin cousins. Wheelbase is some 4 inches longer than either the 308 or 328, to start with. The GTO is wider, too. Noticeable at a glance are the large upright "flag-style" mirrors at each door. Nearly as striking are the bulging fenders, and the sizable spoilers at front and rear. Driving lamps sit at each end of the grille. As in the 328, long indented air scoops that begin at the door tops feed air into the engine bay, ahead of the rear wheels.

The GTO's basic steel body, created at Ferrari's own plant, added a number of fiberglass components—and some made of advanced composite or honeycomb materials. Every last one was painted red, the "traditional" Ferrari color. Ferraris in other hues exist, of course, but one could be forgiven for thinking that red is the one and only choice for any Maranello-built machine.

Under the GTO's rear hatch waits the familiar 4-cam V-8, displacing 2.9 liters and fed by twin IHI turbochargers (from Japan): one for each cylinder bank, each with its own air-to-air intercooler. Weber-Marelli port electronic injection meters the fuel intake to the engine, which was originally developed for use in Lancia rally cars. Instead of the 308/328's transverse engine layout, the GTO turned to a longitudinal position, with the crankshaft in line with the car's chassis. A new gearbox/final-drive transmission also was installed.

Engine output edged into the muscular 400-horsepower neighborhood at a screaming 7000 rpm, with torque hitting its peak (366 pounds/feet) closer to half

that speed. Quite a lively neighborhood. Power hit the rear wheels via a twin-disk clutch and 5-speed transaxle with long (2.90:1) final drive gearing.

How fast was this GTO? One high-speed track run, measured by the company, yielded 190 miles an hour. *Road & Track* magazine's testers managed to run up to 60 mph in an even 5 seconds, and blast through the quarter-mile trap in 14.1, hitting 113 miles an hour. Other evaluators turned in even swifter figures—as little as 12.7 seconds for the quarter-mile.

This was essentially a race car, remember, that happened to be driveable (not without some difficulty) on ordinary roads. Even so, owners could pay an extra $1800 for an option package that included some pleasing amenities: air conditioning, power windows, and an AM/FM stereo system with tape cassette. Initial base price was $83,400, but rose to $125,000.

Oddly, the GTO experiment, which drew from expertise gained in Formula One (single-seater) racing in the early 1980s, never reached the racing circuit. Instead, Ferrari stuck to its single-seat race program, so GTOs took no flags in motor sport events.

The inspired combination of fantastic performance and handling, a glamorous countenance, and the immeasurable Ferrari heritage, turned the GTO into an instant collectible, even while production was still taking place. No surprise, since it was at the time the fastest road car yet built by Ferrari, yielding to no supercar short of (possibly) a Porsche 959. All told, the superstar GTO ranked as close to a purebred racing sports car as is likely ever to be found on an open road. An even more ferocious "Evoluzione" version (of which 20 needed to be made to gain sporting approval) was proposed, but never built.

By the end of 1987, its final season, a total of 271 GTOs had left the Maranello factory (far more than the original GTO of the 1960s). Ranking as a competition vehicle, the GTO never gained certification for sale in the United States. That hasn't kept the car out of the country completely; various examples have been slipping past the import regulations via the "gray market." Such is the way of restricted supercars when somebody wants one badly enough and has the patience—and money—to turn the elusive dream into reality.

As the GTO era drew to a close, Ferrari turned to its F40 supercar to celebrate its 40th anniversary in the motorcar business. Planned for production in slightly greater numbers, the F40 could give just a few more fortunate folks the opportunity to drive a legend in its own time.

FERRARI GTO

SPECIFICATIONS

Manufacturer:	Ferrari S.p.A., Modena, Italy
Body design:	2-passenger, 2-door coupe; steel body with fiberglass/composite components, steel frame
Powertrain layout:	mid-engine, rear-wheel drive
Wheelbase (in.):	96.5
Overall length (in.):	168.9
Overall width (in.):	75.2
Overall height (in.):	44.1
Track, front (in.):	62.5
Track, rear (in.):	61.5
Weight (lbs.):	2557
Approximate price:	$83,400+
Engine type:	twin-turbocharged dohc V-8 (32-valve)
Displacement (liters/cu. in.):	2.9/174
Horsepower @ rpm:	400 @ 7000
Torque (lbs./ft.) @ rpm:	366 @ 3800
Fuel delivery:	Weber-Marelli fuel injection
Transmission:	5-speed manual
Suspension, front:	unequal-length A-arms, coil springs, anti-roll bar
Suspension, rear:	unequal-length A-arms, coil springs, anti-roll bar
Brakes:	front/rear discs

PERFORMANCE

Top speed (mph):	190
0-60 mph (seconds):	5.0
Quarter-mile (seconds):	14.1
mph @ quarter-mile:	113

The GTO (opposite) may be as close to a street-legal race car as one is likely to encounter anywhere in the world. No idle boast, considering that the twin-turbocharged V-8 cranks out 400 horsepower—good for a top speed of 190. The GTO was never certified for U.S. sale; altogether, only 271 were built.

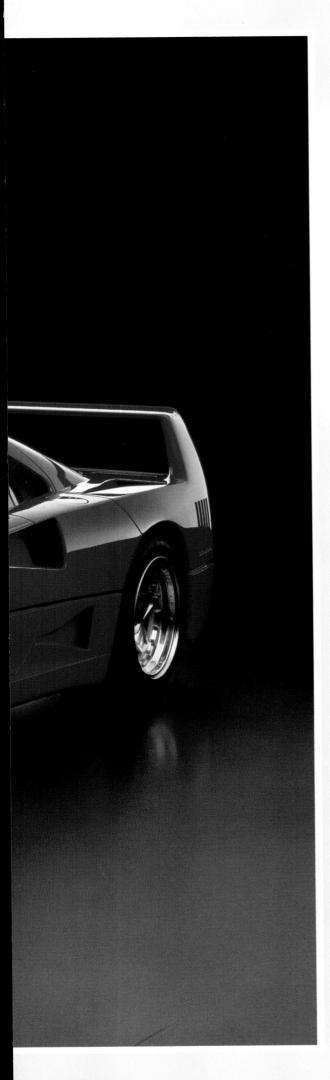

FERRARI F40

That tall wing-style aerofoil spoiler, seemingly waiting for a giant to grasp and lift the back wheels right off the ground, says it all. Here's a dream vehicle built for the racetrack, which just happens to be legal for the street. But not for all streets: American authorities have kept the ultimate Ferrari out of this country, while hundreds of panting supercar fans wait with checkbooks at the ready, prepared to pay just about anything to get one into the garage.

Considering that the handful of examples running in Europe are rumored to be changing hands at prices fast approaching a million dollars—far above the initial $200,000 factory price—that checkbook had better be fat on the day the F40 finally does arrive at U.S. shores. And if you'd like to translate dreams into reality, you're probably out of luck: the 200 to 400 F40s originally intended for American consumption were spoken for long ago. By 1988, in fact, Ferrari had firm offers for at least three times as many cars as it had originally planned to build.

Whether the F40 is the "best" Ferrari is open to dispute, of course. Experts never agree on what's best. More valid, perhaps, would be a claim to the title of "purest" Ferrari. The F40 is the one with the fastest top speed (201 mph), acceleration that defies the imagination, biggest tires (over a foot wide), most startling shape, and loftiest price tag—especially when its initial owner decides to resell.

Ever since the F40 was announced, and even more so after its debut at Maranello, Italy (home of the Ferrari factory) in July 1987, it's become one of two standards of comparison. Porsche's older 959 is the other. Both are the cars against which every supercar must be judged.

Enzo Ferrari, the fabled founder of the company that bears his name, asked his staff in 1986 to come up with a car to remember—one to mark the firm's 40th anniversary. Not an easy task, since every Ferrari built qualifies as memorable. A basis had to be chosen, though, so Enzo told the press he wanted something "reminiscent of the original 250 LM."

If an award were to be given for the "perfect" supercar, Ferrari's F40 just might roar off with that honor. If nothing else, it rivals Porsche's 959 as "most wanted" by Americans. Vents and grilles (above) adorn F40 physique.

Design was based on the GTO *Evoluzione* of 1984, a twin-turbo 650-horsepower beast that had been created for Group B competition, but faded away when that racing class evaporated. Development took place over the next year, so the patriarch had an opportunity to see the result of his dream before his death in 1988. The company wanted to offer to some of its favored customers a chance to drive a Ferrari with racing characteristics, but there's more to the F40 than that. Emilio Anchisi, president of Ferrari North America, called the car a "return to Ferrari's roots."

Once you manage to take your eyes off the F40's aerofoil wing, the next thing you'll notice is how closely its body hugs the ground. Stand back. Let the eye wander over those luscious curves, the low profile, the amalgamation of scoops and NACA ducts and grilles that allow air in and out, the tiny cockpit for two. Squint a bit and you'll spot elements of the original GTO, and even of the more modest 308/328 coupes.

Step closer and you can even take a peek at the mid-mounted 2.9-liter, turbocharged V-8 engine through the transparent cover. What you see is 478 horsepower lurking quietly, waiting patiently for the first opportunity to perform. The engine even *looks* beautiful with its carefully crafted aluminum castings and pattern of braided, stainless steel hoses.

Let's carry our imaginations a giant step further. Take a deep breath before popping the door open and attempting to crawl into the form-fitting seat. Fortunately, three different seat sizes are available, to suit varying human physiques, so we'll assume the correct one is waiting for your visit. And though the bucket seat may be covered in startling day-glo orange material, that's just about the only touch of color you'll see inside. This is essentially a racing car, remember, and racers are austere, not plush. The original Ferraris were designed as race cars, and the interior of the F40 mimics this heritage. That means no carpeting to fondle your feet, no door panels, no sound system. The only entertainment available lies at the base of the accelerator pedal and in the magnificent rumble and clatter of 8 cylinders, 32 valves, and 2 turbochargers. That should be plenty for anyone. Air conditioning is the F40's

only real concession to driving comfort, but don't expect the system to give you more than a moderate cool-down.

Power windows? You don't even get roll-up windows here; just a set of sliding Plexiglas panels so you can reach out to tollbooth attendants, or let in a trickle of fresh air. Visibility to the side leaves much to be desired, and it's worse yet to the rear, where you have to peer through a double layer of Plexiglas. The most wondrous sight to the rear, in any case, is the engine itself, seen through its transparent window. No point letting only the outsiders enjoy such a magnificent view.

Brakes and steering demand real human power from legs and arms. Pedals are traditionally bare metal, including the one for your left foot when it's needed for clutch duties. Waiting for your right fist is Ferrari's familiar shifter with a polished shift gate, hooked to the 5-speed manual gearbox. While most buyers will choose the conventional synchronized transmission, you also have the option of straight-cut (competition) gears, guaranteed to clash unless you're an expert at choreographing the clutch and gas pedal movements.

Sure, some of these austerities help cut down the car's weight (to just 2,425 pounds); but they also add to the race-car look and feel. Pull up to the gas pump, too, and you'll feed fuel not into an ordinary steel tank but a safety bladder that acts like a big rubber-enclosed sponge.

Ferrari claims not only a 201-mph top speed, but acceleration to 200 kilometers per hour (124 mph) in a dazzling dozen seconds. Not quick enough? Some folks are

Foot-wide tires carry the Ferrari F40 to a top speed that blazes past the 200-mph barrier. Created to mark Ferrari's 40th anniversary, the nothing-held-back sports car was also meant to reward favored customers who craved a racing car for the road.

never quite satisfied, so Ferrari even offers an option kit that boosts horsepower beyond 600, using a different set of turbochargers and altered camshaft profile. The "basic" powerplant, using a pair of water-cooled IHI turbos with 16 psi maximum boost and air-to-air Behr intercoolers, will probably please the majority of F40 customers.

A steel-tube space-frame carries the F40's body, made of carbon-fiber and Kevlar (a blend of composite and steel materials) in race-car style. Three-position ride height adjustment lets the car rise to clear a hump in the road, then drop down again either to normal or high-speed mode. At high speeds, in fact, the lowered stance comes automatically.

Technically, the F40 offers little that's new. Instead, it borrows the best of what has gone before, mixing a refined brew of simple, straightforward engineering that stretches the notion of supercar performance to its limit. At the same time, the F40 is designed for driving on real roads, and won't shake you into a frenzy while waiting at a traffic signal or ambling gently along a country highway. Whether in a tame or ferocious mood, the F40 is a car that never fails to be noticed.

During 1988, just 43 of Ferrari's supercars went into customers' hands. Only a trickle of F40s will ever make it into America (if any at all). At this writing, no more than 150 or so have been sold in Europe, and Ferrari is still attempting to have the car certified to meet American safety/emissions standards. The company claims that proven Ferrarists get first choice, and that an F40 will be sold only to "qualified" customers who are capable of handling such a supreme machine.

Even those owner/drivers fortunate enough—and wealthy enough—to purchase one aren't likely to drive them. They surely won't be eager to head for the racetrack, and risk any damage to the car. In a sense, then, when speaking about the cream of the supercars, both their actual owners and the rest of us on the street are dreamers. But what a grand and glorious dream this supercar to end all supercars is.

Flamboyant scoops tucked high and low on the bodyside (opposite page) are there to suck in air—but they also help to strengthen the F40's rough 'n ready image. So does the car's ground-hugging stance and tiny cockpit. The stunning mid-mounted turbo V-8 engine (above), visible through a transparent cover, delivers a whopping 478 horsepower— enough to propel an F40 to 124 mph in a dozen seconds. Not quick enough? An optional power package boosts output to 600 horses.

FERRARI F40

SPECIFICATIONS

Manufacturer:	Ferrari S.p.A.; Modena, Italy
Body design:	2-passenger, 2-door coupe; Kevlar/carbon composite body, steel tube frame
Powertrain layout:	mid-engine, rear-wheel drive
Wheelbase (in.):	96.5
Overall length (in.):	174.4
Overall width (in.):	78.0
Overall height (in.):	44.5
Track, front (in.):	62.8
Track, rear (in.):	63.4
Weight (lbs.):	2425
Approximate price:	$280,000+
Engine type:	turbocharged dohc V-8 (32-valve)
Displacement (liters/cu. in.):	2.9/179
Horsepower @ rpm:	478 @ 7000
Torque (lbs./ft.) @ rpm:	425 @ 4000
Fuel delivery:	Weber-Marelli multi-point fuel injection
Transmission:	5-speed manual
Suspension, front:	unequal-length A-arms, coil springs, anti-roll bar
Suspension, rear:	unequal-length A-arms, coil springs, anti-roll bar
Brakes:	front/rear vented discs

PERFORMANCE

Top speed (mph):	201.3
0-60 mph (seconds):	(est.) 3.5
Quarter-mile (seconds):	11.6
mph @ quarter-mile:	NA

That huge aerofoil spoiler has a job to do in keeping the F40 on the pavement at speed, but also attracts gobs of attention. Don't expect to roll down the window when the interior grows sweaty; a sliding Plexiglas panel provides the only contact with the outside world. Once inside, though, who'd want to leave?

FERRARI
MYTHOS

For the first time, the fabled Pininfarina styling firm declined to showcase its latest creation in Europe. Instead, the company chose Tokyo's October 1989 auto show as the site to debut what may be its most striking design study ever. Created for Ferrari, cementing the decades-long tie between the two companies, the Mythos is no myth, no fantasy. It's a real no-top speedster with a mid-rear 12-cylinder engine. Yet neither does it quite qualify as reality. Not for a while, at any rate.

Although based on the proven Testarossa chassis, Mythos is strictly one-of-a-kind, playing on its own field. And yet, says chief designer Lorenzo Ramaciotti, the car's design can be "adapted to fill the needs of production ... of tomorrow's cars." Now that sounds promising. Sergio Pininfarina, the company chairman, has called it an "advanced research prototype," meant to show that Italian styling is "on the crest of the wave."

Not much doubt about that. Even superlatives seem lacking in vigor when attempting to describe the flowing lines of the Mythos. Best? Smoothest? Most beautiful? Maybe so; but more important, Mythos signals a switch in basic approach to auto design, from the reality-based creations of recent times (which focus on new materials and technologies) back to the dreamy, elemental essences of form. In a word, it's a return to the "purity" of the dream.

Emphasizing the "relationship between volumes," according to the Pininfarina

firm, the Mythos breaks free of the traditional "linked panels." Although made up of two distinct elements, the stylists attempted to meld the pair into a single homogeneous form, one flowing into the other. The main body, containing engine and rear-mounted radiators, serves as one of the two masses; the extension that holds passengers and the car's nose is the other. Unlike the Testarossa, which uses lateral grilles to *minimize* the relation of the two masses, Mythos tries to *emphasize* that contrast—to highlight the obvious fact that they intersect.

Mythos symbolizes a rebirth of the two-seater "barchetta," described by Pininfarina as "very compact, decidedly sporty and extremely spartan." Coupe, targa, and speedster bodies were considered, but the latter took hold because of its race-car connection. That meant neither a solid roof nor side windows had to be dealt with in the design process.

A low but lengthy windshield stretches out steeply, to flow into the projectile-like nose. Wheel arches hug the tires, reaching down close to the pavement. Deeply recessed rectangular headlamps barely break the flow of the fender, from air dam to door. A lower lip at the front end is "echoed" by a touch of bulge that extends all the way back along the lower body, level with the sills.

Monstrous intake holes behind the doors feed air into the greedy Boxer engine; however, there is no Testarossa-style grillework to block the flow. The Pininfarina

The striking Ferrari Mythos, based on the Testarossa chassis, is a reminder of the unique relationship between Ferrari and the Pininfarina styling firm. A 12-cylinder Boxer engine has 390 horses on tap.

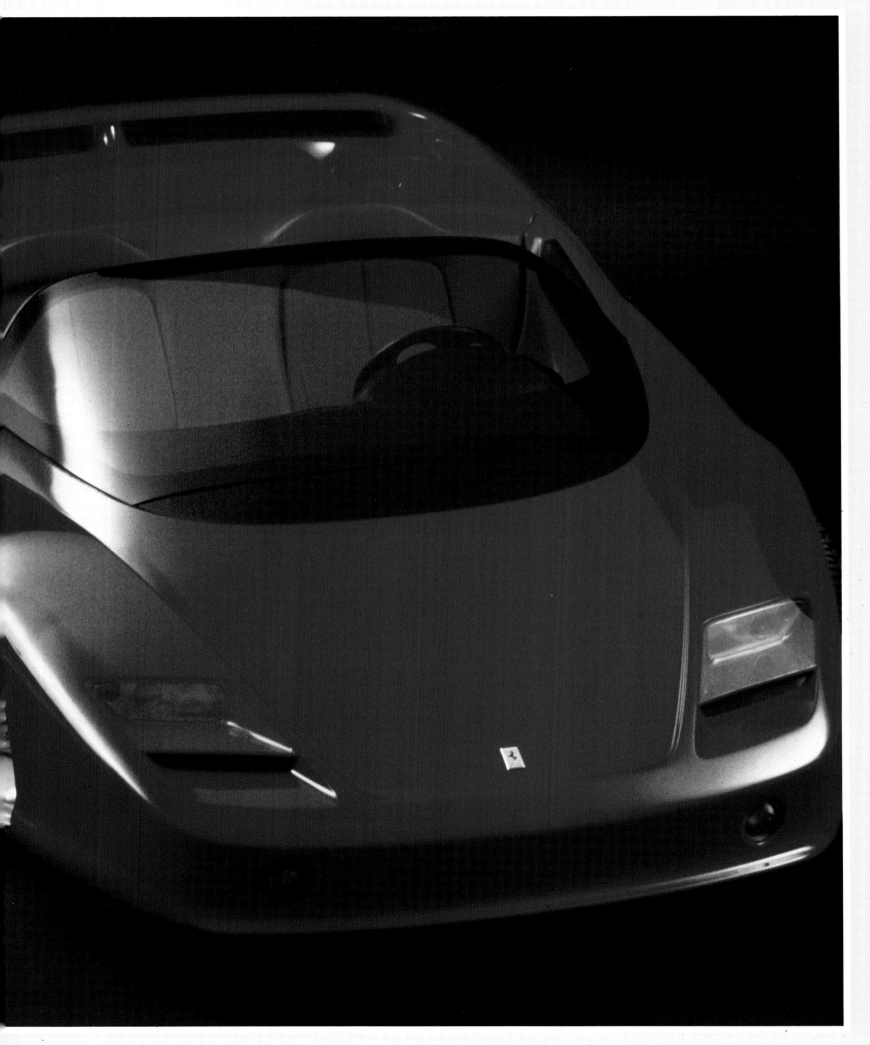

signature and Ferrari crest sit just behind the rear intake, ahead of the back wheel. A rear end that broadens sharply (but ever so gracefully) also rises above the seats, helping to accent the Mythos's wedge profile, whether viewed from the side or above. Rear overhang appears even shorter than a ruler suggests—nearly nonexistent, in fact, going beyond stubby to deliver a sliced-off look. Two pairs of exhaust pipes peek out from the engine-ventilation slit in the back panel, below the taillamp set and above the continuous bumper.

Aggression is evident in such details as the shape of the nose; the small windshield and squared-off tail (both reminiscent of certain Group C racing cars); the steeply-inclined outer edge of the air intake; and the raised front wheel arches, typical of Pininfarina-styled Ferraris. An extension of the windshield glass hides its wiper. Because the car's side planes blend so well, the big rear wing spoiler doesn't stand out nearly as much as in other supercars. Viewed from the top, a link with recent Formula 1 Ferraris is evident in the double "S" section, said to be "similar to the sinuous lines of a ... violin."

Whereas an ordinary Testarossa is wider at the rear than at the front, the Mythos adds 5 more inches to that difference, making the back end 8.2 inches broader than the front. For that reason, the gaping rear air intakes are evident even when viewed from the front of the car. Rear overhang is shorter than Testarossa's, measuring just 25 inches.

Aerodynamics play a key role in the Mythos's design. The rear wing spoiler,

for one, can raise almost a foot (according to speed), to boost the downlift effect. It also rotates 12 degrees, while producing a load of 331 pounds at 155 mph. Instead of the usual correction techniques that affect either the front or rear axle alone, which upsets a car's balance, Pininfarina opted for one at each end. So up front, the retractable lip at the base of the bumper protrudes a little over an inch "to increase the down lift reaction of the dam." Both devices operate electrically, zipping into action at speeds above 62 mph. Each retracts when speed falls below 44 mph.

Ornamentation is about as minimal as in any design in recent memory. Functional elements (bumpers, headlamps, spoilers) are integrated into the overall design, not tacked on later. No surface graphics are needed to identify a car that speaks for itself. Therefore, no space is allotted for such gaucheries.

Within the Mythos lies a symphony of symmetries. Seat bases, for instance, reflect the flowing line of the simple dashboard. The twin-circumference pattern of the analog instruments repeats itself in the steering wheel. Controls sit on symmetrical stalks at the side of the instrument panel. That panel, the steering wheel, and pedals form a single, depth-adjustable block. The lack of window handles allows the door shell to serve as an armrest, while door panels are of the most minimalist nature. Like the body, the two-seat interior, upholstered in red leather, is intended to recapture the spirit of racing "barchettas" of the 1960s. The instrument panel, facia, door panels, and seats are leather-covered shells.

The aggressive stance of the Mythos is partly due to a back end that is more than 8 inches wider than the front. To boost downlift effect, the rear wing spoiler (right) can elevate nearly a foot. A retractable lip at the front bumper (above) helps downlift. The Mythos cockpit (this page) stresses symmetry, with the shape of the analog instrument panel echoed by the steering wheel. The low windshield and interior color—red, of course—are in keeping with Ferrari's racing spirit.

151

The Mythos's dramatic wedge shape and concomitant short rear overhang demanded a revision of the Testarossa exhaust system. Otherwise, the Mythos prototype is based on Testa mechanicals.

Mechanicals come strictly from the Testarossa, including the 12-cylinder, 4942cc flat Boxer engine. Only the exhaust system had to be revised, because of the Mythos's shorter rear overhang. The tubular steel frame is also derived from Testarossa, but reinforced in this application. Hoods, doors, and body panels are made of carbon fiber. Pirelli PZero tires carry the engine's 390-horsepower to the ground: 245/40 ZR17 in front, and mammoth 335/25 ZR17s at the rear. Alloy wheels, derived from the basic Ferrari five-spoke design, display only the familiar prancing horse in their hubs; lug nuts are concealed.

With the creation of the far-from-mythical Mythos, the Pininfarina firm—and Ferrari—reach back to the tradition that brought forth such innovative models as the 250 PS (in 1968), the 512 S (1969), and the futuristic Modulo (1970). Fans of both art and automobiles are sure to welcome a regression of that kind.

FERRARI MYTHOS

SPECIFICATIONS

Manufacturer:	Pininfarina Studi e Ricerche S.p.A., Turin, Italy; for Ferrari S.p.A., Modena, Italy
Body design:	2-passenger, 2-door coupe; carbon fiber body, tubular steel frame
Powertrain layout:	mid-engine, rear-wheel drive
Wheelbase (in.):	100.4
Overall length (in.):	170.7
Overall width (in.):	82.7
Overall height (in.):	41.9
Track, front (in.):	59.8
Track, rear (in.):	68.0
Weight (lbs.):	2756
Approximate price:	NA

Engine type:	dohc horizontally-opposed 12-cylinder
Displacement (liters/cu. in.):	4.9/301
Horsepower @ rpm:	390 (DIN) @ 6300
Torque (lbs./ft.) @ rpm:	(est.) 354 @ 4500
Fuel delivery:	twin multi-point fuel injection
Transmission:	5-speed manual
Suspension, front:	transverse arms, helical coil springs
Suspension, rear:	transverse arms, twin helical coil springs per wheel, anti-roll bar
Brakes:	front/rear ventilated discs

PERFORMANCE

Top speed (mph):	NA
0-60 mph (seconds):	NA
Quarter-mile (seconds):	NA
mph @ quarter-mile:	NA

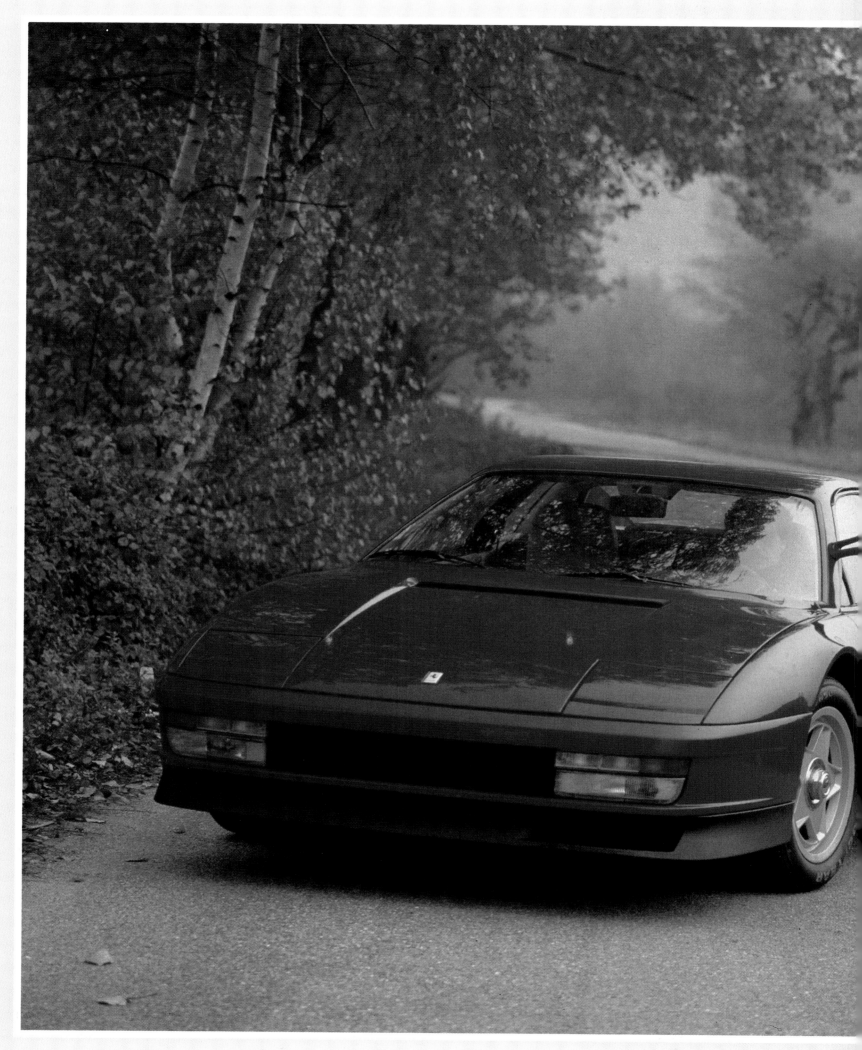

FERRARI TESTAROSSA

Of the three Ferraris currently sold (officially) in the United States, one captures the fancy of automotive dreamers in much the same way as the first examples of the breed. The mere sight of a Testarossa thundering down the highway—or even standing idle in a parking lot—is enough to send shivers down a grownup's spine. It's the heavyweight of the lineup—with big broad shoulders and an earth-shattering 12-cylinder engine.

Back when Ferraris were rarities on American roads, a few fans grew so enamored that they virtually hocked all their belongings for an opportunity to own one. They loved those Ferrari curves, cherished the exhilaration of climbing into the cramped driver's seat, eagerly anticipated each opportunity to take their favorite out on the open road—even if the family had to be left at home for lack of space. No other sports car in the world could satisfy in quite the same way as a Ferrari 250 GTE or 330 GT. Devotees had to have the real thing.

Testarossa is today's equivalent of that irresistible temptation, carrying a legendary name forward into yet another decade. Hardly a production automobile in the world crouches so low to the ground, or looks so poised and ready for action. Tires stand wide apart, like a sumo wrestler's stance as he prepares himself for his opponent's next move. Rear flanks look like they belong on a Formula 1 racer, or even

an Indy car, not something that's sold to ordinary folks—albeit for a healthy six-figure sum.

Sedate is not a word that comes to mind. Neither is small. Sensuous, on the other hand, seems to fit Testarossa like a new pair of string-style driving gloves.

Sports cars do tend to come in two sizes: tiny rough-riding lightweights with screaming, high-winding four-cylinder engines, and big bruisers that mix roaring speed with a slightly higher complement of creature comforts. Both are dashing, both exhilarating, though each in their own ways. But there's no substitute for brute force.

Big and wide enough (almost 6½ feet) to suit any advocate of roadworthy girth, Testarossa is packed with raw, sinewy power. How could it be otherwise, with those six huge horizontal strakes carved into each bodyside, running all the way from the front of the doors to scoops ahead of the back wheels. Oh yes, their ostensible purpose is to send air into the twin radiators positioned just ahead of the rear wheels. But everyone knows that their secondary function, to quicken the pulse rate, is accomplished whether the car is standing still or screaming by at 100 miles per hour.

Add to those flamboyant air-intake ribs the dramatically upswept sides, the massive 77.6-inch breadth that's most evident when viewed from the rear (emphasized by another set of horizontal slats as well as those

Some may call it decadent; others call it love. Either way, today's Testarossa is destined to capture the imagination of anyone whose heart began to pound upon sighting a Ferrari—any Ferrari—for the first time. Like 'em or not, those huge horizontal side strakes are the core of a Testa's personality.

gigantic tires), the quartet of round exhaust pipes below the back panel that emit a siren's song from the mighty 12-cylinder engine. All of this combines in a striking blend of Italian fancy and finely-tuned technology. It's a car that demands to be driven, of course—not merely aimed in one direction or another. Attention must be paid to this dream car, though it's a most enjoyable form of alertness.

You must choose a red one, of course, just as 80 percent of Ferrari buyers do. Other colors are available, including a rather dashing maroon. Motivation researchers learned decades ago, however, that men equate red cars with mistresses. Feminists may decry the comparison, but it's particularly apt when the bright red hue comes in the form of an exotic Italian sports model.

Inside, you'll plunk down in austere yet sensuous comfort, highlighted by fine leather upholstery and complementary carpeting. Gauges are divided between the dashboard and the vertical segment of the center console. Behind the seat, ahead of the engine, you'll find space for a set of fitted luggage, carrying the Ferrari prancing-horse emblem. Additional matching luggage stows into the front compartment. No stereo system is included, but you're free to install your own. Yet any Ferrari owner would rather listen to the rumble of the exhaust, the clatter of the valves, and the zing of the 4-cams.

Like most sports cars, the Testarossa didn't emerge out of thin air when it appeared at the Paris Auto Salon in 1984.

Rather, it's a descendant of the Berlinetta Boxer, and carries the same name as a sports/racing Ferrari model of the late 1950s. The Testarossa nameplate, meaning "redhead," also stems from the bright red color of the engine's cam covers.

Not only designed, but also built by the Pininfarina company, this was the first Ferrari targeted specifically at the American market. It was made to meet federal safety and emissions standards without further modification.

Construction differed from many of its family members, turning to an aluminum body coupled with a steel roof and doors,

Coming or going, a Testarossa commands attention. An aluminum steel body rides the mid-engine chassis. The "redhead" name stems from color of the cam covers on the 12-cylinder engine (below).

which sits atop the customary welded, tubular steel frame. As previously mentioned, the radiators are positioned at the rear, adding some extra luggage space up front and helping the car's interior stay cooler. Those eye-grabbing side slats also send air to the oil cooler, brakes, and exhaust headers. Interestingly, some countries require that large air-intake holes like the Testarossa's be covered by some sort of grillework, hence the need for the menacing slats.

Although similar to the Boxer's powerplant, the flat (horizontally-opposed) 12-cylinder engine held a new 24-valve head on each of its banks and gained 40

horsepower, for a total of 380. That and a torque rating of 354 pounds/feet is what enables a Testarossa to roar up to 60 miles an hour in less than 6 seconds, and streak through the quarter-mile traps in under 14, easily topping 100 mph in the process. Top speed pushes toward 180 mph, or maybe even a hair beyond—quite a feat for a car that weighs in at 3,660 pounds. The engine sits atop a 5-speed transaxle; when servicing is needed, the whole powertrain assembly slips right off the end of the chassis.

Sizable Goodyear Eagle 16-inch tires handle the chore of ground-grabbing: 225/50VR16 up front, and 255/50 cross-section in the back. Rear wheels are

suspended by twin springs and shock absorbers. Massive ventilated disc brakes stand ready to haul the Testarossa to a stop in a hurry, though things could get a trifle tense when coming down from the frightful speeds of which this Ferrari is capable, considering the car does not have anti-lock brakes.

Not everyone loves this far-out "standard" Ferrari. Some think it's a little too much—maybe *far* too much—of a good thing. They scoff at the sight of those half-dozen huge side slats, branding them "cheese slicers." (Admittedly, the grillework does look ready to slice off a huge chunk of Parmesan.) A few observers even decry the

car's civilized comforts, insisting that a super sports car should be stark and tough, and not quite so comfortable inside.

To its ardent fans, though, a Testarossa is the car of never-ending dreams, whether they can be fulfilled in reality or not. To onlookers it's a car that demands rapt attention, rather than merely attracting passing glances; yet it asks for that attention in a joyous manner.

Able to handle low-speed traffic almost as capably as rapid highway travel, the flamboyant Ferrari mixes the exotic with the practical. If imitation is indeed the sincerest form of flattery, the Testarossa has already been praised beyond endurance, as

many of its styling cues—especially those love 'em or hate 'em side slats—have appeared on lesser vehicles.

Only extroverts may want to apply for ownership, though. Driving a Testarossa isn't a solitary experience, but one that brings membership into the larger community of auto worshipers. Suddenly, and perhaps against one's will, even the shyest wallflower becomes Joe (or Jo) Popular. Fire up the V-12 and all ears in the area spring to attention, eager to embrace that sensuous exhaust note. Gapers' blocks begin to form even before the Testa pulls out of its parking space. You'll never be alone until your ride is safely back home.

Poised low, eager for action, a Testarossa (both pages) always looks ready to pounce— barely able to stand still. A broad tire stance adds to the impression of brawn and sinew, coupled with Italian style and sophistication. Built by the Pininfarina firm, the aluminum body carries a steel roof and doors. Although other colors are available, four out of five Ferraris happen to be red—the hue of fire and excitement. Interior comforts stand in contrast to the aggressive body.

FERRARI TESTAROSSA

SPECIFICATIONS

Manufacturer:	Ferrari S.p.A., Modena, Italy
Body design:	2-passenger, 2-door coupe; aluminum/ steel body, tubular steel frame
Powertrain layout:	mid-engine, rear-wheel drive
Wheelbase (in.):	100.4
Overall length (in.):	176.6
Overall width (in.):	77.8
Overall height (in.):	44.5
Track, front (in.):	59.8
Track, rear (in.):	65.4
Weight (lbs.):	3660
Approximate price:	$141,780
Engine type:	dohc horizontally-opposed 12-cylinder
Displacement (liters/cu. in.):	4.9/301
Horsepower @ rpm:	380 @ 5750
Torque (lbs./ft.) @ rpm:	354 @ 4500
Fuel delivery:	twin multi-point fuel injection
Transmission:	5-speed manual
Suspension, front:	transverse arms, helical coil springs
Suspension, rear:	transverse arms, twin helical coil springs per wheel, anti-roll bar
Brakes:	front/rear ventilated discs

PERFORMANCE

Top speed (mph):	180+
0-60 mph (seconds):	5.3
Quarter-mile (seconds):	13.3
mph @ quarter-mile:	107

Testarossa's "trademark" half-dozen air-intake strakes (above), deeply carved into each bodyside, send air to the rear-mounted engine radiators, oil cooler, brakes, and exhaust headers. Practical, yes; but the strakes also add a forceful—indeed unpredictable—aura to the graceful curve above. Additional strakes and vents sit elsewhere on the body (left), while a quartet of exhaust pipes lingers menacingly below the back panel.

161

FORD
SPLASH

Colorful is clearly the word for Ford's playful show car, which rekindles memories of Volkswagen-based dune buggies. Four buddies can squeeze inside, along with scuba and surf gear.

Nobody ever said concept cars couldn't be fun. Ford's free-spirited, youth-oriented Splash concept vehicle flaunts its pleasures brazenly, without a hint of shyness. The colorful four-seater—the creation of a quartet of talented young design students—owes its basic origin more to the Volkswagen Beetle-based dune buggies of California than to humdrum passenger cars, or even to conventional sports cars.

Company publicity, in fact, barely lets on that the multi-purpose Splash was created with motoring in mind. Instead, it's been described as "the ultimate toy for those who like water sports."

Water, in fact, serves as a basic theme. Splash is supposed to be a vehicle that serves as transportation to the beach or the ocean, carrying scuba or surfing gear and as many as four revelers. However, anyone older than 25 is sure to wonder just where those two in the back could possibly squeeze in when the roof panel is in place. Cramped? Sardines would probably cry out for more elbow room.

If nothing else, the Splash is colorful. Flamboyantly so. Youthfully so. No dowdy grays or wilted browns here, to detract from the feeling of wild abandon. Both the body and the interior are decked out in fluorescent blue with magenta accents, intended to deliver a never-ending aura of being out in the fresh, open air. The matching wheels are similarly colored. Upholstery isn't tacky plastic or conventional fabric, but a rubberized material like that used in wet suits. Not much harm could be done if guests flopped down wearing their dripping swimwear.

Wedge-shaped profiles with low front ends and high decks have become standard fare on cars of every stripe, but nothing on the market displays as steep a forward rake as the Splash. Much of it is illusion, though, as the car actually sits fairly level to the ground. A big bubble windshield matches the curved back window. And if you need more than a breath of that sea air, you can remove the windows, roof panel, and hatch to let in all the air you can handle.

As the snow flies, however, windows and a roof will sound sensible indeed, and you may want to tack them on as you pack skis into the Splash for a jaunt to the slopes. Summer or winter, safety is part of the Splash design concept, with its integral roll cage and four-point harness seatbelts for each occupant. Retractable high-mounted, high-intensity driving lamps can be let out for off-roading at night. Mud flaps move upward, out of the way during off-road travel, but can be lowered for highway driving to protect the car's body from stones and mud.

A variable ride-height system adjusts to suit a variety of conditions, so that around town or rolling down the highway, Splash can be lowered to the level of an ordinary automobile. Pull off the road and onto the desert, and it will quickly rise to give the added ground clearance that's needed to prevent bottoming on rough terrain.

Just about every auto enthusiast has scribbled down a design or two for a dream car of some sort—often during high-school study periods. Very few of us ever get an opportunity to let the products of our imaginations take actual shape; certainly not under the auspices of a major auto manufacturer. Yet that's exactly how the Splash came into existence.

Splash was created not by a multi-member professional design team, but by a quartet of transportation students at the industrial design department of Detroit's Center for Creative Studies. Assigned to the project by Jack Telnack, Ford's Vice

President of Design, the students were asked to "design and build a vehicle they would like to use year around as well as on a summer weekend." Work began in the spring of 1988, with the hiring of the four students—Brad Baldonado, Chris Gamble, Warren Manser, and Ricky Hsu—who devoted their summer vacation period to creating a vehicle. The students were given plenty of freedom to decide on the type of vehicle they wanted, how big it might be, and the design theme.

Only one tangible goal was suggested: that it be "flexible, youthful, exciting and just plain fun." Ford wanted to see a vehicle that might appeal to a broad spectrum of young and entry-level drivers, not just to a narrowly-focused group. Like everyone involved in the auto industry, the Ford executives know just how important the

youth market will be to tomorrow's sales picture. The under-25 crowd simply buys too many products—from CDs and movie tickets, to stereo systems and automobiles—for its preferences to be ignored. Everybody wants to attract that segment of the market, but not everyone seems to know what might appeal the most. Splash, then, is just one possible answer.

Actual construction of the prototype began in September 1988, a joint effort of Ford and the Autodynamics Corporation of America. Autodynamics, a prototype engineering firm located in Detroit, had worked on other Ford concept vehicles. Also assisting in the development process were several regular suppliers to the Ford empire, including Goodyear and Kelsey-Hayes.

Although created with the expectation

that it could become a fully operational vehicle with all-wheel drive, the Splash that toured the auto shows in 1989 carried no engine at all. Just a body on wheels, which had to be rolled into the display area. The Splash was not the only concept vehicle on the auto show circuit without an engine. Concept cars tend to be just mock-ups of plastic, fiberglass, and other quickie materials, created to display a fresh form and little else. One must realize that the purpose of the Splash was not to test hardware, but to test public reaction. If it happens to draw enough attention to warrant a drivable version—well, that can always come later.

Will the Splash or a near-clone emerge as a Nineties edition of the dune buggy that proliferated a decade or two earlier, especially in the western states? Probably not, at least for regular highway operation; but the basic idea just might take hold. Ford wasn't the only automaker to come up with a "fun" car to delight auto-show audiences (see the Plymouth Speedster and Pontiac Stinger descriptions later in this book).

With interest in off-roading climbing constantly, a flashy little vehicle aimed at America's younger drivers could conceivably catch on as a new status symbol. If not, it might at least get some of those younger motorists thinking about just what it is that they'd like to see most in a personalized automobile. Not many are likely to be taken as seriously as the four students at the Center for Creative Studies. But a look at what they accomplished might inspire a few modern-day Giugiaros and Pininfarinas to take pen in hand to come up with some fresh creations for automotive fun.

The free-spirited four-seater was penned by young design students, targeted at their peers. Wheels (opposite page) match the bright blue body, while the interior wears hose-it-down upholstery. When skies darken, windows and a roof panel may be mounted.

FORD SPLASH

SPECIFICATIONS

Manufacturer:	Ford Motor Company, Dearborn, MI and Autodynamics Corp. of America, Detroit, MI; student design, Center for Creative Studies, Detroit
Body design:	4-passenger, 2-door roadster
Powertrain layout:	all-wheel drive
Wheelbase (in.):	93.0
Overall length (in.):	143.0
Overall width (in.):	70.0
Overall height (in.):	58
Track, front (in.):	53.0
Track, rear (in.):	53.0
Weight (lbs.):	3100
Approximate price:	NA
Engine type:	none
Displacement (liters/cu. in.):	NA
Horsepower @ rpm:	NA
Torque (lbs./ft.) @ rpm:	NA
Fuel delivery:	NA
Transmission:	NA
Suspension, front:	adjustable ride height
Suspension, rear:	adjustable ride height
Brakes:	NA

PERFORMANCE

Top speed (mph):	NA
0-60 mph (seconds):	NA
Quarter-mile (seconds):	NA
mph @ quarter-mile:	NA

NOTE: The Splash is a design exercise only, with no engine.

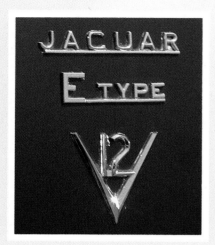

JAGUAR
E-TYPE
SERIES III V-12

Jaguar's E-Type Series III of 1971-75, powered by a new V-12 engine, was a natural outgrowth of the firm's ongoing tradition of performance excellence. Jaguar had stunned the automotive world of 1948 with the XK-120, the first thoroughly modern postwar sports car. Low, sleek, and curvaceous, it was significant for introducing a new twincam inline six-cylinder engine that would prove advanced and adaptable enough to endure for the next four decades. In racing trim, this XK-series engine even carried Jaguars to historic victories at LeMans and elsewhere during the mid-Fifties.

In 1961, Jaguar again set the motoring world on its ear with an even sleeker and sexier dream-car-come-true to replace the 120's evolutionary XK-140/150 successors. Called XK-E in America and E-Type most everywhere else, it shared many styling and technical details with the LeMans-winning D-Type racer, yet offered great long-distance comfort for two, typically British cockpit appointments, a smooth and

tractable powertrain, even decent luggage space. Construction was comprised of a competition-inspired monocoque (unitized) bodyshell bolted up to a multi-tube front structure. Bodywork ahead of the cowl was made up as a unit and hinged at the front to tilt forward for almost unrestricted engine access. The sensational styling was the work of aerodynamicist Malcolm Sayer, making the E-Type the first production Jaguar not shaped by company founder William Lyons. Independent rear suspension (via double wishbones on coil springs, plus an anti-roll bar) and chassis-mounted differential were also new for a production Jaguar.

Though the E-Type used the same front suspension geometry as earlier XKs (double wishbones on torsion bars, plus anti-roll bar), it rode a tighter 96-inch wheelbase and both its 3.8-liter engine and all-disc brakes were uprated. With 265 horsepower and much-vaunted "wind-tunnel tested" styling, an E-Type could reach 150 mph—sensational for the day. All this at a U.S. price of just $5500 made the E-Type the

Based on original E-Type styling by aerodynamicist Malcolm Sayer, the Jaguar E-Type Series III (right) turned plenty of heads when it debuted in 1971. Its appeal has hardly diminished over the years, thanks in part to its imposing V-12 powerplant—good for a top speed over 140 mph.

The Series III's hardworking V-12 brought considerable power, but at the expense of more weight than had to be carried by earlier E-Types. As a result, the Series III abandoned the 2-seat coupe and put the roadster on a 2+2 wheelbase. Frame, bumpers, and brakes were beefed up, but the car remained prone to electrical troubles and other annoyances. Nevertheless, the Series III helped to define the notion of "sports car" in the early Seventies.

automotive equivalent of dollar caviar.

The E-Type was relaunched for 1965 with a bigger-bore 4.2-liter engine that boasted more torque but no more horsepower. A new all-synchromesh gearbox further enhanced low-speed tractability. Brakes and electrical components were upgraded, too. The following year brought a 2+2 coupe on a nine-inch longer wheelbase. It retained its two-seat sister's side-hinged rear hatch but looked more ungainly, thanks to a higher roofline. An exclusive option for it was Borg-Warner's Model 8 automatic transmission. Extra weight and body drag meant the 2+2 could do "only" 140 mph, still more than rapid enough for the time.

U.S. E-Types differed little from British-market models until the revised Series II of 1967, whose styling suffered from federally mandated equipment, including side marker lights, clumsier bumpers, and more upright exposed headlamps (previously mounted behind smoothly faired plastic covers). But there were happier changes, too: larger (and thus more effective) radiator intakes and tail lamps, Girling (instead of Dunlop) disc brakes, newly optional power steering, and a host of other detail improvements, plus a more steeply raked windshield for 2+2s.

Alas, American-market cars began showing the effects of new government emissions limits, and top speed soon fell below 130 mph. But Jaguar soon had an answer for that: a new V-12 engine.

Though originally intended for what materialized in 1968 as the new XJ6 sedan, the Jaguar V-12 first surfaced in a remodeled Series III E-Type, announced in 1971. It stemmed from earlier work on a large-capacity racing twelve, tested in a mid-engine 1967 prototype, the then super-secret XJ13. Massive and complex but beautifully detailed, it employed a 60-degree angle between aluminum cylinder blocks. The same material was also used for the heads and crankcase, with a single overhead camshaft per bank. Combustion chambers were formed in the top of the pistons rather than in the head casting, which was machined fully flat. Aspiration was via a quartet of constant-vacuum Zenith-Stromberg carburetors. With 272 DIN horsepower in European tune or about 250 SAE net bhp in U.S. trim, this 5.3-liter (326-cubic-inch) marvel was far more powerful than the old six, ensuring top speeds of up to 150.

To accommodate the bulkier, weightier engine, Jaguar discontinued the two-seat coupe and put the roadster on the long 2+2 wheelbase. The central monocoque and tubular front sub-frame were beefed up, wider wheels were adopted (slotted steel or center-lock wires), and front brake rotors became vented (instead of solid). Power

steering (still rack-and-pinion) was standardized, and rear suspension was revised by adding trailing arms and having the halfshafts function like the previous upper wishbones. Body modifications comprised a larger hood bulge, re-radiused wheelarches with prominent flares, a somewhat gaudy cross-hatch insert for the "mouth" radiator, the steeper 2+2 windshield for the roadster, triple wipers to clear it and, on U.S. models, big black-rubber bumper guards. A detachable factory hardtop arrived as a new roadster option, while instruments and interior detailing were cleaned up on both models.

The result was an E-Type that not only looked heavier but was: back to XK150 levels, though still sleeker in appearance and much more maneuverable. In fact, the Series III was surprisingly nimble, prompting some to judge it superior to the 1961 original.

There was no disputing performance: at less than 7.5 seconds in the 0-60 mph sprint, the Series III offered colossal acceleration on the order of a Ferrari and Lamborghini— the only other firms then offering showroom V-12s—and for far less money. The U.S. POE price for the basic car was around $8000 in 1972, making the E-Type Series III the world's cheapest 12-cylinder sports car. Moreover, the engine was as smooth and silent as any, though predictably piggish with fuel—in U.S. form, the engine gave just 14.5 mpg or less.

Still, a case could be made that this was just new wine in an old bottle, for most of the familiar E-Type problems remained: vulnerable, unprotected bodywork; tight cockpit; untrustworthy electricals. Indeed, one American magazine summed up the Series III as "a magnificent engine in an outclassed body."

Unique though it was, the Series III was doomed to an early demise by the 1973-74 oil embargo and growing buyer preference for GT-style safety, refinement, and luxury. Jaguar obliged with the four-seat XJS in 1975 after completing the last E-Type roadsters that spring (the 2+2 had been discontinued the previous fall). Series III production stopped at 15,287 units, about a fifth of the E-Type's 14-year grand total.

Clumsy though it may have seemed next to earlier E-Types, the Series III was widely mourned, and many enthusiasts still await another V-12 sports car from Coventry. Prior to being puchased by Ford in 1989, Jaguar had been readying a new "F-Type" sports car for 1992 or '93—though twelve cylinders were less likely than a twin-turbo version of the firm's new-generation AJ6. Should this F-Type appear, let's hope it's at least as good as the underappreciated Series III XKE.

JAGUAR E-TYPE SERIES III V-12
SPECIFICATIONS

Manufacturer:	Jaguar Cars, Ltd. Coventry, England
Body design:	2-passenger, 2-door convertible and fastback coupe; aluminum outer body monocoque inner body with tubular front subframe
Powertrain layout:	longitudinal front engine, rear-wheel drive
Wheelbase (in.):	104.7
Overall length (in):	184.4
Overall width (in.):	66.1
Overall height (in.):	48.1
Track, front (in.):	54.4
Track, rear (in.):	53.4
Weight (lbs):	3230-3450
Approximate price:	$8100 (1971)
Engine type:	sohc V-12
Displacement (liters/cu.in.):	5.4/326
Horsepower @ rpm:	250 (SAE net) @ 6000
Torque (lbs./ft.) @ rpm:	283 (SAE net) @ 3500
Fuel delivery:	4 Zenith-Stromberg 175CD2SE carburetors
Transmissions:	4-speed manual; optional Borg-Warner 3-speed automatic
Suspension, front:	independent; upper and lower wisbones, torsion bars, tubular hydraulic shock absorbers, anti-roll bar
Suspension, rear:	independent; lower wishbones, trailing arms, halfshafts as upper control arms, coil springs, anti-roll bar
Brakes:	front/rear discs

PERFORMANCE

Top speed (mph):	135-142
0-60 mph (seconds):	7.0-7.4
Quarter-mile (seconds):	15.4
mph @ quarter-mile:	93

NOTE: dimensions and performance figures are for U.S.-specification 1972 model convertible.

The Jaguar's V-12 power is hinted at by the Series III's hood bulge (top photos). However, rear badging (bottom photos) spells it out clearly.

JAGUAR XJ220

If a vote were taken on the Big Three sports car makes in history, Porsche, Ferrari, and Jaguar would more than likely top people's lists. Not everyone remembers the impact of the early Jags, but these are automobiles that helped popularize the sports car in America. In addition to their aesthetic qualities, Jags (and MGs) were the affordable sports cars. Some people consider the XK-E to be one of the most beautiful sports cars of all time. Though you might never know anyone who owned a Ferrari, somewhere along life's way, some

friend or acquaintance probably drove a Jag. At least for a while.

No wonder, then, that as the Nineties approached, Jaguar wanted to display a supercar to rival—better yet, exceed—the near-mythical style and performance of Porsche's 959 (evolved from a 1983 show car) and, later, Ferrari's F40. However, they also wanted to incorporate the visual and mechanical traditions laid down by the D and E-type roadsters. Whether the super Jag—called the XJ220—ever reaches the production stage has yet to be decided, but

the show car alone has created quite a stir in the industry. It has also entranced showgoers who had the opportunity to eyeball its astounding profile and peek at the 500-horsepower V-12 tucked inside.

No one had ever seen a Jaguar this low, or this graceful, of course. Rounded contours have been Jaguar's stock in trade, even before the XK120 rocked the sports car world in the early 1950s. The XK-E a decade later took roundness a giant step further along, turning the basic automotive shape into that of a projectile. But this

one—well, *sleek* doesn't begin to do justice to the mathematically and artistically elegant surfaces.

You'd need a calculator to count the number of automobiles with concealed headlamps today, but few approach the exquisite curvature of the oval pop-ups on the XJ220. The w-i-d-e elliptical front air intake is a masterwork of simplicity, perfectly complementing the squared-off opening below, and flanked by a pair of flowing oval recessed openings for the parking lights. Its creators have penned an overall styling theme that obviously stems from earlier Jaguar racing cars, devilishly handsome in their day. But this time they have carried this theme even closer to perfection.

Notice the gentle, barely perceptible flow downward from the front fenders into the wide, swooping nose. To the rear of the door, deeply-carved intake nacelles look eager to suck in all available air for a mile around, spewing the remains out the integrated exhaust pipes at the tips of the lower rear panel. Doors themselves swing

Just as the XK series thrilled a past generation of sports car enthusiasts, Jaguar's proposed XJ220 supercar threatens to steal the thunder from such heavyweight contenders as the Ferrari F40 and Porsche 959. Rounded panels and low, graceful lines are nothing new to Jaguar, of course. Yet the geometric precision of the British supercar's form catapults it far beyond the bounds of its heralded history, and into the realm of the next century.

173

up and out, "jackknife" style, and are power-operated for easy entry and exit.

Beauty and grace don't stop at the top, either. The car's smooth underside forms a pair of venturis alongside the central tunnel, flanking the engine oil pan. A functional design, to be sure, intended to tighten downforce and keep the car low to the ground; but it's also such a pleasure to know that the latest Jaguar flows just as smoothly down below as along the body surfaces above.

While at first glance the XJ220 barely resembles any of its ancestors from Coventry, there's an inherent family tie that binds, at least loosely. Squint your eyes hard and you can see those C- and E-Jag race cars buried in the XJ220's silhouette. Look harder and there's at least a trace of XK-E, and maybe even the old XK120. The graceful side-window shaping, in particular, is Jaguar at its finest.

Although Jaguar's chairman, Sir John Egan, stood proudly beside the XJ220 as it was unveiled at the Birmingham (England) Motor Show in October 1988, the company had distanced itself from the creation process. The brainchild of Jim Randle, Jaguar's director of product engineering, the mid-engine prototype was designed and built over a period of almost four years, by a team of staffers working only in their spare time. As a result of that work schedule, the group soon became known as the "Saturday Club." Company encouragement did not extend to the supplying of either time or money for the project.

To reach the 220-mph goal, pushing a car expected to weigh some 3,400 pounds, a powertrain of phenomenal capacity was needed. Naturally, Jaguar began with its basic V-12 design, which had a long history under the hoods of passenger and racing models. Not only did the new engine's displacement grow from the standard 5.3 liters to a sizable 6.2 liters, but it added a set of four-valve-per-cylinder heads. Those heads actually evolved from a top-secret XJ13 racing project of the mid-1960s. After setting an unofficial speed record of 161.1 miles per hour, the innovative aluminum-bodied, 500-horsepower XJ13 settled into early retirement at the warehouse, never entering the whirlwind of competition. Years later, not only the cylinder heads but a thought or two about aluminum coachwork and shaping emerged as the XJ220 team began its work.

Styling was directed by Keith Helfet at Jaguar, while FF Developments handled work on the four-wheel-drive unit. A Ferguson-type viscous transfer unit sends the engine's power to both axles. A switch at the dashboard selects the height of an adjustable rear wing, to balance downforce as needed. Although ordinary Koni shocks went on the prototype, an electronically-controlled active suspension might appear on a production version. Also, a four-wheel steering, and active anti-roll system may be incorporated into the production version.

Avant-garde as the car is technically, talk constantly revolved around the shape of the aluminum. And that's where the XJ220 shines brightest of all. Not only is it a stunning example of curvaceous metal, but it serves as a showcase for the work of the coachbuilder, located across the Atlantic from Jaguar's home in Coventry.

The Canadian firm of Structures Automobiles Alcan (a division of Alcan Aluminum) in Montreal, Quebec, took on the chore of creating the stressed-aluminum chassis structure. A bonded aluminum unitary frame, or tub, serves as a chassis (actually a 39:1 alloy of aluminum and magnesium). Outer body panels, similarly constructed, are hand-formed and glued together, then bolted into position. Park Sheet Metal, right in Coventry, did the actual coachwork, forming the body panels on wooden templates.

Jaguar's supercar prototype is the first of its kind to take advantage of Alcan's Aluminum Structured Vehicle Technology (ASVT) through the full design process, rather than attempting to duplicate an existing steel structure. The great advantage of this new structure is its adhesive bonding process, which takes the place of welding. Adhesive bonding joins the aluminum components through their entire mating edges. This advanced construction technique lends levels of stability and stiffness to joints that would be impossible to achieve by ordinary riveting or spot-welding, each of which leaves lengthy gaps. Lightweight construction doesn't hurt the potential performance one bit, either.

In addition to the simple urge to offer a supercar capable of matching Porsche and Ferrari, Jaguar had another reason to get the prototype to Birmingham. They wanted a special vehicle to celebrate their 1988 win at Le Mans. So, as showtime drew near, the "club" stepped up its efforts to a frenzy, in an effort to have the car ready for its display stall. Paint and upholstery were plastered on in a hurry, followed by double-curvature Triplex glass. That effort paid off, since the XJ220 proved to be one of the stars of the Birmingham event.

Because the show car was nowhere near ready for running, performance estimates are speculative. The top speed of 220 mph, suggested by the car's badge, is by no means beyond the realm of possibility; and 200 is a virtual sure thing. As for acceleration, Jaguar estimates a 0-60 time of a sizzling 3.5 seconds, hitting a hundred in 8 flat, and going on to 124 miles an hour in a mere 12 seconds. If the production Jaguar carries numbers similar to these estimates, it will be the car to beat in the super-supercar league.

More than a hint of C- and E-Jag race cars lies hazily beneath the surface of the XJ220's astounding shape. Deep-carved intake nacelles ride along the base of each door. Powered "jackknife" doors swing up and out. One of the supercar's goals: to hit 220 miles per hour (hence its name). Helping to make that objective possible is an enlargement of the standard Jaguar V-12 engine (right), mounted at the rear. Raw power hits all four wheels at once. Though no lightweight at 3500 pounds, the XJ220 should require no more than 8 seconds to reach 100 mph, thanks to its 500-horsepower engine.

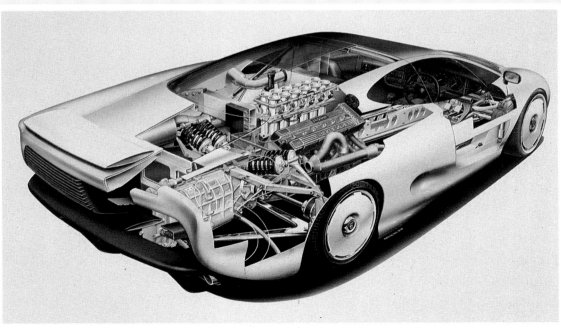

If the prototype is any indication, a production XJ220 would focus as much on comfort as on blast-off performance. Unlike the stark Ferrari F40, or the livable yet modest Porsche 959, Jaguar has a lavish interior in mind—one that features leather upholstery, full climate control, even a compact-disc player.

Production of a thousand super Jaguars isn't out of the question, according to Jim Randle. What would such a Jaguar sell for?

Predictions start at around $250,000, and run as high as three times that figure. Few doubt that the XJ220 could easily become the most costly street-legal sports car of all time. Production wouldn't start before 1991, if at all, and the difficult decision rests in the hands of Ford and JaguarSport, the company's performance division. So it seems that a car which started out as a few men's dream could, one day, become everyone's dream machine.

Not only the form of the XJ220 (left) is new. Instead of conventional welding, the shapely aluminum body—created in Canada—is adhesive bonded, using the latest techniques. Nothing but a gearshift lever sticks up from the console (above). All instruments sit directly ahead of the driver. A production version would have leather, climate control—all the comforts.

JAGUAR XJ220

SPECIFICATIONS

Manufacturer:	Jaguar plc, Coventry, England and Structures Automobiles Alcan, Montreal, Quebec
Body design:	2-passenger, 2-door coupe; monocoque aluminum/magnesium alloy body, bonded to aluminum unitized "tub" frame
Powertrain layout:	mid-engine, 4-wheel drive
Wheelbase (in.):	112.0
Overall length (in.):	202.4
Overall width (in.):	78.7
Overall height (in.):	45.3
Track, front (in.):	NA
Track, rear (in.):	NA
Weight (lbs.):	3439
Approximate price:	(est.) $250,000 (if produced)
Engine type:	dohc V-12 (48-valve)
Displacement (liters/cu. in.):	6.2/380
Horsepower @ rpm:	(est.) 500+ @ 7000
Torque (lbs./ft.) @ rpm:	(est.) 400+ @ 5000
Fuel delivery:	electronic fuel injection
Transmission:	5-speed manual
Suspension, front:	unequal-length A-arms, pushrod/rocker coil springs, anti-roll bar
Suspension, rear:	unequal-length A-arms, coil springs
Brakes:	front/rear ventilated discs, anti-lock

PERFORMANCE

Top speed (mph):	(est.) 200+
0-60 mph (seconds):	(est.) 3.5
Quarter-mile (seconds):	NA
mph @ quarter-mile:	NA

Hard to miss that massive V-12 engine beneath a transparent panel. Stubby front end of the Jaguar supercar suggests how far forward the occupants sit. Part of the decision to produce the XJ220 may rest with Ford, following its acquisition of the Jaguar company in fall 1989.

LAMBORGHINI COUNTACH

Ask most people what they think an exotic car looks like, and they'll probably describe something similar to the Italian-built Lamborghini Countach. Hardly a showcase of smooth contours, its sharp-edged, angular, pseudo-aerodynamic body looks like it contains one or two more pieces than the creator had in mind. Sort of like Han Solo's decadent spaceship in the *Star Wars* saga. "Far out" seems to cover it. Scary, even. If this geometric oddity represents the future, half of us might like to stick around for it, while the other half run off in horror.

Hard to believe that this evident refugee from a future century actually has been sold in the European market since 1974, and arrived in America two years later. Some have called the Countach a vehicle more fit for Darth Vader or Buck Rogers than for anyone who actually has to drive on today's public roads. Others brand the car as evil, sinister, capable of driving calm police officers into a frenzy on sight. Cruising in a Countach down the highway amounts to begging for a handful of traffic tickets, just on general principles. Still others report that its supercar qualities of scintillating performance coupled with precision handling make Countach a car to be admired, no matter how threatening it appears.

If ever an automobile looked like it wanted to tear the local speed limits to shreds, the Countach is a prime candidate. Hell, it looks like it should be able to set its own speed limits. Even when standing still, engine at rest, it looks too dangerous to deal with. With 455 horsepower of V-12 thrust

lurking under the rear engine canopy, a Countach can prove just as vicious as it looks, too. Nobody is likely to doubt its 183 mile-per-hour top speed, or its ability to whip through the quarter-mile in less than 13 seconds. All you need is first gear to edge close to legal highway speeds.

Simply trying to squeeze into a Countach may prove too intimidating for the ordinary person of average dimensions. First, you raise the scissors-style door. Then ease your derriere onto the door sill, before edging backward and slipping (maybe falling) into the low seat. Drag your legs past the tall sill (somehow), watch your head, and you're ready for a driving experience. Provided you don't have to back up, that is. As various testers have noted, driving in reverse may be possible only by raising the door and craning your neck to the rear. That skinny back window isn't likely to show you a thing about what's happening behind you. What you *will* see, though, is a handsome, traditional instrument panel with white-numbered, black-dial gauges.

Comfort and convenience are not Countach's strong points. It's tight in that two-seater cockpit, on either side of the massive center console. Parking can turn into an unexpected workout, perhaps eliminating the need for a session at the local health club. Don't expect a silent episode of easy motoring, either; not with that 5.2-liter V-12 occupying part of the passenger compartment. Unlike its major competitor, the Ferrari Testarossa, which has a sweet-sounding V-12, the Lambo's twelve sounds much more violent and cacophonous.

Whether painted red or a less fearsome color, "brutal" best describes the Countach—the exoticar idea taken to its outer limits. Or beyond. Only a trace of the fabled Italian elegance is evident in the sinister two-seater, which relies on brawn more than beauty.

Those subtle violin passages you expected to hear on the 160-watt stereo will probably disappear beneath its din.

Power windows roll down only a few inches, making fresh air a precious commodity. Once you've calmed yourself after the first ride, climbing out again won't be any easier than getting in. Claustrophobic folks might prefer a Countach with a targa top that could be permanently left at home.

That first ride is likely to produce a surprising sensation of safety rather than fright—at least until you tap the gas pedal a little too hard and suddenly feel like an astronaut blasting off the launching pad. The Countach is designed to hug the road hard, and the huge disc brakes can bring the car to a halt in a hurry. Taking a sharp corner in a Countach at fifty may prove less frightful than doing so at twenty in a lesser vehicle.

Countach's tubular steel frame holds a body hand-formed of thin aluminum, with independent front and rear suspension. High-performance ventilated disc brakes halt all four wheels. Immense Pirelli Z tires (345/45ZR15 at the rear) send the engine's boisterous power down to the road, while a nearly airborne wing-type back spoiler adds additional pressure onto the highway's surface. Plenty of exotic cars have bodyside air intakes, but none are so plentiful or so strangely-shaped as the latest Countach's.

Luggage space? Well, there's a trunk at the back, but don't plan any lengthy journeys unless you're accustomed to traveling light.

Be prepared to answer plenty of questions from passersby. The overly stylized nameplate on the back panel isn't easy to decipher, so everyone will want to know what kind of car it is. And how much it costs, of course. If you're interested, be prepared for a terminal case of sticker shock. Relentless demand and small production quantities have driven actual selling prices far beyond the "official" figure of $145,000.

What a sensation the car must have created when the first prototype Countach appeared at the Geneva Auto Show in 1971. The first production version carried a 3.9-liter V-12, rated 375 bhp. Dimensions grew to 4.8 liters with the 'S' model of 1977, then 5.0, and finally to 5.2 liters in 1985, when a four-valve-per-cylinder head was installed. Since then, its official title has been LP5000S Quattrovalvole. The name

"Countach" (pronounced COON-tahsh) is a slightly risque term in the part of Italy where the car is built, meaning (more or less) "Terrific," or "Wow" or maybe "Good Grief." And to many lovers of exotic automobiles, each of those translations is more than fitting.

Chrysler bought the Lamborghini operation in 1987, creating as wild a marketing mix as any automaker in the world. To mark the 25th birthday of the Lamborghini company, a $145,000 Anniversary Countach appeared for 1989 with a redesigned front air dam, front and side skirting, reshaped air intake grilles along the hood, big flared wheel wells, and a revised one-piece rear bumper. These outward changes gave the car a much cleaner and all-of-one-piece look. Power windows and seats became standard, and seats grew wider. A digital automatic temperature control system regulates interior cooling and heating. All the

Off-kilter angles mix with a bizarre amalgamation of scoops and ducts and pockets to create an evil machine that looks anxious to threaten the serenity of any calm community through which it rides. Countach's tight-fitting cockpit (opposite page) puts occupants in snug cubicles, separated by a huge console.

LAMBORGHINI COUNTACH
SPECIFICATIONS

Manufacturer:	Nuova Automobili Ferrucio Lamborghini S.p.A., Sant'Agata, Bolognese, Italy (a Chrysler company)
Body design:	2-passenger, 2-door coupe; aluminum body, tubular steel frame
Powertrain layout:	mid-engine, rear-wheel drive
Wheelbase (in.):	98.4
Overall length (in.):	170.5
Overall width (in.):	78.8
Overall height (in.):	42.5
Track, front (in.):	60.5
Track, rear (in.):	63.2
Weight (lbs.):	3432
Approximate price:	$145,000
Engine type:	dohc V-12
Displacement (liters/cu. in.):	5.2/315
Horsepower @ rpm:	(U.S.) 420, (Europe) 455 @ 7000
Torque (lbs./ft.) @ rpm:	369 @ 5200
Fuel delivery:	Bosch K-Jetronic fuel injection
Transmission:	5-speed manual
Suspension, front:	unequal-length A-arms, coil springs, anti-roll bar
Suspension, rear:	independent; upper lateral links, lower reversed A-arms, upper/lower trailing arms, dual coil springs, anti-roll bar
Brakes:	front-rear ventilated discs

PERFORMANCE

Top speed (mph):	183.3
0-60 mph (seconds):	4.7
Quarter-mile (seconds):	12.9
mph @ quarter-mile:	NA

comforts of home? Well, a few of them. European versions run with a half-dozen Weber carburetors, while the latest U.S. edition is fuel-injected. Only about 400 of the special-editions were to be built before the Countach name disappears for good.

As if the Countach isn't fast or powerful enough, its replacement, to be called Diablo, is expected to hold an enlarged 5.4-liter (or even 5.7-liter) V-12 engine that produces 480 horsepower or more. A corresponding boost in torque should deliver a top speed near 200 mph.

"A landmark in automotive design." That's how Chrysler describes the final-edition Countach. Speaking to *Car and Driver* magazine, Lamborghini's technical director Luigi Marmiroli dubbed Countach the "king of cars," adding that its demeanor is all male (in contrast to Ferrari's femininity). Undeniably, Countach is one tough-looking cookie.

Practical? Not a chance. Exciting? Definitely! Countach's current engine produces more power than any production car on the globe, and its forbidding shape clamors for incessant attention, carrying the basic automotive wedge shape to the absolute limit. No bashful drivers need apply.

Hard to believe that the mid-engine Countach design (both pages) reaches back to 1971, and that the high-potency sports car has been sold since the mid-1970s. The 5.2-liter V-12 generates more power than any production car around, able to send a Countach speedometer all the way to 183 mph. All that heft is accompanied by raucous sounds from the engine bay, behind the seats. Crawling inside looks easy enough with scissors-style doors raised (left), but it's a battle more suited to contortionists than ordinary folks.

185

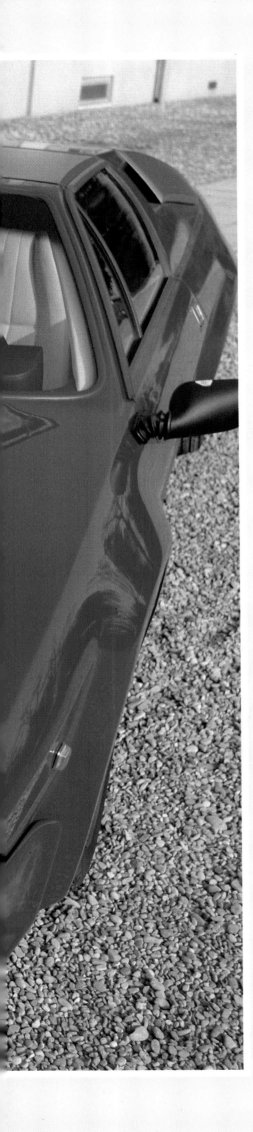

LAMBORGHINI JALPA

Nobody has ever accused Lamborghini of being dull. Usually, it's quite the contrary when speaking of any members of the exotic Italian motorcar family. Metaphors describing this company are as plentiful as air scoops on their Countach.

If the Countach was the radical of the Lambo stable, the Jalpa—introduced nearly a decade later—served as the progressive. The Countach has the role of the disoriented black sheep of the family; Jalpa the handsome, debonair success story that never quite managed to happen. Countach skittered off wildly in every direction, while Jalpa steered a steady course forward as the practical exoticar. Far from tame-looking, this virile yet cultivated Lambo displayed much of the same verve and vitality of Countach, but with a more civilized, even gentlemanly demeanor. Striking enough to draw admiring glances, but not so weird or intimidating that onlookers had to shake their heads in disbelief.

A closer look, however, reveals more than a passing family resemblance between the two. From a distance, the Jalpa cuts a dashing, imposing, figure; no less aggressive than a Countach, but with its own unique style. What's missing from the Jalpa are the extra doodads that, in the opinion of some critics, detract from the Countach's overall appearance. On the other hand, some observers called the Jalpa a little *too* gentlemanly, branding it as a car that never performed as strongly as customers had hoped—even with a 150-mph top speed. But surely the Jalpa never lacked the pedigree to become a dream car.

Jalpa's history began in 1970 with the birth of the graceful, Bertone-styled, four-seat Urraco—the first Lamborghini to carry a 2.5-liter V-8 engine. Six years later came the Urraco Silhouette, which updated the original design into a two-seater with a targa top and sizable B-pillars, as well as a front spoiler. Meanwhile, engine dimensions grew to 3.0 liters. Neither model lasted long. Both the Urraco and Silhouette were gone by 1979, leaving only the bizarre Countach to carry on the tradition of supercars from Sant' Agata.

Early in 1981 an evolution of the Silhouette, named Jalpa, went on sale with a 3.5-liter twin-cam V-8 providing the power. The extra half-liter of displacement over the Silhouette's 2996cc engine dimension promised an extra helping of performance. Sending in the air/fuel mixture was a set of four Weber two-barrel carburetors. Horsepower in European trim was announced as 250 at a near-redline 7000 rpm, with nearly that many pounds/feet of torque produced at a modest 3250 rpm. American editions, when federally certified, earned similar ratings. Lamborghini claimed a 0-60 mph time in the mid-six second neighborhood, though independent testers couldn't manage that pace. Later evaluations, on the other hand, showed even quicker acceleration figures.

Named for a region of Spain where fighting bulls are bred—appropriate since the Lamborghini corporate trademark is a raging bull—the mid-engined Jalpa showed many of the dream-car features of a 1980 show vehicle, the Bertone-penned Athon. The stylist was Marcello Gandini of the

More gentlemanly in appearance and demeanor than its Countach cousin, the Jalpa held back from flaunting its supercar potential. No gimmicks or tack-ons detract from the swooping projectile shape, which evolved from the earlier Bertone-styled Urraco. Only by contrast with Countach can the lesser-known Lambo be branded tame.

Bertone firm, a house that has created the curvatures of nearly all the notable Lambos. A new "flying buttress" roofline extension along either side of the engine bay was the car's most noticeable styling feature, creating a sharp fastback profile. Up front was a revised air dam, with a cutout segment in the middle. *Road & Track* applauded the Jalpa's "rumbling exhaust note" and "swoopy, low" silhouette, adding that the car promised more than its share of excitement for a $58,000 price tag.

Reportedly not the easiest car in the world to drive, the Jalpa came equipped with an extremely heavy clutch and an attractive three-spoke steering wheel that demanded a sizable application of muscle. The gear shifter wasn't the most manipulative, either. Even the gas pedal took a bit more effort than normal. When the driver's muscles got to working properly, however, Jalpas could race to 60 miles an hour in less than 6 seconds and run the quarter-mile in about 14.5 seconds. That and a 150 mph top speed also helped to put it in the near-supercar league. From a more sedate point of view, a Jalpa could move contentedly through traffic better than many other supercars.

Like its Lambo relatives, Jalpa's rearward visibility left a lot to be desired, with a frightful selection of blind spots blocking the view. This could hardly be otherwise, considering the skinny back window and solid, sloping rear quarter sections. Lane-changes are better not imagined, since Lamborghini didn't even bother to provide a right-hand outside mirror to check approaching traffic in the slow aisle. One wonders if they thought each Jalpa would remain in a single lane for its whole driving life.

Luggage space behind the seats comes in handy—but not if the removable targa roof panel has to slip into that spot. Even

so, there was a fair amount of suitcase space in the compartment at the tail end. A full complement of lovely round gauges set into square blocks greeted the driver's eye, as he or she dropped into the low, well-contoured, leather upholstery.

Technical details leaned more toward the conventional than the exotic. The suspension used MacPherson struts, with anti-roll bars at both front and rear. Hefty 16-inch Pirelli P7 tires rode alloy wheels: 205/55 cross-section up front, with a 225/50 design at the rear. Steel unibody construction was used, with strengthening added to reduce flexing at the joints. A separate auxiliary frame supported the mid-mounted V-8 engine.

No more than a few dozen Jalpas reached the United States during each year of its life, even though initial plans called for more than a hundred to arrive soon after the debut. In fact, a mere 410 were built in all. In contrast, more than a thousand Urracos had been produced (but a mere 52 Silhouettes, none of which ever made it to American shores).

By July 1988, production had come to a halt and the Jalpa began its slide into memory. Less-than-sizzling performance has been cited as the major reason for its

Twin "flying buttress" roof extensions (opposite page), flanking the mid-mounted engine, served as a Jalpa trademark. Targa roof panels lift off to let the breezes flow on a summer's day. Four Weber carburetors send fuel into the twin-cam, 3.5-liter V-8 engine (top). Cockpit (above) sports pleasantly-contoured leather seats and a gearshift gate.

189

190

demise, though the speed and acceleration figures don't look so puny at all, particularly when compared to what else was available in the Jalpa's final $65,000 price range. Some critics branded the Jalpa unstable at high road speeds or behind the times in terms of aerodynamic shaping. Whatever the reason, it will be missed by many automotive dreamers, if forgotten by a like number of speed-oriented enthusiasts.

A replacement for the Jalpa, unnamed at this writing, is expected around 1991. Except for the mid-engine, targa-top configuration, it isn't expected to carry on much (if any) of the original's styling cues, and might even hold a V-10 engine.

Jalpa's rearward visibility leaves much to be desired—a bugaboo in many a mid-engine. Recessed instruments (below) flavor the handsome Jalpa dashboard. Appealing lines and an alluring exhaust rumble weren't enough to keep production from halting during 1988.

LAMBORGHINI JALPA

SPECIFICATIONS

Manufacturer:	Automobili Ferruccio Lamborghini S.p.A., Sant' Agata, Bolognese, Italy
Body design:	2-passenger, 2-door targa coupe; steel unibody
Powertrain layout:	mid-engine, rear-wheel drive
Wheelbase (in.):	100.0
Overall length (in.):	170.5
Overall width (in.):	74.0
Overall height (in.):	44.9
Track, front (in.):	61.2
Track, rear (in.):	63.4
Weight (lbs.):	3300
Approximate price:	$65,000 (1988)
Engine type:	dohc V-8
Displacement (liters/cu. in.):	3.5/214
Horsepower @ rpm:	255 @ 7000
Torque (lbs./ft.) @ rpm:	229 @ 3500
Fuel delivery:	4 Weber 2-barrel carburetors
Transmission:	5-speed manual
Suspension, front:	strut/control arms, coil springs, anti-roll bar
Suspension, rear:	strut/control arms, coil springs, anti-roll bar
Brakes:	front/rear ventilated discs

PERFORMANCE

Top speed (mph):	150-155
0-60 mph (seconds):	5.8
Quarter-mile (seconds):	(est.) 14.5
mph @ quarter-mile:	(est.) 93

MASERATI SPYDER

Twin intercooled turbochargers. Now that sounds like raw, bestial power. Where could you find a system of such apparent potency, except atop the engine of a stark, no-frills racing car? Surely not beneath the graceful hood of an Italian dreamboat targeted at luxury-minded couples.

Yet that's exactly where a pair of turbos have been situated since 1982: adding power to the V-6 engine of the Maserati Biturbo, the first twin-turbo production car ever built. In 1989, after two years' absence from the American market, the elegant Maserati Spyder returned, sans Biturbo nameplate but with an equivalent pair of intercooled air-pushers under its shapely hood.

Sensuously elegant is the best way to describe the modern Maserati's gracefully tapered wedge profile, which hails from the renowned Zagato design house. The Spyder is a striking refutation of the belief that luxury, simple beauty, and performance can't merge in a single automobile. The gently rounded edges of hood, grille, and fenders manage to mix the traditional aggressive Maserati look with a friendly, even homey demeanor. Two friendly people can hardly find a more glamorous, or swifter, way to travel the open road than to slide into a Spyder with its top down.

Bodysides are highlighted by a full-length crease, which complements a delicate upper trim line that tapers downward toward the front. The traditional-style grille wears a Maserati trident insignia, which is repeated on the wheel hubs and back panel. Below the thin black front bumper, a large air dam grapples with the wind.

Contrary to popular belief, Ferrari isn't the only Italian automaker with a romantic-sounding name. Nor is it the only one with a long history of sports cars that have delighted both racing drivers and gentlemen motorists. Maserati's history stretches all the way back to 1926, in fact, when Alfieri, one of five automobile-loving Maserati brothers, took first place in the race at Targa Florio. His car wore a Trident logo, based on Neptune's statue in the main square at Bologna, Italy. Victory that day paved the way for use of that very same insignia on Maseratis right up to the present time.

Many other victories followed in the late 1920s and '30s, including back-to-back wins at Indianapolis (1939-40), with Wilbur Shaw at the wheel of a Maserati-based "Boyle Special." Even after the company turned to production of passenger-style sports cars in 1946, racing continued as a

The romance of the road takes on fresh meaning when that road is traveled by two, Italian-style. To create its open-top Spyder, Maserati starts with pure form (best dressed in red), tosses in a liberal helping of luxury—then adds more than a dash of twin-turbo vigor.

Maserati staple, highlighted by a memorable series of first-place finishes earned by the Argentine legend, Juan Fangio, in 1957.

After acquisition by the Citroen company in 1968, Maserati turned out a succession of exciting cars, mostly named for race courses around the world: Ghibli, Indy, Khamsin, Bora, and more. By 1975, however, production had slipped to a couple of hundred cars a year, and the company faced liquidation. Riding to the rescue: both the Italian government and Alejandro DeTomaso, an Argentine entrepreneur and one-time race driver himself.

Dreamily romantic roadster design gives little hint of Maserati's stunning potential on the highway. Spyder's interior (above) fairly radiates rich woods and leathers.

Resurrection of the company began with issuance of the Quattroporte sedan in 1979, followed by the first Biturbo three years later, billed as an "affordable exotic." American fans got their hands on a Biturbo for the first time in 1984, either in closed or convertible (Spyder) form. Elegant inside and out, the Biturbos featured hand-crafted interiors that blended fine woods with hand-sewn Italian leather.

Today's Spyder has all the comforts of the original and more. Rich woods and leathers still line the sumptuous interior. Burled Carpathian elm adorns the gearshift knob, handbrake handle, console, doors,

and dashboard. Sport-style or classic-type seats carry either suede or smooth leather upholstery. While the topside of the convertible top is supple black canvas, with a layer of cozy insulation below, the cabin side is finished in fine hand-stitched suede.

But as we have seen, Masarati is a company founded on racing traditions, and the spyder carries on this tradition well. Beneath the surface, according to the manufacturer, lies a "Maserati racing heart." The single-overhead-cam, 18-valve, 2.8-liter V-6 engine, with head and block constructed of aluminum alloy, delivers a total of 225 horsepower. That's 40 more than the old Biturbo, strong enough to turn in 0-60 times close to 6 seconds, and hit at least 140 miles an hour on the straightaway. Dual IHI turbos with air-to-air-intercoolers force-feed the electronic fuel injection system.

Why two turbos instead of one? Maserati engineers believe that two small units produce less of that annoying turbo lag than a single big one would.

Power hits the rear wheels via a ZF 5-speed manual gearbox which is standard, but a 4-speed automatic is available for those who consider shifting a chore. Light alloy 15-inch wheels carry 205/50 and 225/50 size Michelin tires. Power rack-and-pinion steering is standard, along with vented front disc brakes. Though the Spyder's suspension is less than exotic—just a set of MacPherson struts with anti-sway bar up front, plus trailing arms and Bilstein shocks with coil springs at the rear—it handles like a luxury car with racing pretentions. With a steel monocoque body/chassis, the Spyder weighs in at a comparatively light 2780 pounds.

Maserati calls its contemporary two-seater convertible a luxury car "for the romantic in us all." Because of problems in meeting federal safety standards with the company's two closed models, only the soft-top Maserati came to America in 1989. The U.S. government refused to grant a temporary exemption from the rules, which would have allowed Maserati extra time to fit passive restraints into the 228 and 430 models. Because convertibles were exempt from the existing regulations, the Spyder was permitted to immigrate alone.

Maserati's elegantly simple design demonstrates that dream cars don't have to be bizarre or shocking. Nor do they have to deliver unrestrained shoved-back-in-the-seat performance every time you hit the gas pedal. When you find near-supercar as quick and as (relatively) inexpensive as a Spyder,

the temptation to buy may be too strong too resist.

Oh sure, "real" men might crave a hard-driving Countach, or even a Ferrari or Porsche. Some of us enjoy pain, after all, and don't mind stuffing ourselves into a cramped cockpit only to be jolted and tossed about at speed.

Sensibly romantic men and women, on the other hand, are more likely to fall for Maserati's latest masterpiece of automotive art. They'd rather get a long taste of comfort with their blazing performance; rather like choosing to sip an excellent champagne from a goblet rather than guzzle cheap but potent chablis from a paper cup. Each has its place, but why make life any harder on yourself than it has to be? Tradition has returned, and the Italians haven't lost their touch.

MASERATI SPYDER

SPECIFICATIONS

Manufacturer:	Officine A. Maserati S.p.A., Modena, Italy
Body design:	2-passenger, 2-door convertible coupe; steel unibody
Powertrain layout:	front-engine, rear-wheel drive
Wheelbase (in.):	94.5
Overall length (in.):	159.2
Overall width (in.):	67.5
Overall height (in.):	51.6
Track, front (in.):	59.1
Track, rear (in.):	58.1
Weight (lbs.):	2780
Approximate price:	$46,310
Engine type:	twin-turbocharged sohc V-6 (18-valve)
Displacement (liters/cu. in.):	2.8/170
Horsepower @ rpm:	225 @ 5600
Torque (lbs./ft.) @ rpm:	246 @ 3500
Fuel delivery:	Weber-Marelli electronic fuel injection
Transmission:	5-speed ZF manual or 4-speed automatic
Suspension, front:	MacPherson struts, anti-sway bar
Suspension, rear:	trailing arms, coil springs, Bilstein gas shock absorbers
Brakes:	front/rear discs (front vented)

PERFORMANCE

Top speed (mph):	140-150
0-60 mph (seconds):	6.0
Quarter-mile (seconds):	NA
mph @ quarter-mile:	NA

No bone-jarrer, hardly a rogue, Maserati's deceptively gentle roadster is a rapidly-rolling work of automotive art. Certain dream cars flex their muscles at every turn, demanding to be noticed. Others, like the Spyder, kindly subdue their raw behavior —until the moment it's needed. Maserati's racing heritage has not been forgotten. A V-6 engine (left) with twin turbos churns out 225 horsepower, to hurtle the luxury-laden convertible to 60 mph in about 6 seconds.

MERCEDES-BENZ
300SL

For an entire decade, Mercedes ruled the sports
car world with its 300SL—unbeatable by
anything short of the rare Ferrari.

Like the later Jaguar E-Type, the 1954-63 Mercedes-Benz 300SL was conceived as a sports-racer, not as a road car. Unlike the Jaguar, it proved its mettle on the track before the production model appeared. In subsequent years, 300SLs would also notch an impressive number of rally successes.

But it's neither the car's competition success nor its sophisticated engineering that most captivates people; it's the "gullwing" doors of the initial two-seat coupe. They still seem dramatic despite numerous imitations in the years since 1957, when the closed SL was replaced by a handsome "Roadster" convertible derivative. The Gullwing, in fact, stands as one of those rare coupes that command higher interest— and higher prices on the collector market—than an open counterpart.

Coming from a company that war had reduced to ruins less than a decade earlier, the 300SL was a colossal achievement—a symbol not only of Daimler-Benz's rapid commercial resurgence but a signal that the three-pointed star would go racing again. The 300SL originated in 1952 with a small number of SL ("Super Light") competition prototypes, which won that year's Le Mans 24 Hours and the marathon Carrera Panamericana road race, among other contests. As Stuttgart's first postwar competition machines, they combined suspension and running gear from the then-new 300-series coupe and cabriolet with a light, multi-tube space-frame chassis wearing special closed alloy bodywork. Conventional front-hinged doors would have compromised rigidity in the high-sided chassis, because its tubes were full load-bearing members designed to compress and extend individually. The solution was half-height doors hinged at the roof center to lift upward, which later prompted the "Gullwing" appellation.

Max Hoffman, the import-car impresario of 1950s America, knew a good thing when he saw it. He suggested that Daimler-Benz offer a roadgoing Gullwing, and put his money where his mouth was by ordering 1000 of them. That was enough for D-B, and the production SL duly debuted at New York's International Motor Sports Show in February 1954. Simply put, it was a sensation: a dream car come-to-life, yet a dream that had already proved itself in some of the world's toughest competition. Rarely has a car arrived with such impeccable credentials.

Nor had a car come with such a formidable price: some $7300 in 1956, $500 more than a Cadillac limo. The replacement 300SL Roadster, which used a modified space-frame permitting conventional front-hinged doors, was no less costly, running around $11,400 by 1960. Those lofty figures limited demand as much as the car's painstaking, largely handbuilt construction, so only 1400 coupes and 1858 roadsters would be built before the series was phased out in early 1963. The peak production year was 1955, with 867 units. After 1958, annual volume was only 200 to 250 cars.

Excellence and exclusivity, of course, are never cheap, and the SLs were stupendous: solid, handsome, very fast. In fact, nothing could outpace them except for an occasional Ferrari, which was hardly a "production" car in those days. The one dynamic problem was Mercedes' favored swing-axle rear suspension. On the Gullwing, the swing-axle was the original "high-pivot" type that could mean sudden, vicious oversteer in hard cornering, especially on wet roads. The roadster benefited from the later "low-pivot" arrangement designed for Mercedes' W196 Grand Prix car, with a transverse compensating spring that increased roll stiffness, thus reducing camber change and keeping the back wheels more firmly planted on the pavement.

The coupe had two other drawbacks, both related to its doors: a tendency to allow water leakage, and awkward entry/exit. The latter stemmed partly from the Gullwing design's high, wide door sills and partly from the huge arc the doors scribed, which meant they were impossible to open fully if the car were parked close to, say, a wall. An interesting Gullwing feature that addressed the entry/exit problem was a steering wheel hinged at the base of its hub to tilt almost upside down so as to facilitate wriggling in and out. A clever touch, but not sufficient to make the Gullwing thoroughly practical. Hence the development of the Roadster, which came with a folding soft top and could be ordered with a lift-off steel top much like that of a contemporary Corvette or Thunderbird. The Gullwing and Roadster bodies were made of steel except for aluminum doors, hood, and trunklid, though special all-aluminum competition bodywork was available by special order.

The 300SL engine was basically the 3.0-liter 300-series sohc inline six with

Strakes that stretched backward from the air-extractor vent, plus a gently rounded rear with long trunk lid, helped set a 300SL apart from the pack. Silver paint seemed to do the best job of highlighting body details.

dry-sump lubrication and Bosch mechanical fuel injection, the latter a world first for a production car. The engine was one of the most potent of the day, providing top speeds of 130 to 165 mph depending on gearing. Transmission, final drive, and suspension were all lifted more or less intact from the 300-series.

Appearance, especially the Gullwing's, hardly needs comment, except to note that these SLs were much lower and sleeker than contemporary Mercedes sedans, the somewhat baroque 300-series in particular. Distinguishing features such as the big "mouth" grille with tristar emblem, the wheelarch "eyebrows," and the eggcrate front-fender louvers are well-known. Less obvious, perhaps, is the Roadster's more rounded windshield. Both coupe and convertible were two-seaters with ample stowage space, wind-up windows, and typical no-nonsense Mercedes dashboards dominated by a high-set speedometer and tachometer set amidst plenty of chrome.

More so than the Roadster, the legendary Gullwing has long been the stuff of car-magazine retrospectives. One of the most enlightening from a driver's viewpoint is a September 1989 *Car and Driver* feature by technical editor Csaba Csere, who drove an unrestored '57 model that had logged only 50,000 miles. "Unlike modern cars," he wrote, "the SL doesn't carry a heavy load of sound insulation...Above 3500 rpm, the sounds of the cam chain, the exhaust headers, the intake roar, the injection pump and the valve train drown out all other noises and gradually coalesce into a strident roar. You have a strong sense of driving a machine when you're behind the wheel of a 300SL." But he also found the car "surprisingly refined...The shifter arcs through its longish travel with little pressure and precisely telegraphs the engagement of the gears...The ride is astonishingly plush."

Press harder, as Csere did, and the "steering becomes drastically heavier as you approach the car's limit. On the skidpad, each lap takes about as much effort as a pullup." Lateral acceleration was only 0.65 g, "but remember," Csere cautioned "that Grand Prix cars of 35 years ago made it only into the 1.0-g range...Moreover, the swing-axle suspension was not nearly as diabolical as we expected. The SL's tail did ooze out at the limit, but it could be easily controlled with mild opposite lock. The mythical sudden and uncontrollable oversteer never showed up." Now, think of all this in the context of 35 years past and you begin to understand why the Gullwing was regarded as the best sports car of its day—in Csere's words, "the 1954 equivalent of a Porsche 959 and a Porsche 962 all rolled into one."

In retrospect, the 300SL was a mixed blessing for Mercedes. On the one hand, it was a tremendous symbol of D-B's engineering prowess and a terrific image-leader for the rest of the firm's passenger-car line. On the other hand, the car was never very profitable. Even worse was the tragic spectacle of Pierre Levegh's racing 300SLR flying into the grandstand at Le Mans '55, an accident that hastened D-B's retirement from motorsports.

But none of this has dimmed the luster of the magical Gullwing, long since enshrined in the automotive hall of fame for its performance, pedigree, and sheer impact. It will always be counted among the greats, and that's as it should be.

MERCEDES-BENZ 300SL
SPECIFICATIONS

Manufacturer:	Daimler-Benz, AG Stuttgart-Unterturkheim, West Germany
Body design:	2-passenger, 2-door fastback coupe; steel and aluminum body over steel space-frame chassis
Powertrain layout:	longitudinal front engine, rear-wheel drive
Wheelbase (in.):	94.5
Overall length (in.):	178.0
Overall width (in.):	70.5
Overall height (in.):	51.2
Track, front (in.):	54.5
Track, rear (in.):	56.5
Weight (lbs):	2960
Approximate price:	$7470 (1956)
Engine type:	sohc I-6
Displacement (liters/cu.in.):	3.0/183
Horsepower @ rpm:	219 DIN/243 SAE gross @ 5800
Torque (lbs./ft.) @ rpm:	217 DIN/207 SAE gross @ 5000
Fuel delivery:	Bosch direct mechanical port fuel injection
Transmission:	4-speed manual
Suspension, front:	independent; upper and lower unequal-length A-arms, coil springs, rubber auxiliary springs, tubular hydraulic shock absorbers, anti-roll bar
Suspension, rear:	independent; swing axles, trailing arms, coil springs, tubular hydraulic shock absorbers, anti-roll bar
Brakes:	front/rear drums

PERFORMANCE

Top speed (mph):	140
0-60 mph (seconds):	7.6-8.8
Quarter-mile (seconds):	16.0
mph @ quarter-mile:	89

Mercedes' "Gullwing" coupe (opposite page, bottom) set the sports car world ablaze in 1954. In looks and performance, the stunning gullwing appeared as a renegade from the future. Only the agile could twist gracefully into its cockpit (left), past the tall door sill. An open roadster (top) replaced the coupe in '57.

MERCEDES-BENZ
500SL/300SL

Eighteen years is a long time for a single car design to carry on without a major makeover. However, the Mercedes-Benz 560SL convertible was a car whose character, like that of a fine wine, grew greater each year. So, when plans for a new convertible were released, Mercedes fans eagerly awaited its arrival.

Few would argue that the lusciously smooth, freshly shaped 500SL and its 300SL counterpart were not worth the wait. Rather than a hasty makeover, or even a sizable revision, Mercedes turned to an all-new platform on which to mold a thoroughly modern body. The family heritage is easy to trace, starting with the familiar grille, long hood, and functional little air-extractor vents ahead of the doors —which are borrowed from the original 300SL, introduced 35 years earlier. But this modern, near-supercar has moved beyond its predecessor's shadow to carve out a personality all its own.

Bumpers, for instance, are so carefully integrated into the body that you hardly realize their function—or notice them at all. The square, angular profile is gone. Instead, the overall look is taut, uniform, flush-fitting. Mildly curvaceous elements flow together to create virtually a one-piece impression.

Steeply raked windshield pillars blend pleasantly into the front fenders, and low-curvature front glass is flush-mounted. The body line curves gently upward through the doors, reaching toward a compact, softly contoured tail section. Because the body itself keeps lift down to a minimal level, there is no need for a tacky, add-on spoiler. Crouch down and you'll see that attention has even been paid to the underbody, where careful planning has made it smoother, allowing air to flow more efficiently from front to rear.

If the 500SL's predecessor was starting to look a little fatigued, barely staggering out of the corner for its final round, the upstart seems to be crouched down low, aching for a fight. Capable, too. The newest SL has turned into quite a dazzling performer, echoing its early origins with a V-8 that ranks with the most powerful on the production-car market.

Handsome but heavy at 4163 pounds, the 500SL takes its power from an aluminum dual-overhead-cam V-8 (code M119), evolved from the former SL's but with new 32-valve head configuration. Displacement is 4973cc, or 303.5 cubic inches, and it delivers 322 horsepower. At the same time, the 500SL powerplant is rated at an eye-popping 332 pounds/feet.

Familiar yet totally modern, an SL duo for the Nineties streaked into life as the prior decade ended, ready to retire the aged 560SL. Steering-wheel airbag (above) is one of many safety features.

An electro-hydraulic mechanism adjusts valve timing automatically to give the best of both worlds: higher torque at lower speeds, but more horsepower at the upper end.

A 4-speed automatic transmission is standard, but exceptional in that its top gear is a direct ratio rather than overdrive. Ample, if undramatic, 225/55ZR16 tires ride 8.0 J × 16 light alloy wheels. Like other luxury makes, Mercedes had planned for a "smart" (adjustable) suspension to further finesse ride on rough roads, but that won't be available until 1991. Automatic rear level adjustment is standard now. So is

anti-lock braking, which Mercedes helped pioneer in the mid-1980s.

Nearly identical in appearance except for its identifying badge on the trunk lid, the 300SL differs considerably in motive power. An inline 6-cylinder engine (code M104), also with four valves per cylinder, churns out 228 horsepower. That's nearly a hundred less than the current V-8, though equivalent to the 8-cylinder power of the departed 560SL. Unique to the 300SL is a choice of two 5-speed transmissions: manual or automatic. The 5-speed automatic is a first for Mercedes. The automaker hasn't

offered a 5-speed manual for nearly 20 years, and that should tell you something about the mission of 300SL. This lighter and therefore nimbler roadster is the enthusiast's car in the line-up. A less-powerful 12-valve 6-cylinder SL is sold only overseas, and is not available in North America.

Reaching beyond the striking new design, the SL carries an intriguing selection of innovative technical features. Most clever (and sensible) is the integrated, padded rollover bar. So subtly mounted that you'll barely know it's there, the bar is ready to leap up automatically by spring action—in

a minuscule three-tenths of a second—if sensors determine that a rollover accident is likely to occur. That happens when the car's position goes beyond a specified roll angle, and the suspension detector reveals that one wheel is about to lose contact with the road. Seat belts lock at the same time, while doors unlock (but remain latched), in case you need to get out in a hurry.

With the convertible top down, the bar need never break the car's flowing front-to-back lines; but it's always there waiting, ready when the need is urgent. The bar can also be raised or lowered by the driver at will, by touching a rocker switch on the console.

When Mercedes finally decided to turn to a power-operated top, they didn't hold back on convenience. Raising and lowering a soft top has rarely been so easy or so graceful. No need to fool with a tonneau cover or unhook a series of latches. All you do is hold the button down. The hydraulic mechanism handles the whole procedure in about half a minute, including the opening and closing of the neat tonneau cover.

Wind noise won't keep you from enjoying a conversation with the top

Angles and edges of the past disappeared, replaced by rounded corners and a fluid shape in the new 500SL (both pages). Operative air-extractor vents ahead of the doors hark back to the original 300SL. Under the 500SL hood lies one of the most powerful V-8s around. The automatic rollover bar (bottom) is hardly visible—but leaps into action if computer senses an imminent rollover.

down at speed if your SL is equipped with an optional fabric net system. Hook it onto the rollbar to divert the breezes from your freshly-coiffed hair, and hold in more of the heater's warmth as the sun drops over the horizon. When the seasons change, a removable 74 pound aluminum hardtop can be installed.

Mercedes is serious about safety, striving for occupant protection rivaling that of a sedan. Seats are plush and comfortable, of course, but conceal their most useful secret. They're made of die-cast magnesium, with frames that deform in the event of a side impact. You'll get both visible and audible warnings, too. If the seatback is unlatched, it latches automatically as the car gets rolling. A passenger-side air bag replaces the customary glovebox. Naturally, the driver has one too. When rain comes, a single wiper blade clears more than 90 percent of the windshield's viewing area.

Mercedes buyers expect a full complement of luxury appointments, and they won't be disappointed by the latest SL. Ten-way power seats, for instance, come with a three-position memory that also adjusts the steering wheel and all three mirrors. Tilt steering is a first for Mercedes. Six speakers deliver 100 watts of stereo sound, and there's central locking for all inside compartments. An electrostatic filter for the heating/air-conditioning system works to keep dust and pollen out of sensitive noses. Heated seats and orthopedic backrests are available at extra cost.

Design studies for the latest SL began as early as 1973, not long after its predecessor went on sale, and included some consideration of a mid-engine setup. The project faded away for a while, returning in 1982. By autumn of 1984, the final design was selected, in a configuration that would again be front-engine/rear-drive. Bruno Sacco served as chief designer for the SL project, dubbed R129. Both a conventional modification of the prior (R107) SL series, and a futuristic creation, were rejected in favor of a new concept "with a touch of tradition." At first glance, nothing other than those little air-extractor vents appears reminiscent of the first of the SL line: the "classic" gullwing 300SL coupe of 1954. Closer inspection, scanning from every angle, reveals a few subtle ancestral connections tucked here and there, including the view from above.

Introduced in the spring of 1989 at the Geneva Motor Show, the SL of the Nineties went on sale in Europe the following summer and was released in the U.S. later that year. If sales follow the lead of its predecessor, we can expect to see some 12,000 a year emerge from the plant at Stuttgart, Germany. Proof positive that dream cars need not come in small quantities.

When autumn winds begin to blow, it's time to remount the SL's hardtop (opposite page). Safety seat frames (top) are built to deform in case of a side impact. An optional net (above) lets occupants talk with the top down.

MERCEDES-BENZ 500SL/300SL

SPECIFICATIONS

Manufacturer:	Daimler-Benz AG, Stuttgart, Germany
Models available:	500SL (V-8), 300SL (6-cylinder)
Body design:	2-passenger, 2-door roadster; R129 steel body/frame
Powertrain layout:	front-engine, rear-wheel drive
Wheelbase (in.):	99.0
Overall length (in.):	176.0
Overall width (in.):	71.3
Overall height (in.):	51.2
Track, front (in.):	60.3
Track, rear (in.):	59.9
Weight (lbs.):	(300SL) 3975, (500SL) 4163
Approximate price:	(500SL est.) $73,500
Engine type:	(300SL) dohc inline 24-valve 6-cylinder, (500SL) dohc 32-valve V-8
Displacement (liters/cu. in.):	(300SL) 3.0/181, (500SL) 5.0/303
Horsepower @ rpm:	(300SL) 228 @ 6300, (500SL) 322 @ 5500
Torque (lbs./ft.) @ rpm:	(300SL) 201 @ 4600, (500SL) 332 @ 4000
Fuel delivery:	fuel injection
Transmission:	(300SL) 5-speed manual or 5-speed automatic, (500SL) 4-speed automatic
Suspension, front:	struts, coil springs on wishbones, gas shocks, torsion bar stabilizer, anti-dive control
Suspension, rear:	independent multi-link, coil springs, anti-squat/lift, torsion stabilizer, level control
Brakes:	front/rear discs (front vented), anti-lock

PERFORMANCE

Top speed (mph):	(300SL) 143, (500SL) 155
0–60 mph (seconds):	(300SL) 8.3, (500SL) 6.3
Quarter-mile (seconds):	NA
mph @ quarter-mile:	NA

Bumpers flow so smoothly into the SL body (both pages) that they're hardly noticed. A 6-cylinder engine powers the lighter, more agile 300SL roadster.

MITSUBISHI HSR

Science-fiction writers long ago concocted a future consisting of dramatically low, bubble-topped vehicles traveling along at 200 miles an hour on super-safe superhighways. Families, the writers predicted, would be able to pop into a car that looked more like a spaceship, and head for destinations hundreds of miles away at velocities approaching those now reserved for airplanes. Maybe drivers would still be guiding their cars themselves; or maybe they would follow a guideline embedded in the road, aided by radar, with little human intervention. Either way, they'd expect to journey long distances without fretting much about such mundane irritants as flat tires, boiled-over engines, or semi-trailers suddenly roaring out from the car's blind spot.

For a variety of reasons, that scenario never materialized, even though the technology to make this possible now exists. Practical considerations, such as a decaying highway system, continuing public resistance to higher automotive speeds, and a continuing propensity to drink and drive, have kept triple-digit speeds largely in the province of fiction writers. As the 1990s

emerge, though, Mitsubishi's High Speed Research concept vehicle tries to suggest that such a future might not lie so far ahead after all.

It's no secret that Japan has led the race into electronic-assisted technology for automobiles. Mitsubishi bills its concept car as an "unprecedented union of advanced technology, efficient power and fluid, aerodynamic design." The ultimate goal, they say, is to enable average drivers to "travel long distances quickly and confidently."

HSR development proceeded from the basic assumption that the "needs of ordinary motorists will soon outstrip the capabilities of current automobiles." Mitsubishi chose to respond by creating a vehicle that could provide "safe and predictable high-speed driving," incorporating a helpful blend of communications and navigation equipment and computer monitoring.

First unveiled at the Tokyo Motor Show, the fully-drivable HSR proved to be a virtual show-stopper. Audiences at American exhibitions in 1989 cast a similarly excited eye at the bubble-topper's organic, functional shape. Near-future drivers, they learned, might be "enclosed in

Bubble-top space-age shaping is no accident. Mitsubishi's High Speed Research vehicle is meant to predict what cars will be like when (or if) drivers and highways grow capable of 200-mph velocities. Unlike many show cars, the HSR is ready to perform.

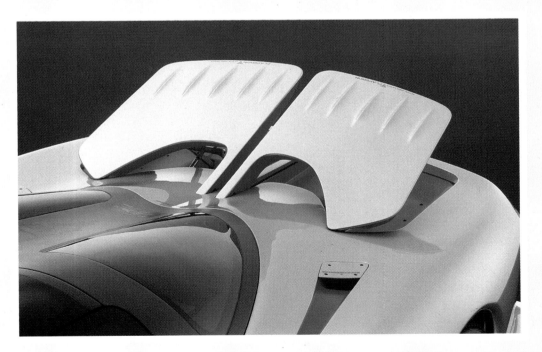

With the help of raised flaps (above), an HSR will hug the ground tighter as speed hits triple digits. Because Mitsubishi is also a technical leader in electronics, it's no surprise that the cockpit (top) is packed with video displays. Computers deliver data on running conditions and map out routes.

a reinforced, space-age skin, with expansive visibility all around." Better yet, they would revel in a "solid sense of confidence and well-being."

Aerodynamics had been the buzzword in the auto trade for several years already, so the HSR appeared to be the next logical step forward. Even showgoers who knew (and cared) little about a car's coefficient of drag, not to mention the coefficient's impact on high-speed stability and fuel efficiency, could imagine a vehicle like this barreling down tomorrow's open highway—and probably without having to stop at every other gas pump along the way.

Sounds great, in theory. Onlookers might be excused for temporarily forgetting the traffic jams and crazed drivers they might have encountered on the way to the auto show. Dreams can't be bothered by such tiresome realities.

In fact, what Mitsubishi created is not quite as futuristic as it appears. Many of its elements and features aren't "maybe" devices at all, but real technological developments that are close to completion. Several already exist in some form on today's cars. A number of HSR's powertrain and suspension components, in fact, are shared with the company's Galant and Eclipse models.

Mitsubishi's Eclipse coupe, for instance—built at the new Diamond-Star plant in Illinois—benefited from the same research that produced the HSR. According to the company, the Eclipse gained a startlingly low drag coefficient of 0.294, along with the lowest frontal-lift coefficient of any production car.

Drag coefficient of the HSR itself drops to an unheard-of figure of 0.2, an amount more appropriate in an airplane than a road vehicle. Moreover, the flowing form creates a useful down-force that increases road-hugging capabilities at high speeds. It actually holds tighter as speed rises, maneuvering as precisely at 200 miles an hour as at more modest velocities.

A Nazca hummingbird—as pictured in lines cut into the Peruvian plateaus—served as the initial abstract image for the HSR's shape. The lines in that image are supposed to represent the linkage between the vehicle's systems, as they reflect the "speed, grace and mobility of the hummingbird" itself. The curved form is also intended to portray the motion of an ocean wave.

The circular glass bubble-top sets atop a luscious collection of curves and protrusions. Ground-effects-type spoilers, practically running-board size, wrap almost completely around the vehicle, and are punctuated only by a sizable notch at the front. The rear spoiler appears to glide right off the deck. Ground clearance is so snug that the body appears to fall perilously close to dragging on the pavement.

Technology is by no means limited to the car's powertrain and aerodynamic aggressiveness. The HSR contains a futuristic system for communications and navigation, as well as computerized monitoring of its functions. A space-age complement of optical gyro fibers, cathode-ray tubes, and other electronic devices let you (and your navigator) pinpoint where you're located on a map, set and follow a desired route, gather traffic information along the way, and communicate with other vehicles or along-the-road stations. Mitsubishi claims its system comes close to what might be found on an aircraft's instrument panel.

The "super-intelligent" overall Operating Control System (OCS) offers assistance and advice related to the actual running, steering, and braking of the car. A "g" sensor and other gadgets send facts to the multi-purpose central computer. Quickly digesting that information, the microchips spit out instructions or a summary of what's happening at every step of the trip. Mike Nash, Vice-President of Marketing Services, says the system is designed to assist owners "with average driving skills to both safely and comfortably sustain cruising speeds in a diverse range of driving environments."

A bit less fanciful, though certainly not low-tech, is the HSR powertrain: a 2.0-liter, double-overhead-cam 4-cylinder engine that transmits its power to a full-time 4-wheel drive system. A combination of strength and light weight is the secret to any future-car's performance. For that reason, the HSR wears a body made of Kevlar and polycarbonate.

Independent suspension at all four wheels is electronically-controlled, able to adjust automatically in response to changing road conditions. Such systems are beginning to appear in one form or another on a number of recent luxury and performance automobiles. Anti-lock braking is standard, along with a supplementary hydraulic air brake. Nothing too shocking in any of that list—just a harmonious mix of what already exists.

Dream-car designers of the past didn't always focus much on safety. Or efficiency. Flashy bodies and super-powered V-8s under the hood were enough to set new-car customers to salivating. Not anymore. Tomorrow's motorists will still crave performance, but automakers are discovering that safety is likely to become a primary selling point.

It's true, the highway system isn't yet ready for a real-life descendant of the HSR. But few drivers, for that matter, are likely to be capable of handling speeds beyond 200 miles an hour, regardless of Mitsubishi's claims of aiming toward the motorist of "average" skill. Nevertheless, the dream of swift, near-silent cross-country travel—whizzing from Chicago to Los Angeles in a matter of hours rather than days—has never faded from the minds of automotive designers and futurists.

Meanwhile, the lessons learned on futuristic vehicles like the HSR are applied to the cars that enter the real-world marketplace each year. Even if none of us live long enough to see a world of bubble-tops blurring across the landscape, we surely will all benefit from the advances today's engineers devise for tomorrow's dream cars.

Ground-effects spoilers the size of running boards are part of the HSR's appeal. A rear-view video monitor (below) is just one of many future-think gadgets inside the cockpit. A later edition, HSR II, sports even more gadgetry.

MITSUBISHI HSR
SPECIFICATIONS

Manufacturer:	Mitsubishi Motors Corp., Tokyo, Japan
Body design:	2-passenger, 2-door coupe; Kevlar/ polycarbonate body
Powertrain layout:	front-engine, 4-wheel drive
Wheelbase (in.):	102.4
Overall length (in.):	181.1
Overall width (in.):	71.3
Overall height (in.):	46.7
Track, front (in.):	58.5
Track, rear (in.):	56.7
Weight (lbs.):	2160
Approximate price:	NA
Engine type:	turbocharged dohc inline 4-cylinder (16-valve)
Displacement (liters/cu. in.):	2.0/122
Horsepower @ rpm:	295 @ 8000
Torque (lbs./ft.) @ rpm:	244 @ 5000
Fuel delivery:	fuel injection
Transmission:	5-speed manual
Suspension, front:	independent, electronic control
Suspension, rear:	independent, electronic control
Brakes:	front/rear discs, anti-lock; hydraulic air brake

PERFORMANCE

Top speed (mph):	200+
0-60 mph (seconds):	NA
Quarter-mile (seconds):	NA
mph @ quarter-mile:	NA

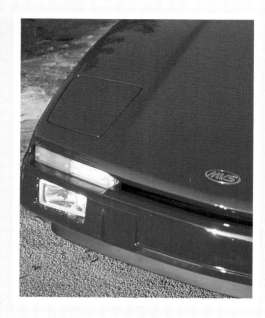

MVS VENTURI

You say Ferraris have grown boring? Porsches are just too, too common in your neighborhood? Then what you need, my friend, is a mid-engined newcomer from France called the Venturi!

Whether you're in a buying mood or just dream-shopping, you're not likely to find one either on the road or in the showroom just yet. The first examples didn't reach America until late 1989. Only 150 or so are expected during the first year, even if sales manage to take off as well as the car's Florida-based distributor hopes.

Though fresh and sassy to American audiences, the MVS Venturi has been around in Europe, at least in some form, since the mid-1980s. An early engine-less clay mockup appeared at the 1984 Paris Auto Salon, riding a Volkswagen platform. Two years later a running prototype arrived, powered by a Peugeot 4-cylinder engine. When that anemic powerplant failed to excite journalists invited to a test drive, the fledgling company quickly switched to a Renault V-6 for the next Paris show. Actual production began in 1987. By late 1989, more than 300 cars had reached the end of the assembly line at the factory in Brittany (in northwest France) and found European buyers.

Not many sports cars display cleaner lines than the sprightly Venturi, even if its overall shape is less than startling. Neither raucously bizarre like a Countach, nor loaded down with grillework like Testarossa and its clones, the Venturi presents a down-to-business demeanor. Nothing flashy,

nothing frightful; just a smooth shape matched by stimulating V-6 power.

A deep bodyside crease running all the way from fender tip to back panel delivers a neat break to the smoothly curved surface. Rear side windows are low and long, matching the front glass to add to the impression of length. The roofline angles downward only modestly, to lead into a high rear deck. Entry handles tuck snugly into vertical recesses to the rear of each door.

Concealed headlamps are ready to pop into nighttime position, but are barely noticeable during the day. Driving lights reside in recessed housings farther below. At the rear, twin exhaust-pipe outlets are integrated into the back panel.

Unlike some exotics, you don't need to be a contortionist to climb into the roomy coupe's cockpit. Doors are cut high enough to allow entry with some semblance of gracefulness, aided by the low door sills. Inside you'll find a simple, yet plush layout with leather upholstery and a beautifully-finished walnut-veneer dashboard. Pedals are straight ahead rather than angled toward the center, as in a number of supercars. An evaluator for *Sports Car Illustrated* called the Venturi's interior "the best of any exotic I have seen." *Automobile* magazine declared the whole car "pretty, well made, and a pleasure to drive." The Venturi is a supercar that doesn't sacrifice for performance; it incorporates both performance and comfort in one attractive package.

Just about all the common comforts and

pleasantries of the road, at least for a two-seater, are available for your driving pleasure. Air conditioning is standard. So are power seats and windows. All-around visibility is much greater than expected for a mid-engine car, though there isn't much room for more than a briefcase inside. A luggage area at the tail end is available, but it might be prudent not to plan any week-long journeys.

To turn out the most efficient product, company founder Claude Poiraud and stylist Gerard Godfroy enlisted the aid of various outside advisers. A group headed by one-time Le Mans winner and race-car builder Jean Rondeau contributed to the original development. Aerodynamicist Robert Choulet worked with the car's creators to finesse the form into a 0.31 drag coefficient, better than quite a few rivals in the supercar league. Michelin assisted in developing an adjustable suspension, with help from former racing driver Mauro Bianchi.

Borrowing from a technique common in the early days of the automobile, the company relies heavily on outside suppliers for components, rather than manufacturing

Rarely in recent memory has a French firm tried to capture a sizable morsel of the supercar pie. MVS sets its corporate eye squarely on Ferrari and Porsche fans with the debut of a pretty—and potent—Venturi coupe.

its own. The brakes and transaxle come right off Renault parts shelves; taillamps from BMW. Other companies handle welding and machining duties, too. The fiberglass body comes from the shop of Heuliez, which turns out similar work for other French automobile companies. Otherwise, the MVS Venturi is hand-assembled.

Advertisements claim the Venturi is the "first premium sports car to embrace aerospace and race car technologies." The car's racing origins are evident in the basic layout: fiberglass body bonded to a rigid, spot-welded, pressed-steel platform. Suspension is more conventional than exotic, with ordinary, but quite capable, double wishbones at the front. Attaching the rear coil springs are parallel lower links, a separate upper link, and two trailing arms. Each wheel is damped by concentric-mounted Koni shock absorbers and halted by vented disc brakes. Michelin MXX tires ride cast-alloy 16-inch wheels. The car weighs in at 2820 pounds.

A turbocharged all-aluminum 2458cc V-6 engine is similar to that used in the Renault 25 and Alpine GTA. Rated at 182 horsepower (SAE), it's mounted longitudinally ahead of the rear wheels. A Garett T3 turbocharger with intercooler helps shove in the fuel-air mixture, via Bendix electronic fuel injection. The 5-speed gearbox extends past the back axle.

A top speed of 152 miles per hour is claimed by the manufacturer. Acceleration from a standing start to 100 kilometers per hour (about 62 mph) takes just under 7 seconds. An MVS can travel through 400 meters (about ¼ mile) in 14.6 seconds.

Early testers praised the engine's performance, as well as the car's overall handling and roadholding skills. They also report that the bodywork displays a high level of fit and finish. On the other hand, some have complained of noisy behavior at the high end of the rpm spectrum, and had a hard time finding neutral with the short-throw gearshift lever. As with most mid-engine exotics, service access to the engine isn't the best.

A convertible prototype was unveiled during the Venturi's official world premiere at the 1988 Paris Auto Show, with a solid top that disappears completely into the tail end. It's likely to enter production eventually. A higher-horsepower version is also contemplated. Before either of those could arrive on the American market, the importers have to evaluate the appeal of the basic Venturi.

Poiraud and Godfroy named their company *Manufacture de Voitures de Sport* (MVS), which translates to the refreshingly straightforward Sports Car Manufacturing Company. They're ready to deliver a limited-production sports car that performs near the level of Ferraris and Porsches, at a comparatively tempting price. Prospective dealers were invited to take a look

during the National Automobile Dealers Association convention in 1989, and perhaps claim one of the "limited number" of dealerships available.

At this writing, the Venturi has passed its governmental tests, but hasn't yet received U.S. government certification. A spokesman reports that American dealers have shown "lots of interest," but none have been appointed so far. The distributor expects to sign up 30 or more, and hopes to have begun selling the car to American customers by the time you read this.

Whether customers in the U.S. will show as much interest as European buyers is not yet certain. But it just could be that these French automakers will give the Italians and Germans a run for their money in the race for sports car supremacy.

A French aerodynamicist helped shape the Venturi's fiberglass curves (both pages), which ride a platform that springs from aerospace and racing. Venturi's interior has drawn raves comparable to the applause for its crisp, no-nonsense body.

MVS VENTURI

SPECIFICATIONS

Manufacturer:	Manufacture de Voitures de Sport, Cholet, France
Body design:	2-passenger, 2-door coupe; fiberglass body on steel platform
Powertrain layout:	mid-engine, rear-wheel drive
Wheelbase (in.):	94.5
Overall length (in.):	161.0
Overall width (in.):	67.0
Overall height (in.):	46.0
Track, front (in.):	57.7
Track, rear (in.):	57.9
Weight (lbs.):	2820
Approximate price:	$68,900
Engine type:	Renault turbocharged sohc V-6
Displacement (liters/cu. in.):	2.5/150
Horsepower @ rpm:	182 (SAE) @ 5750
Torque (lbs./ft.) @ rpm:	214 (SAE) @ 2250
Fuel delivery:	Bendix electronic fuel injection
Transmission:	5-speed manual
Suspension, front:	unequal-length A-arms, coil springs, anti-roll bar
Suspension, rear:	upper arm, parallel lower arms, upper/lower trailing arms, coil springs, anti-roll bar
Brakes:	front/rear vented discs

PERFORMANCE

Top speed (mph):	152
0-60 mph (seconds):	6.5
Quarter-mile (seconds):	14.7
mph @ quarter-mile:	95

OLDSMOBILE AEROTECH
I, II, and III

A.J. Foyt drove Aerotech I (both pages) to a record-breaking 267 mph in 1987. Twin spinoffs soon evolved from the original design.

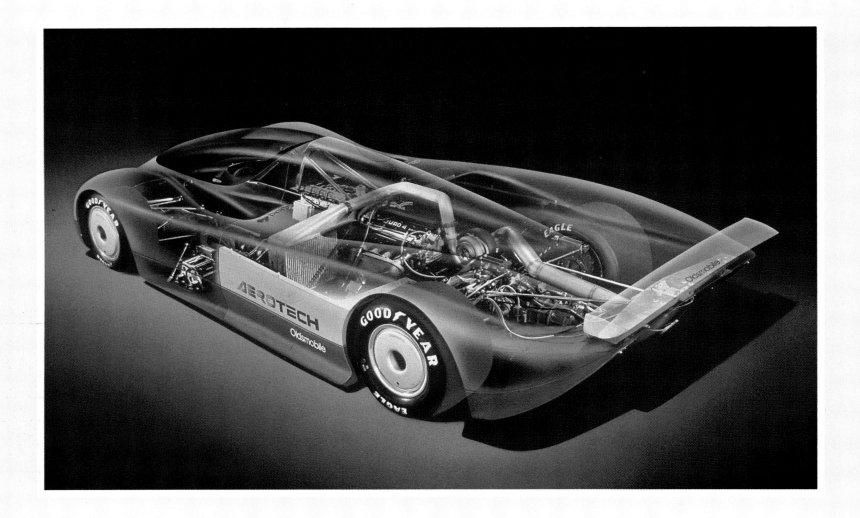

The path from concept car to possible production car can take many forms. When the fantastic original Aerotech I carried A.J. Foyt to record-breaking speeds in August 1987, it was more of an engineering project than a design exercise. A year and a half later, a pair of spinoffs made their debut at the North American International Show in Detroit. Oldsmobile's goal: to apply some of the techniques used in the 260-mph single-seat Aerotech I to realistic vehicles that might carry passengers onto real highways.

Aerotech II, a hybrid coupe/wagon on a lengthened GM-10 platform, looks like it belongs in the 21st century. Ties to the original racing model are evident in its flowing lines. The Aerotech III sedan, on the other hand, is a lot closer to earth and might well be the forerunner of the next generation of Oldsmobile's Cutlass Supreme.

If nothing else, many of the II's high-tech features are expected to appear on real-life Oldsmobiles as they're perfected. Some of the electronic helpers, in fact, are merely advanced versions of gadgetry that's already being produced. The head-up driver's information display, for instance, which projects speedometer figures onto a holographic simulation that appears to float at the car's front end, is a future version of the system offered in some Cutlass Supremes. And the color visual information center is similar to the one used in newer-model Toronados. Aerotech's version includes advanced navigation functions, using compact discs to program map information.

At first glance, the Aerotech II looks like a coupe of tomorrow with a gigantic rear spoiler sticking up at the very tail—even taller than the Ferrari F40's. Looking closer, you realize that glass spans the gap between the roof and the "spoiler." The latter is actually the back frame for the massive glass panel that turns what is evidently a coupe into the equivalent of a station wagon. In addition to creating an unforgettable design cue, the extended roofline expands interior volume for luggage, as well as headroom for back-seat passengers. The back compartment is easily accessible through a pair of center-hinged, tinted-glass hatches that lift upward from each side of the car, like a pair of wings.

A continuous, unbroken line extends from the smoothly-molded front bumper, up the short nose, across the huge glass windshield and into the 4-foot-tall roof—then on toward the far rear of the tail section. Oldsmobile calls the car's silhouette "purposely bullet-like to pierce the wind with the least commotion." An array of low-profile quartz-halogen "mini-cube" headlamps hide behind fold-down covers during the day.

John Perkins, chief designer at Oldsmobile's Studio One, has described the Aerotech II as a "sportsman's vehicle," and even a form of "shooting brake." Rear bucket seats fold to take long or bulky objects (skis, for instance) into the big rear cargo hold.

Long, flowing lines and soft curves continue inside the Aerotech II, creating an inviting space for driver and passengers. Molded dash contours extend all the way into the rear compartment, making functional surfaces accessible to all passengers. Switches and controls are flush-mounted. Lap and shoulder belts protect all four occupants, while the front pair get air bags. The low-profile steering wheel tilts electrically out of the way for easy entry into the car, then returns to a preset position—signaled by computerized memory—at the touch of a button. Radio and climate-control switches are built into the steering wheel. In addition to the head-up instrument display up front, a ceiling-mounted holographic device projects a red 3-dimensional warning onto the rear glass panel whenever brakes are applied.

Although the prototype Aerotech II isn't drivable, it was created to hold a supercharged version of the original's 2.3-liter Quad 4 engine, rated 230 horsepower and feeding an automatic transmission. Electronic traction control

In record-setting tune, the mid-mounted Quad 4 engine in Aerotech I (both pages) eked out some 850 horsepower, using twin turbos. A toned-down Quad 4 later went under Cutlass Calais hoods.

will eliminate wheel spin on slippery surfaces, while anti-lock brakes do similar duty when stopping.

If Aerotech II represents a taste of the future, Aerotech III is a moderate evolution of Oldsmobile products that could be coming soon in a touring sedan. Like the original Aerotech, the concept sedan shows off a low nose and tallish tail end. Triple horizontal bodyside ribbing wraps around the front and rear of the car, but fades away toward the center, at the doors. A functional front air dam and a lumpy aerofoil on the stubby rear deck help cut down on aerodynamic lift and drag forces. Up front are experimental "mini-cube" headlamps. And hugging the ground, low-profile tires on 17-inch aluminum wheels.

Reclining bucket seats carry all four Aerotech III passengers in comfort, with air bags protecting those in front. A sliding security shelf gives clearance for reclining the rear buckets, while at the same time allowing access to the trunk. Added storage space comes from a center console that runs the full length of the interior. A power tilt system automatically moves the steering wheel aside as you enter or depart, and it returns to a memorized position at a button's touch. For ease of use, radio and climate-control switches reside in the steering wheel hub.

Similar to the coupe/wagon, the Aerotech III has a head-up display that projects vital operating information into the driver's line of sight. The electronics however, go a giant step further, with a sophisticated rear-obstacle detection system. A compact rear-facing radar unit monitors the area immediately behind the car, giving audible and visual warnings whenever the car approaches a fixed obstacle.

Tentative powerplant for the Aerotech III is the same as the II's, namely a supercharged Quad 4; but a 5-speed manual gearbox replaces the automatic transmission used in the Aerotech II.

True enthusiasts will appreciate the achievements accomplished by Bill Porterfield, the engineer in charge of the original Aerotech high-speed project. The engine was producing about 850 horsepower when A.J. Foyt set the record pace at Fort Stockton Test Center in Texas. Two versions were built: a long tail (LT) with twin turbos, and a short tail (ST) that ran a single turbocharger. The LT reached a peak of 278 miles per hour in one direction, 257 the other way, for an official average of 267.399 mph in the "flying mile." The car could run through the quarter-mile trap in around 8.1 seconds, reaching 181 miles an hour. Chief engineer Ted Louckes noted that Aerotech I was designed around the Quad 4 engine, to demonstrate its capability "in an extreme testing environment," and no one can deny that 267 miles an hour is extreme!

226

Long Tail version (foreground and right) of the Aerotech I set the "flying mile" record in Texas. The Short Tail design (background) ran with a single turbocharger and wing spoiler.

Aerotech wasn't a single-company production. A large number of subcontractors were employed for the record-setting Aerotech I project, including one that provided the cockpit's Lexan cover. A carbon-fiber body sat upon a specially-designed ground-effects Indy-car chassis, and the whole vehicle weighed just 1600 pounds. High-speed racers need to stick close to the ground and the Aerotech I was no exception, with an inch or less of airspace between its lowest body point and the ground surface.

A replica of the original Aerotech I toured the 1988 auto shows, while a subdued edition of its Quad 4 engine emerged under the hood of the Oldsmobile Cutlass Calais. This new engine was the first multi-valve powerplant to come from Detroit in recent times. As designer John Perkins says, "concept cars stretch the imagination" and show the public what stylists have in their minds. Oldsmobile hit the jackpot with its Aerotech trio, delivering a record-breaker, a high-tech car of the future, a sedan to whet potential customers' automotive appetites, and a surprisingly muscular little engine that's found its way into a broadening selection of GM vehicles.

OLDSMOBILE AEROTECH I
SPECIFICATIONS

Manufacturer:	Oldsmobile Division, General Motors Corp., Lansing, Michigan
Body design:	1-passenger, no-door coupe; carbon-fiber body on steel frame
Powertrain layout:	mid-engine, rear-wheel drive
Wheelbase (in.):	111.3
Overall length (in.):	192.2
Overall width (in.):	86.0
Overall height (in.):	40.0
Track, front (in.):	66.0
Track, rear (in.):	63.0
Weight (lbs.):	1600
Approximate price:	NA
Engine type:	turbocharged Quad 4 inline 4-cylinder
Displacement (liters/cu. in.):	2.3/140
Horsepower @ rpm:	approx. 850
Torque (lbs./ft.) @ rpm:	NA
Fuel delivery:	fuel injection
Transmission:	5-speed manual
Suspension, front:	NA
Suspension, rear:	NA
Brakes:	front/rear discs

PERFORMANCE

Top speed (mph):	267.4
0–60 mph (seconds):	NA
Quarter-mile (seconds):	approx. 8.1
mph @ quarter-mile:	181

NOTE: Four-passenger Aerotech II and III concept cars are designed for supercharged (230-bhp) Quad 4 engine.

Is it a coupe or a station wagon? Oldsmobile's hybrid Aerotech II concept car (above and opposite page) comes closest to the racing original in appearance, but wears a vast glass rear panel. Center-hinged rear hatches lift up like wings. High-tech extras include a head-up instrument display and visual information center. A compact-disc system displays maps on screen for navigation. Except for "mini-cube" headlamps, the subtler Aerotech III (left) looks fit to join the next Olds lineup.

PEUGEOT OXIA

Nobody has to look twice before realizing that Peugeot's latest concept vehicle, spotlighted at the 1988 Paris Auto Show, is meant to be a high-performance touring coupe. If ever a show car looked like it just drove in from a race track—maybe a track of the 21st century—then this was the one. It could have, too, because unlike many prototypes and concept cars, the stunning Peugeot was fully operational. And by operational, we're talking about a twin-turbo V-6 churning out a whopping 670 horsepower at an ear-splitting 8200 rpm. Even with all that superpower the Oxia isn't a bone-shattering racing machine, but a comfortable, well-behaved motorcar.

"Dramatic" barely begins to define the car's sharply angular profile. Wheels pushed all the way out to the corners of the body, reducing front and rear overhang to a minimum. The short, plunging line of the hood—led by slatted air intakes—blends serenely into the vast windshield, with its generous and steeply angled expanse of glass. The roofline's smooth curve continues rearward to blend at an elegant tangent with the tail. At the rear, a variable aileron looks ready to carry the Oxia off the ground—perhaps into outer space, or maybe to send it burrowing down into the ground.

No less unique is a view of the car from the top, which shows a body that widens at the rear rather than remaining of similar breadth throughout its length. The cockpit narrows sharply toward the roof. Beautifully curved door windows edge into tiny triangular quarter panes. Thin-edged spoilers scarcely clear the ground, and the bodysides are highlighted by deep cutouts

in the lower regions. It takes a bit of squinting but, as interior stylist Paul Bracq has pointed out, there's a definite family resemblance between the Oxia and real-world Peugeots—and not just the corporate insignia at the center of the slatted grille.

The Oxia may look like it belongs in outer space, and at least that's where its name comes from. Oxia Palus is the name of a region on the planet Mars that happens to be situated at latitude zero and longitude zero: the starting point for geographic measurements. Peugeot's Oxia, too, described as "making its earthly debut" in Paris, may be viewed as a starting point for performance vehicles in the coming century.

Created at Peugeot's La Garenne research center in France, the Oxia is packed with futuristic technology but isn't really as far-out as it appears. Senior engineer Jean Derampe calls it "more than a showpiece. By synthesizing functional reality with advanced Peugeot technologies," he insists, "we've built a car that can be driven in the real world."

The super-powered, transverse-mounted, 2849cc V-6 lives behind the passenger compartment and has four valves

per cylinder, operated by twin overhead cams on each bank. The Bosch Motronic management system uses two seperate computers (one for each bank). A hydraulic twin-disc clutch engages the 6-speed gearbox, which leads to limited-slip front and rear differentials completing the 4-wheel-drive package. All four wheels steer, too, using a mechanical variable-assist system that "enhances maneuverability at all road speeds." The electrically-adjustable rear spoiler changes angle according to road speed, to deliver peak stability at each velocity, all the way up to the conservatively claimed 187-mph limit (as we'll later see).

An electronic tire monitoring system measures both the temperature and pressure of the 17-inch Michelin tires, which are mounted on magnesium alloy wheels. If its sensors detect a problem, the system even indicates the maximum speed that can be safely driven until a repair is made.

However, that's only part of the Oxia's complement of electronic helpers. Doors are unlocked and opened to the ajar position, either separately or simultaneously, via an electromagnetic locking system. The car's communications center includes a

Extroverts who don't mind being stared at might be the best choice to drive Peugeot's dramatically different concept touring coupe, which looks like a refugee from a 21st century race course. In theory, at least, this show car is fully drivable—and frightfully fast.

radio-telephone to receive weather and traffic bulletins, as well as route and destination information. A built-in personal computer with color display screen, tracker ball, and keyboard can handle either travel, business, or personal chores. Key in information about your departure location, destination, and points along the route, and a road map appears on the screen to display your progress. The map's scale depends on the speed of the car. Databases might even deliver facts on hotel accommodations in upcoming cities, or schedules for public transit.

Computerized air conditioning makes sure that the selected temperature and airflow stay constant, regardless of external conditions. When the car is stopped, this system draws power from 18 solar cells, to maintain airflow through the passenger compartment.

Getting into the two-seater isn't so easy, since you have to climb over a tall sill. Once inside you'll find a blend of traditional leather and future high-tech. The tall console sweeps downward, with a high gearshift lever in easy reach. A steel-blue anodized finish decorates the aluminum dashboard. Electrically-adjustable seats contain a 5-point safety harness. Carpets are bright blue; trim is a colored mix of anthracite gray and steel blue. Electrically powered mirrors stand right at eye level, aligned with the inside mirror to produce a wide field of view. As for entertainment, the Oxia's stereo system comes with a compact disc player. Both the driver and passenger have an entertainment-selection keyboard located on the door panel.

Body construction borrows considerably from race-car techniques, combining light weight with rigidity. An outer skin of carbon and Kevlar-epoxy resin composite is bonded to an aluminum honeycomb structure. The entire chassis assembly weighs only 180 pounds.

Peugeot is no stranger to dramatic concept cars, or to memorable production cars. After years of offering rather sedate passenger vehicles, the company suddenly came up with the speedy 205GTI in 1984. A year later, a turbocharged twin-cam 16-valve 205 Turbo 16, with 4-wheel drive, won the World Rally Championship.

At the 1985 Paris Auto Show, Peugeot displayed its futuristic Quasar concept sports car, which had been designed in-house, even though the legendary Pininfarina had styled many Peugeot production models. No less than the later Oxia, the fanciful Quasar had a science-fiction quality about it. Doors pivoted forward and up from the sculptured body, in the manner of Lamborghini's Countach. Immense side intake ducts adorned the body, while occupants sat inside a massive glass canopy. Twin megaphone exhaust

Oxia's dashboard (top) looks ordinary enough but is packed with innovations, including a computer and a map display that shows travel progress. Comfort and swiftness form a tantalizing mix.

pipes blared out the back end. The Quasar also belted out a mean 600 horsepower, not far short of its later cousin, and was packed with electronic gadgetry from the Clarion company of Japan. A computer system stood ready to map out travel routes, perform a standard safety check, and warn of road and traffic conditions ahead.

Next year came the Proxima concept vehicle. In 1988, a Peugeot 405 Turbo 16

rally car with 4-wheel-steering made a record-breaking run up Pikes Peak. Peugeot teams have also fared well in World Cup Championship racing, prompting the development of a race car to enter the new Sports-Prototype World Championship, which includes the 24 Hours of Le Mans. The company has also been active in the electric-vehicle field, with a number of small fleets running in Europe. In

1989, Peugeot was the only full-scale automaker among seven finalists in a bid to bring electric vehicles to the Los Angeles Department of Water & Power. Unfortunately, sales of conventional Peugeots in the U.S. haven't kept pace with the company's other successes, declining each year since 1984.

Interior styling chief Paul Bracq, as reported in *Automobile* magazine,

compared the Oxia with exoticars of decades past, calling it "my idea of a Delage, Delahaye, or Talbot for the 1990s." Though it won't ever see service on real roads, certain features may well appear in Peugeot racing models—and perhaps in production cars as well.

To demonstrate that Oxia is more than a showpiece, Peugeot invited

journalists for a ride around a French track. With a Michelin test driver at the wheel, the supercoupe reached a speed of 217 mph, well above the company's claim.

Peugeot describes its Oxia creation as "the very essence of the dreamer which lies hidden deep in the heart of modern man." It's the car that "all would like to own but nobody can."

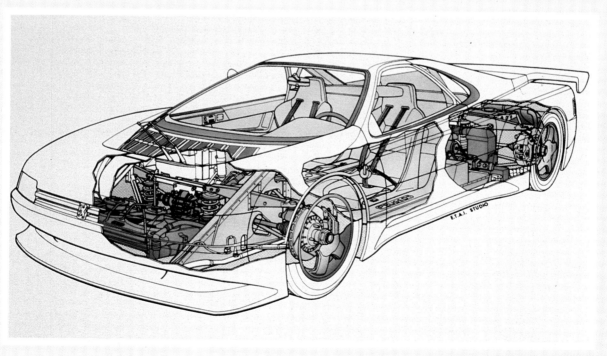

PEUGEOT OXIA

SPECIFICATIONS

Manufacturer:	Automobiles Peugeot, Paris, France
Body design:	2-passenger, 2-door coupe; carbon-fiber and Kevlar body on aluminum structure
Powertrain layout:	mid-engine, 4-wheel drive
Wheelbase (in.):	110.2
Overall length (in.):	181.5
Overall width (in.):	79.5
Overall height (in.):	44.5
Track, front (in.):	68.3
Track, rear (in.):	66.3
Weight (lbs.):	3000
Approximate price:	NA
Engine type:	twin turbo-charged dohc V-6 (24-valve)
Displacement (liters/cu. in.):	2.8/174
Horsepower @ rpm:	670 @ 8200
Torque (lbs./ft.) @ rpm:	535 @ 4500
Fuel delivery:	Bosch Motronic fuel injection
Transmission:	6-speed manual
Suspension, front:	superimposed wishbones, coil spring/ shock assembly
Suspension, rear:	superimposed wishbones, coil spring/ shock assembly
Brakes:	front/rear vented discs, anti-lock

PERFORMANCE

Top speed (mph):	217
0-60 mph (seconds):	under 5.0
Quarter-mile (seconds):	NA
mph @ quarter-mile:	NA

A variable aileron helps make Peugeot's Oxia (both pages) look ready to take off for Mars—the source of the car's name. A long wheelbase gives the radical body little overhang at either end. Blazing acceleration and 200-mph speeds sound almost reasonable with 670 horsepower tearing forth in Oxia's twin-turbo V-6 engine, mounted behind the occupants (opposite page). All that power drives all four wheels. Sadly, Peugeot doesn't plan to produce its angular exoticar.

PLYMOUTH
SPEEDSTER

What do you get when you cross a car and a motorcycle? Plymouth's cute little Speedster 2-seater, of course, ready for a day of fun.

Four wheels do not a car make. Not always. Plymouth's concept Speedster rides on four wheels, all right, but it's a spry little mix of motorcycle and automobile, geared more toward fun than humdrum transport.

Pondering how it might be possible to climb inside the speedster, no one would be surprised to learn that it is aimed clearly at the 18 to 25 year-olds so prized by the marketing mavens. Demographers and marketers love the under-25s, shrewdly calculating that young people have loads of surplus cash, with which they are eager to purchase products of every kind. Naturally, one of those products is an automobile. So just about every automaker (except for those who specialize in luxury vehicles) struggles to appeal to the elusive tastes of the youngest drivers.

Fun and frolic, surf and swim. According to the analysts, that's how young people utilize their free time. And that's the basic theme of the Speedster, which, if produced, would be expected to carry laughing loads of teens and young adults to beaches and ocean vistas. One trade paper described the Speedster as "whimsical." Some might brand it frivolous. Yet who can say what kind of narrow market niches might emerge as the Nineties get underway?

Pontiac tried a similar approach with its Stinger (also described in this book). Both concept vehicles made the rounds of the auto-show circuit during 1989. Maybe both companies have finally found the car they need to draw young folks to their more pedestrian wares, even if this pair never drops off the end of an assembly line.

Not surprisingly, there isn't much about the Speedster that could be called conventional. If you expected an ordinary round steering wheel, for instance, you're in for a surprise. The little funster is supposed to serve as a merging of high-performance motorcycle with open sports car, so it has more of the feel of a two-wheeler than might be imagined. All the major controls and instruments are mounted on a movable, rectangular steering control fork. Instruments could have come off a motorcycle instead of an automobile. Driver and passenger seats are in fixed positions, but the foot controls move forward and backward to suit drivers of different physiques.

Front fenders and hood combine to form a motorcycle-type fairing that wraps around the front, reaching all the way to the doors. As well, this car does not incorporate ordinary headlights: Contained within that fairing are pop-up upper and fixed lower light bars. The low wraparound windscreen is like a cross between a motorcycle's air deflector and a downsize roadster windshield.

Speedster's gray two-seat body is actually a simple molded plastic tub, with a lighter-gray roll bar for safety's sake. It

almost looks ready to float out to sea, like the old Amphicar of the 1960s. The wedge-shaped profile is led by a rounded nose, with near-ground level rocker panels that look almost like old-time running boards. Splashes of color are added by bright green wheels that look like they could have come off a performance 'cycle. The exhaust pipes also appear to have a motorcycle pedigree, and the front turn signals form an integrated assembly with the car's mirrors.

No need to worry about keeping the Speedster clean and tidy. When the molded plastic interior grows grimy with the deleterious effects of leftover hamburger wrappers and other byproducts of the youthful Good Life, cleanup is a breeze. All you have to do is sweep out the big stuff and hose away the rest. The fixed seating surfaces are upholstered with removable foam pads, covered in unique neoprene "wet suit" material; nobody has to bother changing from swimwear to motoring togs. Just plop your dripping bod down on the seats and drive off, letting the sea air and sun handle the drying-off chore. Lots more fun that way, anyway.

Specialty cars don't have to be big. The Speedster is a shorty, in fact, riding a wheelbase of just 81.7 inches and measuring only 130 inches from stem to stern. Chrysler Pacifica, the corporation's design studio in Carlsbad, California, handled the styling assignment. Two major goals were set: The car had to appeal strongly to those favored 18 to 25ers, and it had to be light in weight. No one had to make any plans for likely—or even possible—production on a real assembly line. Or to imagine what dealers might think of such a creation.

Old fogies (those of us over age 25) are sure to spot one unpleasant drawback right off the bat. The Speedster doesn't just happen to have its top in the down position. It happens to have no top at all. When it rains, you get wet. When dust storms appear, you grow dusty. Sudden snowflakes become part of the wild and wacky motoring experience. In short, you get most of the disadvantages of a motorcycle, but probably not too many of its benefits, such as heart-stopping acceleration. Not unless Chrysler would pop a potent turbo-powered four into the engine bay, or even a V-6. And that doesn't seem to be in the cards.

Like many of Chrysler's concept vehicles, the Speedster is merely a steel-and-plastic styling mockup, with no powertrain installed. Not unless some serious feedback results from the car's appearances at shows would Chrysler begin to ponder the merits of one engine or another.

Appearing at 1989 auto shows along with Plymouth's cycle/car were two other

notable Chrysler concept vehicles: Dodge's potentially super-powered Viper which called onlookers back to the (supposedly) good old days of fast cars and easy living, and Chrysler's safety-oriented Millennium, that looks toward the likely future, when performance and good looks will have to be tempered by occupant protection and good sense. What does the Speedster look toward? Just plain fun, it seems. And it's hard to find anything wrong with that, even if we can't quite picture ourselves grappling with that quasi-motorcycle steering fork.

PLYMOUTH SPEEDSTER
SPECIFICATIONS

Manufacturer:	Chrysler Corporation, Highland Park, MI
Body design:	2-passenger, 2-door roadster; molded plastic tub body
Powertrain layout:	NA
Wheelbase (in.):	81.7
Overall length (in.):	130.2
Overall width (in.):	61.2
Overall height (in.):	45.2
Track, front (in.):	53.5
Track, rear (in.):	53.5
Weight (lbs.):	NA
Approximate price:	NA
Engine type:	none
Displacement (liters/cu. in.):	NA
Horsepower @ rpm:	NA
Torque (lbs./ft.) @ rpm:	NA
Fuel delivery:	NA
Transmission:	NA
Suspension, front:	NA
Suspension, rear:	NA
Brakes:	NA

PERFORMANCE

Top speed (mph):	NA
0-60 mph (seconds):	NA
Quarter-mile (seconds):	NA
mph @ quarter-mile:	NA

NOTE: The Speedster is a design exercise with no engine.

Missing from the Speedster's cockpit (opposite page) is a conventional steering wheel. In keeping with the motorcycle motif, controls and instruments ride a movable rectangular steering fork. Front seats don't move, but the foot pedals do. A molded plastic tub forms the roadster's boatlike body.

PONTIAC BANSHEE

Look closely, because what you are seeing may be the next-generation Firebird. That's what plenty of experts have been predicting ever since the blazing Banshee hit the auto shows in 1988. No concept vehicle ever goes from display stand to assembly line intact, of course. Still, it's highly possible that a sizable element of the Banshee's shape, as well as its mechanical features, might emerge as the F-car of late 1992 or '93.

Like all concept cars, part of the Banshee's purpose was to enhance its creator's image. In Pontiac's case, that meant a long-standing image for "sporty, fun-to-drive personal transportation." At the same time, it let the company toss out styling ideas in 3-dimensional form, then listen to public reaction before committing to a real-life design. Pontiac admitted Banshee's test-bed role from the beginning, noting that it was a "futuristic performance coupe with realistic design and engineering features that could appear in the next generation of the popular Firebird."

Sure, the pointy-nosed, sleekly-sloped Banshee looks extreme, even radical, when standing next to a Firebird of yore. Yet a closer look reveals nearly all the expected Pontiac styling cues, albeit in futuristic dress. The familiar Pontiac front-end vee-motif, for example, takes on gigantic form, serving as the centerpiece for the hood.

Banshee's gaping mouth, created by the presence of a "floating wing" near ground level, looks ready to suck up all the available air anywhere near its path, after the sharp nose slices its way through the atmosphere. In tandem with the outboard aero sponsons, the front end displays a fresh interpretation of the traditional Pontiac split-grille formation. The movable wing has a function, too, altering the airflow into the cooling system.

Dual gaping cutouts at the tapered tail end are no less dramatic, even if their purpose is less evident. Pontiac claims they "direct air from under the vehicle." They also allow a peek at chassis components, if you're so inclined. Atop the rear deck stands a pair of wraparound, super-thin wing-style adjustable spoilers, separate from each other and extending all the way forward into the doors. At rising speeds, they can adjust to a position that increases

Pointy beak of the Banshee show car carries the familiar Pontiac "vee," grown to huge proportions. This could be the next Firebird.

downforce, giving traction a boost. Tail lamps are mounted right in the split wings, rather than tacked onto the back panel.

Throughout, the profile is an imaginative blend of graceful curves and assertive angles. John Folden, head of Exterior No. 2 Studio, says the potential F-car "had to be low and slippery with an intensely provocative personality." Furthermore, the traditional front-engine/rear-drive layout had to be maintained, since the public would expect Pontiac-level performance from the car.

Like many concept vehicles, the Banshee body is made up of fiberglass skin stretched across a tubular frame. Smoothly flowing bodysides are devoid of breaks or interruptions. Not even a mirror or a door handle blocks the line from front to rear. Doors open in response to a signal from a wristwatch-size remote control unit. Flush-mounted glass and doors add to the one-piece effect. So do the concealed headlamps.

Under the futuristic front hood lies a 4.0-liter double-overhead-cam aluminum V-8 engine, capable of producing 230 horsepower. Because of the engine's integral block/head design, which needs no head gaskets, it's not the strongest bet for evolution into a production powerplant. The design is actually a leftover from an engine program that was abandoned.

A 5-speed manual gearbox feeds power to the *rear* wheels, as it has been on Firebirds for more than two decades. Chassis features include independent suspension all around, but twin control arms replace the current Firebird's MacPherson struts up front. At the rear is a composite leaf spring, not unlike Corvette's. Four-wheel disc brakes come with an anti-locking system. Goodyear 17-inch tires handle the ground-hugging duties with wheels that look sharp and ready for the next century. But a closer look reveals that they're merely fiberglass covers atop everyday aluminum wheels. Such is the way of concept cars.

Inside you'll find a blend of today and tomorrow: high-tech gadgetry and conveniences, but based on technology that already exists. A head-up instrument display (HUD) projects a holographic image ahead of the windshield, so the driver can check speed, fuel level, turn signals, and the like without looking down at the dash. The HUD appears to float at the front edge of the hood, just below the horizon line, visible in the driver's peripheral vision.

Projected below the HUD information is a virtual image display (VID) that shows an optically-enlarged 3-D portrayal of the analog cluster (speedometer, oil pressure, temperature, voltage). This one appears to lie just a little closer than the HUD. Closer

No mirrors or handles mar the boisterous Banshee's smooth bodyside contour, led by its vast, far-reaching windshield. Design elements, if not the complete car, may be "coming soon" on a real-world Firebird. A movable front wing, near ground level, controls intake airflow on the drivable prototype.

Looks normal at a glance, but Banshee's instruments aren't just on the dashboard (left). Head-up and virtual image displays project clones of the gauges and view-to-rear into the windshield. The unusually "busy" steering wheel is packed with pushbuttons. An ETAK navigation system could show a computer-generated view of the road ahead—traffic, terrain, even a suggested speed.

yet is an image of the shift indicator and rear-view monitor. These in-the-windshield images are optical tricks, of course, since the instruments themselves are inside the car.

Wraparound front seats have a center pivot, and differ from the ones on which we normally park our posteriors. The contoured lower portions hook onto the floor and console, in the normal manner. Swing-away backs have a cantilever-type hookup to another portion of the console, and don't appear to be fixed in place at all. Well, you probably have to sit in them to get

the full picture.

Seats adjust only up and down, but pedals and steering wheel complete the personalization. Set the memory switches for your favorite position and the steering wheel, pedals, and seat pull themselves into perfect alignment. Banshee's steering column tilts and telescopes electrically. Pedals adjust fore and aft, while both front seats have position-memory.

Controls to adjust the radio, interior climate, and other functions are at the flick of a wrist, being located on the steering

wheel hub. Headrest-mount radio speakers contain individual volume, tone, and balance controls. Mobile entertainment includes a CD player with remote-control disc storage in the car trunk.

Video plays an expanding role in driving convenience. Rear-view monitors replace the customary mirrors, for starters. Banshee's ETAK navigational system also uses a TV monitor, ready to display weather data, road conditions—even a computer-generated overhead view of the road ahead. When fully developed, the system will give

PONTIAC BANSHEE
SPECIFICATIONS

Manufacturer:	Pontiac Division, General Motors Corp., Pontiac, MI
Body design:	2+2-passenger, 2-door coupe; fiberglass body on tubular steel frame
Powertrain layout:	front-engine, rear-wheel drive
Wheelbase (in.):	105.0
Overall length (in.):	201.0
Overall width (in.):	80.0
Overall height (in.):	46.2
Track, front (in.):	NA
Track, rear (in.):	NA
Weight (lbs.):	2990
Approximate price:	NA
Engine type:	dohc V-8
Displacement (liters/cu. in.):	4.0/244
Horsepower @ rpm:	230 @ 5600
Torque (lbs./ft.) @ rpm:	(est.) 300 @ 4000
Fuel delivery:	port fuel injection
Transmission:	5-speed Getrag 290 manual
Suspension, front:	unequal-length A-arms, coil springs
Suspension, rear:	independent; 4-link leaf spring
Brakes:	front/rear discs, anti-lock

PERFORMANCE

Top speed (mph):	55 (governed for test purposes)
0-60 mph (seconds):	NA
Quarter-mile (seconds):	NA
mph @ quarter-mile:	NA

a picture of the surrounding terrain and traffic, data on incoming cars, and even suggest the best speed for current conditions.

Banshee is a fully operational prototype, but because test drivers have been limited to a governed 55-mph speed, performance predictions are speculative at best. With the right powertrain under that shapely skin, though, we'd bet that they prove mighty tempting. *Hot Rod* magazine estimated a

development cost of $1.5 million for the Banshee project, and the result looks well worth the investment.

Although rumors have suggested that Pontiac's F-car might fade away rather than be replaced by a Banshee derivative, Firebird's popularity seems likely to prevail into one more generation. Even before such a switch, a handful of styling cues from the '88 concept car are likely to appear on mildly modified 'birds for the early 1990s.

Matching twin spoilers (above) adjust to add downforce at higher speeds, giving Banshee an extra jolt of traction. Rear cutouts let passersby peek into chassis, but also send air out from under. Following Firebird tradition, Banshee must deliver the goods, Pontiac-style. Not a problem with the 4.0-liter V-8 (right).

246

PONTIAC STINGER

Year after year in the late Eighties, Pontiac's auto-show display was a big hit with critics and customers alike. The 1986 multi-purpose vehicle, the Trans Sport, evolved into the GM trio of minivans three years later. For 1987, the performance-oriented Pursuit displayed both styling cues and technical features likely to appear on Pontiacs in the Nineties. Then came Banshee (profiled elsewhere in this book), predicting what the next generation of Firebirds might look like.

What to do for an encore in 1989? Turn to something completely different, of course; something like the rapidly emerging sport-utility vehicle marketplace. And do it in a way that suggests the great outdoors, fun and frolic in the sun. Send a message to young people that Pontiac has their unique interests and lifestyles in mind.

The result was the Stinger, and you don't need a second look to realize that it's a youth-oriented sportster, guaranteed to capture the attention mainly of lively singles. Pontiac's general manager, J. Michael Losh, described it as "spirited, great-looking transportation for the under-35 car buyer or the young person in all of us."

Kinship to the old Volkswagen

Beetle-based dune buggy is unmistakable—but radically updated in concept to take advantage of tomorrow's technology, stretching some of the techniques to their limit. For example, an active suspension system is designed to withstand tough all-terrain driving, delivering as controlled a ride as possible under rigorous conditions. Anyone who's nearly flown off the seat of a Bug buggy is likely to welcome any improvement in that area.

Pontiac's goal was to create a car that mixes elements of an automobile, a jeep, a truck, and a van, aimed not only at the young but at the sports-minded who lead busy lives. Stinger is supposed to lead a dual life: serious during the week, but ready for fun as the weekend arrives. Designer Dave Ross says the design studio calls it "an attitude car." If produced, it would be a "new form of transportation that is personalized and adaptable." Tough but not crude, a production Stinger might appeal to off-roaders, to pickup and van fans, even to motorcyclists. With the right complement of features and accessories, it just might attract surfers, campers, rock climbers—outdoorspeople of every persuasion.

In fully assembled form, the Stinger

More a collection of accessories than a mere motorcar, the Pontiac Stinger aims for youthful fun in the sun. Extras, if the car were produced, might include a camp stove, first aid kit, binoculars, sewing kit, compass, picnic table, vacuum—everything in its place.

offers a comparatively traditional design. Nothing shocking, at least not until the glass panels begin to come off in an automotive strip-tease every bit as titillating as the human version. By the time all five have left the car, you're left with a (literally) open-air sport vehicle: topless, windowless, fully exposed to the elements.

Even the big panel in the center of each door is ready for a quick pop-out at any moment, to let fresh air flow across everyone's legs. But wait, the thoughtful folks at Pontiac declared, why let that space go to waste as nothing more than an airflow entry? Let's plug the gap with a beverage

cooler, so there will always be plenty of refreshing cold drinks on hand when the revelers hit the beach.

The cooler is just the beginning. Indeed, not many vehicles of *any* kind have come with an accessory list to match Stinger's. Tucked in nooks and niches throughout the interior you'll find a pull-out radio (with handy carrying case) for entertainment in the sand, a portable hand vacuum to clean off that sand after it's traveled from swimsuit to seat, a camp stove, and a flashlight. Also incorporated into the Stinger's unique shape are a first aid kit, a fire extinguisher, a toolbox,

and even a hose.

No need to search for a picnic table on crowded weekends, either; Stinger brings its own, ready to fold out for under-the-sun dining. A built-in utility seat within the front passenger seat slips out for use as a camp chair. Look a little further and you'll unearth an extension cord, binoculars with carrying case, sewing kit, compass with magnifying glass, umbrella, tote bags, brush and dustpan—even a calculator to total up gas mileage or the day's expenses. Inside a pull-out drawer sits a cellular phone, so even a day at the beach might not excuse tomorrow's young executives from an

Stinger delivers more than a hint of two-wheeler feel and outdoor excitement, eager to blaze along the beach or bush, courtesy of 4-wheel-drive. A movable back windshield (above) offers rear-seat riders a little protection. Instrument panel (top) looks a lot more conventional than the car itself. Rear passengers are guaranteed a tight fit in colorful seats (center). Back-seat storage area (right) holds camping gear, while tools pack neatly into a rear box.

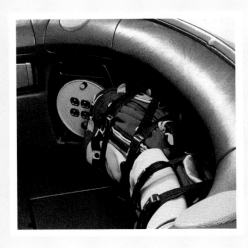

electronic tether to the office.

In short, the stylish sport-utility for tomorrow contains all the gadgets an automaker might provide for a young person's weekend of fun. The goodies are thoughtfully arranged, too: Nothing dangles dangerously. Everything is strapped securely into place. Head designer Terry Henline has called Stinger "a piece of sports equipment" in itself. *Popular Science* magazine described it as something akin to a "Swiss army knife on wheels."

Light weight is another design theme, so Stinger turns to a carbon-fiber body. Headlamps and fog lights are integrated into the surface of the front end. The smoothly flowing windshield continues upward to a removable roof panel, and back to the space-frame roll bar, which also contains roof lights and an adjustable spoiler. Non-scratch paint is the perfect choice for "blasting through the bushes." Sizable rocker panels offer more than a hint of the running boards of yesteryear.

Marietta Kearney, senior designer of Stinger's interior, says she envisioned "hot California young people starting their weekend after a week of work; an atmosphere of freedom and vitality." That thought led to a solid look in the interior, rather than plush comfort; and to a touch of motorcycle in the Stinger's "feel" and controls. Upholstery and trim follow the same gray/green color scheme as the outer body. Gray seats with bright green accents are made from wet-suit material that looks hosed-down even when it's nowhere near water. Radio controls are oversized and the steering wheel is bigger than expected. Six-way power seats have a memory, plus an inflatable bladder system for form-fitting comfort up front.

Passing a parade? Want to get an unobstructed view of the crowd at the beach? Maybe your back-seat passengers just crave a better view of the surrounding scenery for a moment. All you do is raise the two back seats to the handiest height. They extend 15 inches above the normal position when Stinger is at a standstill—and when the transparent rear roof panel is off the car, of course. At nightfall, or for daytime naps, the bucket seats can be folded flat, creating a bed of sorts.

Part of the rear glass can even flip upward to serve as a rear-mount windshield, almost like an old-fashioned rumble seat. Curious how some of those touches from our automotive past keep cropping up.

Performance hasn't been forgotten, either. Not with a 3.0-liter, 16-valve four under the front hood, whipping out 170 horsepower. Four-wheel drive is standard, of course, along with a 3-speed automatic transmission and anti-lock braking. The active pneumatic suspension offers adjustable road height. Upon request, the whole car

With all of its lift-off panels left at home (above), gentle breezes waft past the Stinger's joyful passengers. So do hearty gales and stinging rains. Either a glass side panel or a cooler and case (opposite page) can slip neatly into the door openings. Five panels are removable, including the rear glass. Rising above the seats (left) is a roof light-bar and spoiler.

No-scratch paint and hose-it-clean interior should help keep the Stinger neat and tidy. A pneumatic system can raise the whole car 4 inches for off-roading—part of the active suspension. Few off-roads are likely to hold Stinger back, with a 170-horsepower engine (opposite page) tucked up front. Most surprising, Pontiac is reported to be considering production.

rises by 4 inches—a virtual necessity when rolling along shifting terrain. Goodyear tires measure 295/55R16 in front, with equivalent-dimension 18-inchers at the rear. An attitude gyro on the instrument panel shows the degree of vehicle tilt, so you can restrain yourself from going past its logical limit. An electric compass could prove handier yet when you've wandered a little too far off the road.

Pontiac's planners believe there's a definite market for a free-spirited, all-season Stinger-like vehicle, and that it could be profitable. They point to the success of such vehicles as Suzuki's Samurai and Sidekick, Dodge's Raider, and similar products. Whether production ever becomes a reality depends upon public reaction and the whims of Detroit. Those of us who wouldn't mind playing all weekend after a long week at work might be tempted.

PONTIAC STINGER
SPECIFICATIONS

Manufacturer:	Pontiac Division, General Motors Corp., Pontiac, MI
Body design:	2+2-passenger, 2-door roadster; carbon-fiber body on steel frame
Powertrain layout:	front-engine, 4-wheel drive
Wheelbase (in.):	98.0
Overall length (in.):	164.8
Overall width (in.):	73.7
Overall height (in.):	58.8
Track, front (in.):	61.6
Track, rear (in.):	61.6
Weight (lbs.):	approx. 3000
Approximate price:	NA
Engine type:	inline 4-cylinder (16-valve)
Displacement (liters/cu. in.):	3.0/183
Horsepower @ rpm:	170 @ 6500
Torque (lbs./ft.) @ rpm:	200 @ 6000
Fuel delivery:	fuel injection
Transmission:	3-speed automatic
Suspension, front:	independent, pneumatic active
Suspension, rear:	independent, pneumatic active
Brakes:	front/rear discs, anti-lock

PERFORMANCE

Top speed (mph):	NA
0-60 mph (seconds):	NA
Quarter-mile (seconds):	NA
mph @ quarter-mile:	NA

PORSCHE 911
CARRERA CABRIO

With or without its big spoiler,
the current Cabrio carries on the form
of the first Porsches.

Few sports cars deserve the title of "classic" car more than Porsche's 911. Directly descended from the Type 356, which awed critics and the general public alike in the early Fifties, the 911—once thought destined for extinction—carries on the Porsche tradition of big performance in a small package with a new spirit of youth.

If a closed 911 is classic, the open-topped Cabrio is nothing short of sheer pleasure. A joy to watch, a joy to drive, a joy to imagine. Who wouldn't want to slide into the driver's seat, take down the top, and hear that flat-6, rear engine sing its throaty melody along the open road.

Like every Porsche, past and present, the 911 offers irrefutable evidence of their maker's Teutonic expertise around the machine shop. From the beginning, the low-slung Porsches were seen as expertly engineered. Curvaceous forms attracted the eye, of course, but solid drivability is what earned the company its reputation for quality. Porsche engineers are always learning, always refining. After four decades on the road with similar mechanicals and form, the 911 keeps getting better and better.

Although 911 history began officially in 1965, its roots reach back 15 years earlier, to the emergence of the first Porsche 356. Along with the Jaguar XK120 and MG TD, the 356 was responsible for turning thousands of young Americans away from Detroit iron, and transforming them into lifelong lovers of sports cars. Carrying its flat engine in back rather than in the "normal" front position, Porsche served with distinction on the track as well as the road, bringing Germany a Le Mans victory in 1951. Volkswagen shared a similar configuration, and both makes helped to convince American drivers of the 1950s that the Detroit way wasn't the only way to travel.

In 1963 a modification of the 356 appeared, styled by Ferdinand "Butzi" Porsche, grandson of the company's founder. Called 901 when in prototype form, it switched to the 911 title for 1965 production. Prior Porsches had run with 4-cylinder horizontally-opposed engines (which continued with a new 912 model). However, the 911 switched to a 6-cylinder edition that displaced 2.0 liters—quite a jump from the original Porsche's 1131cc size.

By 1974, engine dimensions had taken several more upward leaps, reaching 2687cc. That year, American fans could buy a street-legal Carrera version that wore a rubber-rimmed "ducktail" rear spoiler—sometimes called a "whaletail." And they did buy. More than half of all Porsches built headed for U.S. shores by the mid-1970s. A Turbo edition entered Europe in 1975, sufficiently different that the company insisted on calling it model 930. A year later it crossed the Atlantic with the name Turbo Carrera.

A fifth jump in engine size came in 1982, this time to 3.2 liters (and 200 horsepower), reviving the Carrera name once again. That title saw on-again, off-again life on Porsche models beginning in 1953. Horsepower got a boost to 214 for 1987, but the engine has retained the same dimensions.

Mechanical improvements and new features have arrived with pleasing regularity. Power brakes became standard in 1979, air conditioning and power windows a no-cost extra a year later, halogen headlamps the following season.

Standard fittings today include an electric sliding roof, heated mirrors and headlight-washer nozzles, leather-rimmed steering wheel, and partial leather reclining front seats with electric height adjustment. Electronic cruise control replaced the former pneumatic variety in 1988. Blaupunkt "Reno" stereo sends 100 watts of power into eight speakers (six in the convertible)—enough to blast unwanted occupants out of the cozy back seat. Forged alloy wheels carry 205/55ZR16 tires in front, and larger 225/50ZR16 rubber in the back. Power-assisted disc brakes are internally vented. The 5-speed manual gearbox is mounted in the rear transaxle.

Front and rear spoilers are optional. If you crave the appearance of a Turbo 911,

but don't really need the extra jolt of performance, there's always the Turbo-look package, available with or without the requisite spoilers.

The Cabrio top is fully padded, with an automatic tensioning system for a snug fit and smart appearance when up. Touch-button power operation is an option. With that feature, you don't even have to open or lock the latch clips yourself. Not everyone cares for wind-in-the-face motoring, of course, so Porsche gives you three choices: all the way open in the Cabriolet, halfway in a Targa version, or the traditional closed coupe. Targa roof panels lift out and store in the luggage compartment, or behind the

seats. Whatever the body style, you may have to choose small friends or limit yourself to a single passenger. Not many 2+2s hold more than a pair of youngsters or a bit of luggage behind the front seats, and the 911 is no exception.

Performance has long been Porsche's strong suit. Today's normally-aspirated 911 is capable of 149 miles an hour, according to the manufacturer, and can get to 60 mph in 6.1 seconds. Not many of us need anything swifter.

Comparing today's 911 Cabrio with a 911 from 1967, *Road & Track* found a marked improvement in handling. While the old edition could turn a trifle scary now

Slicing the top off the basic 911 coupe design, to create the Cabrio, adds an extra dash of ecstasy to open-road Porsche motoring—without sacrificing the "classic" profile. The rear-mounted flat-six engine has grown from 2.0 to 3.2 liters since the 911's birth in 1965. With 214 horsepower waiting at the rear, summer breezes may approach gale force as the throttle opens wide.

Targa (above) and closed-coupe models join the open 911 Cabrio to create a tantalizing Carrera trio. Roof panels slip behind the seats, or into the luggage area. Few sports car designs have lived as long as the 911's.

and again, its modern-day successor held the road with a vengeance. Porsche has finally found a way to keep the 911's inherent rear weight bias in check. And the new model felt better the faster it went, easy to drive under any conditions.

The classic 911 profile has become almost synonymous with the concept of sports cars—one basic form of sports

car—for at least one generation of enthusiasts. Today's sophisticated version doesn't look quite as much like an inverted bathtub as the original 356 did, but it carries an equivalent complement of delicious curves. Even when the vastly different 928 appeared in 1978, as the 911's intended replacement, the 911 clung to life. *Car* magazine (in Britain) later declared it

PORSCHE 911 CARRERA CABRIO

SPECIFICATIONS

Manufacturer:	Dr. Ing. h.c. F. Porsche AG; Stuttgart, West Germany
Models available:	coupe, targa, cabriolet
Body design:	2+2-passenger, 2-door coupe; steel unibody
Powertrain layout:	rear-engine, rear-wheel drive
Wheelbase (in.):	89.5
Overall length (in.):	168.9
Overall width (in.):	65.0
Overall height (in.):	52.0
Track, front (in.):	54.0
Track, rear (in.):	55.3
Weight (lbs.):	2756
Approximate price:	(coupe) $51,205, (targa) $52,435, (cabrio) $59,200
Engine type:	sohc horizontally-opposed 6-cylinder
Displacement (liters/cu. in.):	3.2/193
Horsepower @ rpm:	214 @ 5900
Torque (lbs./ft.) @ rpm:	195 @ 4800
Fuel delivery:	fuel injection
Transmission:	5-speed manual
Suspension, front:	independent struts, longitudinal torsion bars, stabilizer bar
Suspension, rear:	independent; semi-trailing arms, transverse torsion bar, stabilizer bar
Brakes:	front/rear vented discs

PERFORMANCE

Top speed (mph):	149
0-60 mph (seconds):	6.1
Quarter-mile (seconds):	approx. 14.3
mph @ quarter-mile:	approx. 94

virtually "immortal," adding that no rival sports car "inflames the passions as much as a Porsche 911 does."

Timeless designs never die. The best of anything never really disappears. But Porsche sales in general, it must be noted, have declined markedly since the mid-1980s. Scarcely half as many of the cars from Stuttgart-Zuffenhausen tempt American buyers today, compared with sales a few short years ago. The reasons for this sales slump range from rising prices to the increasing cost of insurance. But, Porsche remains undeterred, and wants to push the notion of "sport" in its sports cars even harder. If that plan bears fruit, Porsche's timeless 911 profile seems destined to keep rolling on, straight into the next century.

PORSCHE 911
CARRERA 4

Four-wheel drive has enjoyed a sudden upsurge of popularity in the late 1980s. Not so long ago, it was mainly the powertrain of choice for off-roaders and rural motorists. Traction at two extra wheels became quite desirable when ambling down rutted country paths, slogging across the mud, or attempting to maneuver through a sudden blizzard.

Then car manufacturers discovered the merits of having each wheel grab the road, following the lead of race vehicles. Sports cars were the first to receive the 4WD technology, followed by mid-level performers, and before long, it seemed like every manufacturer was pushing a 4WD model of some sort.

Porsche headed in the four-wheel direction full-bore in spring 1989, with the introduction of the Carrera 4. Not that 4WD was something new to the German company. Far from it. The super-powered engine of the 959 supercar drives all four wheels. A 911-based all-wheel-driver

appeared at the Frankfurt auto show in 1981. And to cite an example from way back, an ancestor of Porsche used all-wheel drive at the turn of the century. That one happened to be an electric car, with motors in each wheel hub. Still, it goes to prove that the idea of adding stability and traction with 4WD has been around for some time.

Based on the "classic" 911 design, the Carrera 4 debuted with considerable hoopla at the 1989 North American International Auto Show in Detroit. This wasn't any old 4WD car, of course—this was a Porsche. Customers anticipated the opportunity to enjoy all the greatness of the famed 911, and the most modern drivetrain, too. Although the Carrera 4 and 911 look surprisingly similar, only 15 percent of the cars' components are shared. Porsche described the 4WD coupe as "virtually all new under the skin." Suspension was new and though the engine remains in the horizontally opposed 6-cylinder configuration of the 911, it does

Four-wheel drive entered Porsche's closed coupe (top) first, joined later by Cabrio (center) and Targa-top (bottom) models. The fully automatic 4WD system isn't meant to send Porsches into dense jungles and underbrush, but to help it hug tightly to the pavement.

so with larger dimensions. This one measures 3.6 liters and churns out 247 horsepower at 6100 rpm. That makes it the most powerful non-aspirated engine ever found in a 911-based production car. Twin spark-plug ignition is adapted from Porsche's PFM 3200 aircraft engine.

Aero refinements have subtly altered the familiar 911 body shape, to the extent that it's a total restyle, with a taste of Porsche 959 (profiled in this book) here and there. Bumpers and front/rear aprons are completely different than those on the 911. The floorpan is all new, evolved from the 959's. As for the suspension, rather than the traditional torsion bars, the Carrera switched to coil springs with cast aluminum wishbones. Otherwise, the suspension is the same as that of a standard 911, with front struts and rear semi-trailing arms. Sixteen-inch alloy wheels carry 205/55ZR tires in front and 225/50ZR in the rear.

For the first time in a 911, power steering and Bosch anti-lock braking are available, and as standard equipment. Insulation has been increased for quieter running. Porsche insists, however, that the change will only "soften" the traditional 911 sound, not eliminate it. So all who appreciate that particular brand of noise need not fear its demise.

At 50 miles an hour, the retractable rear spoiler rises to assist in creating downforce and keep the Carrera tight against the road. At 6 miles an hour, the spoiler drops down again. On the highway, then, the Carrera displays no aerodynamic lift. In addition to boosting high-speed stability, the spoiler (when extended) doubles the size of the air-intake grille. The aero body alterations reduce coefficient of drag by 15 percent, allowing the Carrera to slide through the air a little easier than a basic 911.

Progressive as the 959's four-wheel-drive system was, the Carrera's is said to respond three times as fast. The technology was developed, tested, and proven in competition, through 911 and 959 models that ran in Paris-Dakar rallies. Experience with the 961 at the 24 Hours of Le Mans offered additional guidance. Carrera's "intelligent" four-wheel drive is also less complicated than earlier versions: A 959 driver must select a torque-split program, but the Carrera's is fully automatic.

Many ordinary 4WD systems simply transmit equal or predetermined amounts of power to the front and rear wheels, regardless of load or road surface condition. Others use a viscous coupling to provide a variable torque split of a sort, but only when the primary drive wheels lose traction. Carrera's full-time system uses multiple sensors and two hydraulically-actuated multi-disc clutches. Sensors detect acceleration forces forward and sideways, along with differences in wheel-rotation speed (as little

Appearances deceive. Even though Porsche's 4WD Carrera (both pages) looks much like the rear-drive 911, they share only a modest number of parts. Elements of the 959 supercar also pop up in the Carrera's profile, and in its basic floorpan. Coil springs replaced the customary torsion bars. A retractable rear spoiler (left) rises at 50 mph, then drops when slowing to 6 mph. Not only does the spoiler help hold the car down, it doubles the capacity of the air-intake.

as 0.6 mph), to show traction loss. Then, they instruct clutches to engage the center and/or rear differential as needed. Normal torque split is 31 percent to the front wheels, 69 percent to the rear. But in response to the sensor signals, the system delivers more power to the wheels that have the traction to use it best, and reduces power sent to those that don't.

Minor wheel-speed differences (when turning a corner, for instance) won't cause a response. Differentials disengage, too, when ABS is activated, so nothing weird is likely to happen during a panic stop. You can also flip a switch to get full engagement when needed, as when preparing to start up a snowy incline.

Drivers experienced with the 911 or its predecessors need no explanation of the 4WD system's big advantage. Let up on the gas during a high-speed maneuver in a 911 and its back end is likely to lurch to the side, not where you wanted to find it at all. No more: The four-wheel drive grips tight at all four corners.

Standard features are similar to those in a two-wheel drive 911: partial leather reclining bucket seats (with electric height adjustment), heated power mirrors, power windows, cruise control, and an electric sliding sunroof. Air conditioning has automatic climate control and the top-notch stereo radio/cassette system is by Blaupunkt.

Porsche's goal was to create a new sports car "in the 911 tradition," and take advantage of emerging technology. *Car and Driver* calls the Carrera the "most technically sophisticated 911 ever," adding that the 4WD sports car is also "astonishingly easy to drive."

Professor Helmuth Bott, Porsche's retired Vice-President for Development, was responsible for much of the firm's 4WD progress over the past decade. Since 1982, in fact, he's had a four-wheel-drive 911 available for daily trips. Bott is convinced that the Carrera 4 "will win all-wheel drive fans for [Porsche], who might never have been moved to try an all-wheel-drive car." He also predicts further 4WD projects from the company.

The latest Porsche is assembled at a new plant in Stuttgart-Zuffenhausen, Germany. Inside the company, it's called the 964. During the 1990 model year, both Cabrio and Targa versions join the Carrera 4, offering the same trio of body styles as the two-wheel-drive 911.

In contrast to the super-rare, astonishingly expensive Porsche 959, more than a thousand four-wheel drive Carreras will be waiting at dealers' showrooms each year, luring dreamers with their real-world prices. Few of us will ever see a 959, but the Carrera 4—inspiring in its own right—remains an accessible dream.

With all four wheels grabbing the tarmac, there's no longer a risk of the rear end snapping to the side when rounding a turn. Result: it's a snap to drive. Sensors and hydraulic clutches respond to acceleration forces and wheel speeds, to decide which wheels get the most power. Power steering is standard for the first time; anti-lock braking, too. Bigger than 911's, the flat-six engine qualifies as the most potent non-turbo ever installed in a production Porsche.

PORSCHE 911 CARRERA 4

SPECIFICATIONS

Manufacturer:	Dr. Ing. h.c. F. Porsche AG, Stuttgart, West Germany
Body design:	2+2-passenger, 2-door coupe; steel unibody
Powertrain layout:	rear-engine, 4-wheel drive
Wheelbase (in.):	89.5
Overall length (in.):	167.3
Overall width (in.):	65.0
Overall height (in.):	52.0
Track, front (in.):	54.3
Track, rear (in.):	54.1
Weight (lbs.):	3197
Approximate price:	$69,500
Engine type:	sohc horizontally-opposed 6-cylinder
Displacement (liters/cu. in.):	3.6/220
Horsepower @ rpm:	247 @ 6100
Torque (lbs./ft.) @ rpm:	228 @ 4800
Fuel delivery:	Bosch Motronic port fuel injection
Transmission:	5-speed manual
Suspension, front:	independent struts with lower wishbones, coil springs, stabilizer bar
Suspension, rear:	independent with semi-trailing arms, coil springs, stabilizer bar
Brakes:	front/rear vented discs, anti-lock

PERFORMANCE

Top speed (mph):	162
0-60 mph (seconds):	5.7
Quarter-mile (seconds):	approx. 13.6
mph @ quarter-mile:	approx. 102

PORSCHE 959

As the summer of 1989 approached, the collective moan of more than two dozen avid American supercar fans might have been heard from far afield. These saddened individuals had just learned that Porsche's ultimate supercar would not be certified by the government for sale in the United States. And they'd been among the potentially fortunate handful whose names sat on the waiting list, deposits paid, ready for the day when a small load of 959s finally rolled onto the docks.

Ever since rumors of the 959 began to waft through the rarefied air of automotive conversations, everybody wanted one. Not everybody could get one, of course. Only 200 were to be built—just enough to qualify for Group B racing status (until that category faded away). An opening price of $130,000 climbed swiftly into the quarter-million-dollar neighborhood and beyond.

Beneath the 959's striking bodywork lies the tried-and-true 911 design (which itself evolved from the original 356). Resemblance is strongest at the roofline and windows, but evaporates farther down, even though each car rides on the same wheelbase.

Mathematics comes so quickly to mind when running the eye over a real live 959. First the statistics: top speed pushing toward 200 mph, standing-start to 60 miles an hour in 3.7 seconds, breaking the 12-second mark through the quarter-mile traps, hitting 150 mph in a mere 21.5 seconds. Then you start to note all those beautiful surfaces and their relationships to the whole. It's all so perfect, so correct, so—mathematical.

Topology is the name given to the scientific study of surfaces, and the 959 is nothing short of an amateur topologist's dream. The vast protruding ground-effects rocker panels, for example, shaped as exotically molded running boards, deserve careful scrutiny. Lots of supercars have air intakes on their bodies, but none more luscious than the 959's gracefully curved grille-less openings to the rear of the doors. What do they resemble most? Nothing other than the opening of a Klein bottle—a mythical container with only one side, created by folding a Möbius strip into the next dimension. Though real enough in theory, Klein bottles fall closer to the province of science-fiction than into academic topology. Still, the feeling for such a perfect shape stands right before the eye that's beholding this super Porsche, even if the mind behind that eye has never given a moment's thought to higher math. Another example of the 959's exquisite lines is its spoiler. Nearly all supercars have rear spoilers, but none quite like the 959's graceful wing.

Moving inside the rear compartment, we come to the heart of the 959: its flat-six engine. Although only 2850cc (174 cubic inches), it blasts out a dizzying 450 horsepower at 6500 rpm. Torque of 369 pounds/feet peaks at a surprisingly rapid 5500 rpm, helping to account for the out-of-a-cannon experience if you hit the gas pedal hard at mid-level speeds. Two-stage turbocharging also contributes to the 959's reputation as a performance standard. Initially, exhaust gases help only the primary turbo boost the intake manifold pressure. But as soon as you enter the 4000-rpm range, a second turbo joins the circulation route, and bumps manifold pressure up even higher. Two big intercoolers sit at the engine's flanks to keep the turbos from seizing-up in all that exhaust heat. Although the engine block is air-cooled, in conventional Porsche rear-engine style, the cylinder heads have water coursing through their cooling passages.

Four-wheel drive has become almost expected on supercars, and the 959 uses a computerized variable system. Depending on the program selected (Traction, Ice, Wet, or Dry) and the opinion of the computer at any moment, the torque split might be an ordinary 50/50; or as much as 80 percent might be transmitted to the rear wheels.

Simply breathtaking in both form and performance, Porsche's ultimate supercar has hundreds of Americans clamoring to pay far more than its initial price for the privilege of ownership. They could have a long wait.

Wheel-mounted speed sensors are part of the anti-lock braking system.

Power reaches the wheels through a 6-speed gearbox, but that's not quite as helpful as it sounds. The sixth (ultra-low) gear ratio isn't much use except for off-road driving, and is even identified as the *Gelande* (terrain) gear.

If you happen to wander off-road, an adjustable suspension can raise ground clearance by 2.5 inches. By the way, the car lowers itself automatically at high speed, just in case you forget to drop down when you return to smooth pavement. Seventeen-inch VR tires are big enough to handle a little rough riding, too: 235/45 cross-section at the front and 255/40 on the back wheels. Early 959 prototypes made a good showing in tough Paris-to-Dakar rallies, winning two, so it seems that the production 959 is likely to offer similarly vigorous performance.

Fiberglass-reinforced Kevlar makes up the 959's body skin. Completing the blend are aluminum doors and front lid, and a polyurethane nose cap. The whole thing sits on a safety-cell framework of galvanized

Kinship to traditional 911 design is most evident above the beltline. Farther down, the 959 (above) is a gorgeous blend of geometric shapes and surfaces, accented by a passel of grilles and spoilers. The ultra-light body contains Kevlar, aluminum, and polyurethane. Computerized 4-wheel drive varies the power sent to each wheel by the mid-mounted engine (right). Small in size, the 450-horsepower twin-turbo flat-six (opposite) helps send the 959 into a supercar class by itself.

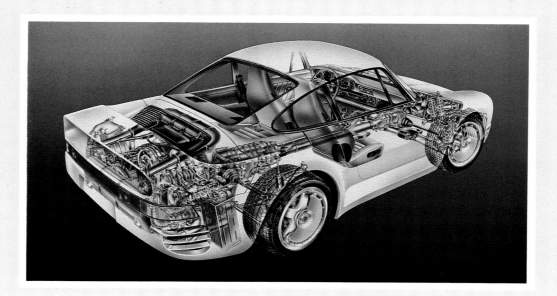

steel. A flat pan underneath contributes to the 959's no-lift characteristic.

Step inside and you'll feel familiar enough, if you've ever sat in a 911. Actually, the interior is all new, but there are no dramatic departures from the classic 911 layout. Leather trim matches the body color. For weight considerations, a Sport version lacks such niceties as air conditioning

and back seats. Power, performance, and a distinctive body—what more could you want? How about everyday driveability? Definitely. Comparing the 959 with a selection of supercars, Phil Hill noted that "everything comes so easily to the car," and even at high triple-digit speeds "it feels like a normal car speeding along the freeway." Porsche's goal, in fact, when the project first emerged around 1980, was to create a vehicle that edges into race-car performance, but could actually be driven reasonably by the average motorist.

Zero lift helps give the 959 such impressive high-speed stability—and safety. The car stays tight on the ground and *feels* like it's on the ground, not ready to fly off into space if you nudge the throttle a trifle more. Visibility to the rear is excellent—far better than that of typical mid-engine supercars. Steering is light and easy, since the 4-wheel-drive system stops sending power to the front wheels when you're trying to squeeze into a parking space (assuming, of course, that anyone would risk parking this beauty on a public street).

High-speed cars demand higher-speed tires. Not only are the Bridgestone RE71 tires something special, but the magnesium wheels on which they rotate are just as advanced. Their spokes are hollow, thus able to hold part of the air that's pumped into each tire. More air translates to a more comfortable ride, as well as secure handling. Puncture worries dissipate, too, because the tires can be driven when flat for 50 miles or so, and a sensor will warn you of pressure loss. For that reason, the 959 carries no spare.

Early prospects for importing those few 959s looked promising. Renowned race driver Al Holbert planned to handle the distribution, in concert with Porsche Motorsport U.S. But Holbert's death in late 1988 seemed to signal a similar fate for the supercar.

Not that the Environmental Protection Agency (EPA) acted without cause. Enthusiasts wanted the 959 to be classed as a racing car (illegal for street driving). But the EPA noted that Porsche's official race version was the 961. Officials reasoned that you couldn't have two cars occupying the same category. Then too, they worried that some lenient states might see fit to license an imported 959 for the road, EPA rulings notwithstanding. Modifying the car to meet emissions requirements probably would have been possible, but bumpers couldn't meet crash and height requirements without major alterations. Ferrari has continued to pursue the import course for its F40, but Porsche abandoned its efforts.

In a way, dreamers are better off than those luckless souls who'd counted on owning one of Porsche's standards of comparison. Even dreamers may catch a glimpse of a 959, for at least two examples

have been floating around the country, displayed periodically. None can be driven on a public road; their owners had to sign waivers guaranteeing that fate. For the most part, the cars are *pushed* around like roving museum pieces: loaded and unloaded from trucks, and hauled to the next site.

Price tags in the realm of $400,000 have been bandied about for the 959s that exist in Europe, and even higher estimates for the handful that have entered the U.S. under limited approval. If real certification would ever come, you'd hardly find a better—or more thrilling—investment.

PORSCHE 959

SPECIFICATIONS

Manufacturer:	Dr. Ing. h.c. F. Porsche AG, Stuttgart, West Germany
Models available:	Sport, Comfort
Body design:	2-passenger, 2-door coupe; Kevlar/ aluminum body on galvanized steel frame
Powertrain layout:	rear-engine, 4-wheel drive
Wheelbase (in.):	89.4
Overall length (in.):	167.7
Overall width (in.):	72.4
Overall height (in.):	47.2
Track, front (in.):	59.2
Track, rear (in.):	61.0
Weight (lbs.):	(Sport) 2977, (Comfort) 3190
Approximate price:	(est.) $400,000
Engine type:	twin turbocharged (two-stage), dohc horizontally-opposed 6-cylinder
Displacement (liters/cu. in.):	2.8/174
Horsepower @ rpm:	450 @ 6500
Torque (lbs./ft.) @ rpm:	369 @ 5500
Fuel delivery:	Bosch Motronic fuel injection
Transmission:	6-speed manual
Suspension, front:	upper/lower A-arms, coil springs, anti-roll bar
Suspension, rear:	upper/lower A-arms, coil springs, anti-roll bar
Brakes:	front/rear vented discs, anti-lock

PERFORMANCE

Top speed (mph):	193+
0-60 mph (seconds):	3.7
Quarter-mile (seconds):	approx. 11.9
mph @ quarter-mile:	NA

PORSCHE
928

Traditionalists scoffed but others cheered when a reshaped, front-engined Porsche arrived in 1978. The 'S4' suffix faded away by 1990.

Purists were not entirely thrilled when Porsche strayed from its origins to present a new face to the world in 1978. That face took shape in a dramatic new 928 model, barely recognizable at a glance as a member of the Porsche family. Even more shocking, its engine lived up front, not in the rear, and it was cooled by water, not air. Enthusiasts wondered how could this be a "real" Porsche?

Few imagined in the early 1970s, when the idea for a new model began to bud, that the traditional 911 would hang on much longer. Why, its styling dated back virtually to the beginning, rooted in the Volkswagen-based Type 356 of the early 1950s.

Now, as the Nineties emerge, the "old fashioned" 911 is *still* here, and so is its presumed replacement. Both have been modified and revamped since the Seventies, but appear remarkably similar to the originals. And both still rank among the most sought-after of the dream cars that actually exist in dealer showrooms.

When the 928 first appeared at the Geneva Auto Show in 1977, some hailed it as sleek and futuristic, yet another

legendary sports car destined to carry Porsche strongly into the Eighties. European journalists voted it Car of the Year. But critics branded the fresh 2+2 hatchback shape bulbous and paunchy, with an oversize and overweight look. In fact, it was bigger than the 911, and considerably more plush.

The 928 was also the first model designed strictly as a Porsche, from the ground up, with no Volkswagen platform or powertrain to think about. The Porsche 924, introduced more than a year earlier, displayed a similarly fresh shape and configuration but was based on VW/Audi components, and carried a 4-cylinder engine under its front hood. For the 928 a 90-degree V-8 was created, displacing 4.5 liters and dishing out 220 horsepower.

Why a front-mounted V-8? Porsche engineers believed that, with the rear-mounted flat engine, it would soon become difficult to meet international governmental regulations that favor front-engine cars. At the same time, a front-engine layout made it easier to build in traditional comforts and extra refinements. Quieter, too. Peek under

the hood, though, and you might mistake that V-8 for the old flat six, since its cam covers are nearly vertical. Extensive use of aluminum in the block and cylinder heads has kept weight down.

Although the 928's coil-spring suspension looked ordinary enough, it was something new for a Porsche. Double wishbones up front worked with coil-spring struts. At the rear was a similar arrangement, but with a Weissach axle that used an upper lateral arm and lower semi-trailing arm on each side. Porsche insists it helps maintain the best possible wheel geometry when cornering, so the 928 tracks precisely around curves even if you lift your foot off the gas. (Owners of early-model 911s know only too well how risky that maneuver can be in high-speed corners.) Either a 5-speed manual gearbox or 3-speed automatic was available, the latter supplied by Daimler-Benz.

Doors, hood, and front fenders were made of aluminum, yet the restyled Porsche was no lightweight, weighing in at 3300 pounds. Today's edition goes a couple of hundred pounds higher yet. Pop-up headlamps lie flat, just below the

274

hood/fender surface; a design that soon would become *de rigueur* in sports cars of all sorts.

Porsche anticipated buyer resistance to the new design, which had been penned largely by Anatole Lapine, the American-born chief stylist. The company even gave dealers lists of responses to make when a prospect expressed any misgivings. They were advised to explain the car's improved aerodynamics, its generous rear headroom, its luxury appointments, the diverse aesthetic niceties of curvaceous lines—plus its continuing kinship with the original 911 design.

Later on, the V-8 grew in size: up to 4.6 liters in 1980 on the European edition, while Americans got a new "S" version in 1983 with that enlarged engine. By this time, a top speed of 146 mph earned Porsche the title of fastest street-legal production car sold in the United States.

Two years later, the 928 S grew to 5.0 liters and added a second set of camshafts to drive new four-valve-per-cylinder heads (which evolved from Porsche's 956 racing experience). That helped produce a jump

from 234 to 288 horsepower. Anti-lock brakes also became standard.

Today's 928 S4 appeared in 1987, with 28 more horsepower than its predecessor. The "4" has no profound meaning, merely indicating that it's the fourth series. A mildly revised body features a reshaped nose and deep front airdam that hold a set of driving/fog lights. The former lip-style rear spoiler, mounted at the window base, was replaced by a bigger "detached" version, aimed straight off the back of the hatch. Wraparound flush tail lamps add to the smooth look of the tail end.

If performance was dazzling before, the current edition reaches even further into supercar figures with a top speed of 168 miles per hour and acceleration to 60 mph

in less than 6 seconds with the manual gearbox. Automatic-shift adds a few tenths to those times, as usual—but not enough to turn away many customers.

The current 928 rides 225/50ZR16 (front) and 245/45ZR16 (rear) tires on forged alloy wheels. Light Emitting Diodes in the door lock buttons show when the alarm is engaged—a sensible feature since Porsches are popular with car thieves. The instrument cluster moves up and down with the adjustable steering column, so you can adjust for the best view and feel at the same time. Both mirrors and the driver's seat slip into their preselected positions via a Positrol memory system. A driver information/diagnostic system uses a text and symbol format to report on 21 different

More posh than earlier Porsches, the 928 hatchback drew a fresh legion of admirers— for both its shape and its blistering speeds. Boldly curved doors, pop-up headlamps and lengthy triangular quarter windows make the 928 series easy to spot from a distance.

operating details. Leather upholstery is standard, and even the back seat passengers get sun visors. Mirrors and windshield-washer nozzles can be heated during the winter, and headlights can be automatically spray-cleaned.

Two things stand out about the 928's profile. First is the extreme curvature of the entry door, especially at its rear edge. A door with that kind of shape just has to lead into something extra special. Second is that long triangular quarter window, positioned so carefully below the endless roofline. Throw in the long sloping nose, the smooth and straightforward bodyside with subtle horizontal ribbing, and the cute rear end. All of this may not be traditional, but it's a car that draws the eye and, with a big V-8 beneath that shapely front, is one that's ready to roll with the swiftest of the lot. During a short-lived 1989 sales program,

purchasers of a 928 even got a bonus of two days' training at a race-driving school.

Porsche's original goal of offering "very high performance in a comfortable environment" was reached long ago, then refined with each 928 improvement. Brochures call it the "highest performing luxury car ever built." *Automobile* magazine has placed the 928 "in a class of its own," while *Motor Trend* goes so far as to call it the

"finest car in the world." High praise indeed; but thousands of owners (and even more admirers) are sure to agree.

Oh, a few lingering purists might still shun the curviest Porsche. Nearly everyone else has taken to its elegant mix of rounded lines and sizzling performance. How pleasing it is to have more than one beautiful Porsche to dream about, to talk about, to ogle at the dealer's showroom.

Unlike the 911, which rose from a VW platform, this curvy Porsche was designed from the ground up. Recent versions carry a "detached" spoiler (above). Not only did the engine (right) move up front for 928 duty, it turned into a V-8. More startling yet, water rather than the traditional air courses through its cooling channels.

PORSCHE 928

SPECIFICATIONS

Manufacturer:	Dr. Ing. h.c. F. Porsche AG; Stuttgart, West Germany
Body design:	4-passenger, 2-door coupe; steel unibody
Powertrain layout:	front-engine, rear-wheel drive
Wheelbase (in.):	98.4
Overall length (in.):	178.1
Overall width (in.):	72.3
Overall height (in.):	50.5
Track, front (in.):	61.1
Track, rear (in.):	60.9
Weight (lbs.):	3505
Approximate price:	$74,545
Engine type:	dohc V-8 (32-valve)
Displacement (liters/cu. in.):	5.0/302.5
Horsepower @ rpm:	316 @ 6000
Torque (lbs./ft.) @ rpm:	317 @ 3000
Fuel delivery:	LH-Jetronic port fuel injection
Transmission:	5-speed manual or 4-speed automatic
Suspension, front:	unequal-length A-arms, coil springs, hollow stabilizer bar
Suspension, rear:	independent Weissach with upper links, lower A-arms, hollow stabilizer bar
Brakes:	front/rear vented discs, anti-lock

PERFORMANCE

Top speed (mph):	168
0-60 mph (seconds):	5.7
Quarter-mile (seconds):	14.1
mph @ quarter-mile:	NA

PORSCHE PANAMERICANA

Receiving a car as a birthday present isn't too farfetched, especially for the owner of a car manufacturing company. Getting one specially built to mark the occasion— now that's a tad more exciting. That's precisely what Professor Dr. Ferry Porsche received for his 80th birthday: a striking new two-seater concept study, shown to the public for the first time at the 1989 International Motor Show in Frankfurt, West Germany. Arriving without prior fanfare, the Panamericana stole the show, drawing surprised (and admiring) sighs from ordinary motorists and industry observers alike.

Neither Ferry—the son of the company's founder, Ferdinand Porsche—nor anyone else might have much of an opportunity to drive this wild, low-cut machine, since there are no plans for production. Even so, it demonstrates once again the future-oriented thinking, creativity, and technical competence that have for the past four decades identified the Porsche organization at Stuttgart.

This is a free-spirited, free-thinking Porsche, bursting loose from the final constraints of traditionalist thought. It's a Porsche to tempt the aficionado—the driver who's seen them all, driven them all. Even more than Porsches in general, the Panamericana combines the best elements of high-tech while spurning faddish gadgetry.

More exciting yet, Porsche advises that the racy concept car just might "indicate the potential of future developments for the 911." Perhaps, then, this prototype won't fade away like so many show cars, after the enthralled early observers have had their fill, but could metamorphose into a 911 of the 1990s. Considering that in some well-to-do neighborhoods, Porsches have become a little too popular—indeed, almost common—a bold two-seater guaranteed to turn the heads of the most jaded onlookers is sure to be snapped up in a hurry.

Virtually every Porsche produced since 1948 stands above the crowd. Yet the Panamericana is unlike any Porsche on the street—or in most anyone's dreams, for that matter. Its body is an amalgamation of striking—even bulbous—curves, cut by the occasional sharp edge. What stands out from the very first adoring glance, though, is the car's low and completely transparent top. Apart from a narrow structural band around the perimeter that leads into the rear engine access cover, it's all glass above the driver and single passenger. And if that's not enough openness, both the roof and rear window slip off for open-air motoring.

Moving down from the clear top, the next styling touches to strike the eye are the startling open wheel arches. Massive cutouts in the body's contour completely expose both the front and rear wheels, with plenty of open space ahead of and behind

*Traditional restraints shattered into memory
with the development of this two-seater concept
Porsche, presented as an 80th birthday gift to
the son of the company's founder. Only the best of
future-tech mates with a luscious blending of
Porsche body cues, to create a drivable show car
with a personality all its own. The fastback
top is transparent and removable.*

each tire. The front arch reaches over the wheel to form a sharp crease that fades away as it enters the door panel. Farther back on the door begins yet another assertive crease. That one flows backward to form a jutting bulge above the back wheel, before curving serenely into the rear panel.

The Panamericana's imaginative design works through a mix of fantasy and freedom, stretching beyond the normal confines imposed by "legislative limits." More than one observer at the Frankfurt debut commented on the car's similarity to a dune buggy. Could be, but if so, it's a dune buggy with more power than the typical desert racer would ever expect.

Styling, according to the company, is meant to serve as a reminder of the renowned Carrera Panamericana, the legendary endurance road race of the early 1950s. A demanding and harrowing trek through Mexico, the annual race featured cars that had to be "as fast on asphalt as on a loose surface." One such entrant was Porsche's 550 Spyder, which gained international fame as a result of its distinguished competition in Mexico in the 1953 and '54 events. That twin-cam Spyder engine went into Porsche sports-racing models in 1954, carrying the Carrera designation as a mark of the car's racing origin.

Today's Panamericana design is a clear evolution of the traditional 911 shape, but adds a vibrant personality of its own to suggest the future of that classic profile. A nearly straight, flat tapered line reaches from the windshield to the end of the rear deck, above sharply tapered quarter windows, to form a fastback profile that really looks fast. Stand back, squint your eyes a bit, and you can discern elements of other modern Porsches in its makeup. The shape of the front end, for instance, isn't so far removed from that of Porsche's 959 supercar. Viewed from the rear, with a full-width red panel joining the wraparound taillamps, there's a touch of 928. A shapely oval exhaust outlet is built into the back panel. Heavy-looking 6-spoke wheels display an over-and-under design, and carry the oversize tires that are expected on a car of this caliber.

Mechanically, the Panamericana is based on the all-wheel-drive Carrera 4, introduced in 1989. Their kinship ends at the body skin, which in this case is carbon

fiber and glass rather than the customary metal. On the modern-day racing circuit, steel bodies are going the way of the dinosaur. Even aluminum panels are disappearing, replaced by materials that originated in aircraft technology and the space program, then made their way to the auto race courses. So the Panamericana's creators turned to a high-tech carbon fiber and glass blend, formed into a "sandwich" that combines light weight with structural rigidity.

Beneath that skin, however, lies a conventional Carrera 4 powertrain, with a horizontally-opposed 6-cylinder engine driving all four wheels. Performance, of course, should be just as spectacular as the Carrera's. That translates to a top speed in the 160 mph neighborhood or beyond, and

acceleration to 60 mph in under 6 seconds. Even so, the car is all stock and roadworthy, right down to the "environmentally-friendly, three-way catalytic converter." The exotic turquoise-blue Panamericana, says Porsche, serves as a clear statement that the company "will continue to be able to provide answers to the demands of the times in the future, using pathfinding technology and intelligent detail solutions." Responsibility for its creation lies in the hands of Dr. Ulrich Bez, who'd been at Porsche for only a year but had formerly lent his talents to the creation of BMW's Z1.

A vision of pure motoring pleasure for two, the passionate Panamericana is clearly a future-coupe for the open road, not for frenzied rush-hour expressways or traffic-laden city streets. Everything is designed

with the driver in mind, from the suspender-style shoulder harnesses that reach back to the rear panel to the functional, no-nonsense instrumentation.

Whether the prototype evolves into the real-life Porsche of the future, or fades away like so many short-lived stars of the European and American auto-show circuits, remains to be seen. Meanwhile, we can all imagine the envious eyes that would follow our course in a ramble down Main Street, if only we could slip behind the wheel of this inspired Stuttgart creation. If nothing else, the Panamericana demonstrates the inevitable trend toward super-light, super-strength construction techniques that are coming soon to the supercar arena—and even to everyday automobiles as the 21st century nears.

While the body below the beltline borrows from the finest Porsche models, especially the classic 911, Panamericana's low, straight, fastback roofline attacks the eye first. Both the roof and back window may be removed.

Both the name and appearance are meant to rekindle memories of the Carrera Panamericana, which blazed through Mexican road races in the 1950s. Mechanicals are shared with the Carrera 4, but the shapely body (above) is made of carbon fiber and glass. Huge open arches expose the muscular six-spoke wheels and massive tires (opposite page). Wraparound taillamps meet a full-width red panel in a luscious back end that resembles the 928's. Design elements could wind up in future 911s.

PORSCHE PANAMERICANA

SPECIFICATIONS

Manufacturer:	Dr. Ing. h. c. F. Porsche AG, Stuttgart, West Germany
Body design:	2-passenger, 2-door coupe; glass/carbon fiber body, steel frame
Powertrain layout:	rear-engine, 4-wheel drive
Wheelbase (in.):	89.5
Overall length (in.):	164.4
Overall width (in.):	74.6
Overall height (in.):	(with roof) 52.2
Track, front (in.):	54.3
Track, rear (in.):	54.1
Weight (lbs.):	3197
Approximate price:	NA
Engine type:	sohc horizontally-opposed 6-cylinder
Displacement (liters/cu. in.):	3.6/220
Horsepower @ rpm:	247 @ 6100
Torque (lbs./ft.) @ rpm:	228 @ 4800
Fuel delivery:	Bosch Motronic port fuel injection
Transmission:	5-speed manual
Suspension, front:	independent struts with lower wishbones, coil springs, stabilizer bar
Suspension, rear:	independent with semi-trailing arms, coil springs, stabilizer bar
Brakes:	front/rear vented discs, anti-lock

PERFORMANCE

Top speed (mph):	approx. 160
0-60 mph (seconds):	less than 6.0
Quarter-mile (seconds):	approx. 13.6
mph @ quarter-mile:	approx. 102

RENAULT MÉGANE

Slide open the door—any door—of Renault's concept sedan and you're bound to feel that you're about to step into someone's small but elegantly appointed living room. First of all, those wide doors slide all the way apart, crossing right in front of the fenders. As the doors separate, they reveal a pillarless entryway with four armchair-like seats beckoning you in.

May as well sit down. After all, as soon as the remote control requested the doors to open, the seat swiveled to the side in greeting. To refuse this invitation seems almost impolite. How about trying out the back compartment? Plenty of space in there—but if it's still not enough, just ask the driver to touch the right button. Then watch as the frameless back window moves itself rearward more than a foot on concealed rails, transforming the basic notchback sedan into an even roomier hatchback with an all-new silhouette.

If you've suddenly felt the urge to nap after sinking deeply into that plush seat, the back tilts down and, for your weary feet, recliners extend outward. After a relaxing nap, maybe you're ready to peek inside the refrigerated mini-bar, tucked conveniently into the rear center console. If you're in the mood for quiet conversation, perhaps the front passenger would like to swivel that seat all the way around, to face rearward. Easy enough; the seatbelt travels right along with it.

Meanwhile, the driver has been enjoying his or her own brand of comfort and convenience. Of course, the engine wouldn't even start until the remote-control unit had been plugged into the slot to the left of the dash. Mounted in the front console is an Atlas touch-screen, which takes the place of many ordinary buttons and switches. Developed over a 5-year period by Renault and TDF (Television Diffusion de France, a French television-broadcasting company), it offers navigational assistance as well as status checks. You might even consult an on-screen edition of the owner's manual, check on hotel vacancies ahead, get tourist

All four doors in Renault's luxurious concept sedan slide apart to reveal a no-pillar entryway, leading to a plush and spacious room for riding—nearer to a living room than a motorcar. Comfy back armchairs recline for easy legs-stretched relaxation.

information on the nearby area, or study parking regulations in the next town— whatever data can be programmed onto a compact disc. In the event that dashboard warning lights come on to signal trouble, the Mégane would never leave you stranded—the Atlas screen can offer advice on the proper procedure to follow.

Also in the front compartment is an audio/video system developed by Philips, featuring a radio that's controlled from the steering wheel. Messages received via radio signals might be seen on the Atlas screen, rather than heard. Two fold-down color LCD screens are built into the roof, aimed at rear-seat passengers. These lucky travelers can get images either from the Atlas system or from ordinary TV stations. A no-hands telephone waits in the front section, while rear passengers have to make

do with a conventional hand-held model.

The mirrors, however, do not have power adjustment. In fact, they don't have to be adjusted at all. All rear-viewing is accomplished by video, which gives full, all-around visibility. A dashboard switch selects the image from either the rear or right-side camera. Mégane's body lacks not only mirrors, but protrusions of any sort. No door handles, no knobs, no trim, no antennas—just smooth, uninterrupted surfaces.

If you want a little fresh air along the road, you're out of luck. There's no button or crank to roll down the window because all the windows are fixed. The only openings are a pair of small, electrically operated panels in the front windows, which can be opened for paying tolls and similar temporary duties.

Air conditioning is controlled by the Atlas touch-screen. On those frosty mornings, a transparent conductive layer in the windshield delivers quick de-misting and de-icing. Only a small amount of information appears on the dashboard, within round needle-style gauges. Everything else is part of the Atlas system.

Where's the gearshift for the automatic/ manual transmission? Just to the right of the steering wheel, in the form of a miniature lever. Even though there's no clutch pedal, the transmission can be shifted manually, by simply moving the selector. The clutch disengages as soon as the lever moves. The clutchless system, according to Renault, lets drivers adopt the "sporting" style of shifting gears, using the left foot to operate the brake pedal. Automatic shifts may also be made via the Valeo electronic control system.

A transverse-mounted, Garrett turbo-charged, 3.0-liter V-6 produces 250 horsepower, eager to haul the two-ton Mégane all the way past 160 miles an hour. From a standing start, the car can reach 100 kilometers per hour (about 62 mph) in 8.3 seconds. All four wheels transmit power to the pavement. As if that were not enough, all four wheels also steer—the back ones are moved by hydraulic jacks, and steer either in the same direction as the fronts (at high speed) or opposite (low speed). An electronically controlled adaptive suspension starts with one of three settings: soft, normal, or hard. Variable-rate shock absorbers then alter their stiffness automatically according to the road surface and car speed. Try to steer around an obstacle at high speed and the shocks shift immediately into "hard."

Michelin run-flat ATS tires can be driven for up to 60 miles at highway speeds following a puncture. Foam expands to fill the tire's interior almost completely. A Michelin system also keeps track of tire pressure.

After Chrysler took over American Motors in 1987 and abandoned the Renault-styled (but Wisconsin-built) Alliance and Encore, Renault almost disappeared from the American motoring mind. The company's all-out concept vehicle, first seen at the Paris Auto Salon in autumn 1988, demonstrates that Renault is still very much alive in Europe. Not only have profits hit record levels in the wake of financial weakness during the mid-1980s, but the revived company (owned by the French government) is eager to flex its motorcar muscle and show what it can do in futuristic style and technology.

Mégane's appearance is meant to demonstrate that Renault "means business in the difficult upper end of the market." Rather than turn to a super sports car concept on the order of Ferrari's F40 (profiled elsewhere in this book), the company chose instead to create a shape never seen before, "plump yet not appearing so, a completely new form." In addition to aesthetic appeal, the Mégane's unique aerodynamic shape slices neatly through the air, with a drag coefficient as low as 0.21. That's close to aircraft levels.

Renault describes its first real concept car as "a supercar for living." Most amazing of all, the Mégane went from idea to drivable vehicle in just eight months. Patrick le Quement, formerly with Ford and Volkswagen but now design director for Renault, told *Automobile* magazine that he had three priorities in mind: an "attractive shape, a convincing concept, and...driving pleasure." Not many people will have an opportunity to experience the latter, but on the first two counts, at the very least, Renault has hit a bull's-eye.

Arriving at your destination, you won't have to strain your back to reach all the luggage stuffed into the Mégane's rear compartment. A sliding platform pulls out like a drawer, for easy access from the sides as well as the back. One section of the compartment is also reachable from inside.

Pretty heady stuff. And we haven't even begun to talk about the unusually long look of the car, with wheels positioned far apart on a 122.5-inch wheelbase. Nor have we flipped up the hood to glimpse the powertrain. This is a running prototype sedan, not an idle mockup.

Mégane's gracefully romantic body holds a big surprise. Slide the rear window back a foot and—voila, the notchback sedan turns into a hatchback, with more space inside. One luggage area is handy to passengers, while hard-to-reach cargo slides out on a platform. Non-opening windows heighten the supercar's streamlined shape, with aerodynamic qualities that rival some airplanes.

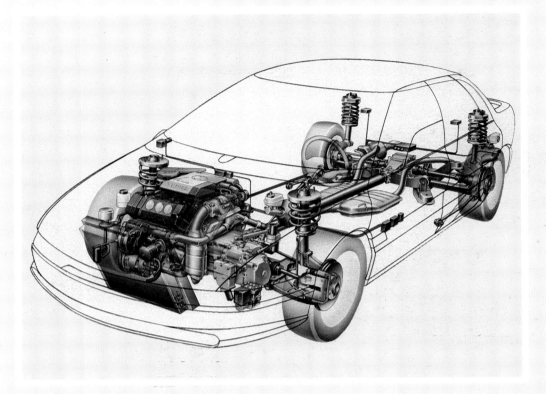

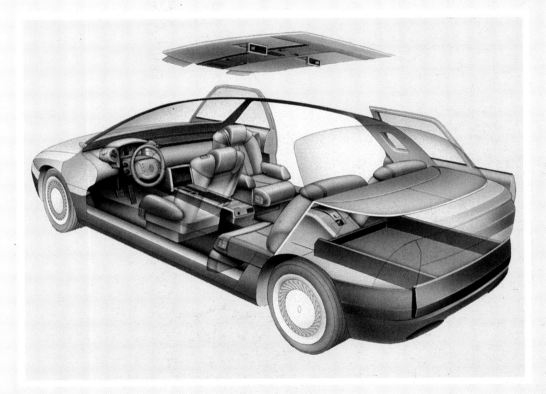

RENAULT MÉGANE

SPECIFICATIONS

Manufacturer:	Regie Nationale des Usines Renault, Bourlogne-Billancourt, France
Body design:	4-passenger, 4-door sedan; steel monocoque
Powertrain layout:	front-engine, 4-wheel drive
Wheelbase (in.):	122.5
Overall length (in.):	195.0
Overall width (in.):	74.8
Overall height (in.):	55.9
Track, front (in.):	62.2
Track, rear (in.):	59.8
Weight (lbs.):	3968
Approximate price:	NA
Engine type:	turbocharged sohc V-6
Displacement (liters/cu. in.):	3.0/181
Horsepower @ rpm:	250 (DIN) @ 6000
Torque (lbs./ft.) @ rpm:	257 @ 2000-4000
Fuel delivery:	multipoint fuel injection
Transmission:	5-speed manual
Suspension, front:	MacPherson struts, lower wishbone, anti-roll bar; electronically-controlled
Suspension, rear:	modified MacPherson struts, anti-roll bar; electronically-controlled
Brakes:	front/rear ventilated discs

PERFORMANCE

Top speed (mph):	161.5
0-60 mph (seconds):	less than 8.3
Quarter-mile (seconds):	16.0
mph @ quarter-mile:	NA

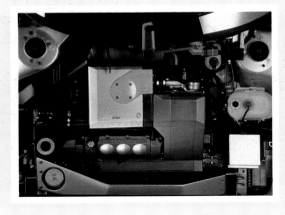

Beauty reaches beyond Mégane's lovely body. A turbocharged V-6 engine, mounted up front (top), drives all four wheels, and all four steer. A 3-way electronic suspension adapts the car's ride to road surface and speed. Video displays (left) offer travel and navigation guidance, as well as "no-mirrors" views to the rear.

ROLLS-ROYCE CORNICHE II

There are convertibles and then there is *the* convertible. When Rolls-Royce introduced its two-door Corniche in 1971, it was presenting far more than a topless Rolls. It was a restatement of the company's past, as well a shift into more contemporary times. The Corniche helped remind the company of its roots—of all the years when its cars were, quite simply, the best that could be found.

Not that an "ordinary" Rolls is less than best, either. Still, the sporty/stately Corniche serves as the prime example of the British company's commitment to excellence. A mere glance reveals its handcrafted qualities. You just know that here is a quiet motorcar. Plush. Perfect—or as close as any automaker is likely to get to that lofty goal. Expensive, too, with a price tag that tops $200,000.

Corniche II is the latest "enhanced" version of the convertible that many consider to be the most glamorous of all Rolls-Royce motorcars. It's also the one designed and built specifically for U.S. customers, offering an American-oriented selection of accessories, and is therefore sold only in North America. Robert Schwartz, president and CEO of Rolls-Royce Motor Cars Inc., calls the Corniche a "classic [that] has been designed for the person who wishes to combine top-down motoring with the ultimate in elegance and luxury."

Each Corniche requires five months of meticulous craftwork by specialists in leather, metal, and cabinetmaking. Only four emerge from the plant at Crewe, England, each week: just 200 or so a year. Virtually all of the details are crafted by hand, with bodies created by the master coach builders of Mulliner Park Ward (London).

Rolls experts have claimed that only 10 men in the world can properly hand-build a Rolls-Royce grille. Although the exquisite vertical-bar design looks a lot like silver, it's stainless steel, hand-polished for five hours.

Some people think the stories of stethoscopes used by quality-control engineers during the Rolls' 8-hour engine tests are apocryphal. Not so. Rolls-Royce history is filled with tales of coins that could be balanced on end atop the exposed radiator of an early model as the car stood idling. Any vibration at all was simply intolerable. There's no reason to believe today's Rolls would fare any worse in such a test. The unseen details, too, are impeccable. Exhaust noise, for instance, is muffled by six separate silencer boxes, each tuned to eliminate a specific frequency range.

During production, one engine in every hundred is totally torn down and inspected for even the slightest wear. Each engine is hand-assembled by one person, who takes final responsibility for its performance, to the point that the worker's signature appears on the engine's visible surface.

Sweeping body lines carry on the long tradition of Rolls-Royce style and craftsmanship, which began soon after the turn of the century. Sculpted fender tips, pushing past the separate headlights, hold elegantly simple parking lamps. Dual hood creases aim toward the traditional grille with its "Spirit of Ecstasy" ornament, as though nothing had changed since the days of exposed radiators and separate fenders. The side profile of the Corniche shows a modest bulge as it reaches the rear deck, with an even bigger bulge of oversize tonneau that contains the soft top.

Perfection, long the goal of the Rolls-Royce marque, edges close to reality in the open-topped Corniche II. It's the legendary firm's masterful melding of genteel sport, traditional beauty, and stately demeanor. Every component, down to the nameplate and taillamps (above) shows loving attention to detail.

Rich woods adorn the elegant Corniche dashboard (above), sweeping down into a dramatic console. Each sweep and swirl of the graining stands out in the crossbanded pattern of burled walnut veneers. Traditional round gauges are joined by automatic bi-level air conditioning and a cellular phone, as Corniche II aims at American tastes.

Window frames and wheel-arch moldings are made of stainless steel. So are the Corniche wheel covers. Paint is hand-sprayed and hand-rubbed, up to a dozen times. When complete, the total paint coating measures up to 2.5 times the thickness found on lesser automobiles.

Corniche's power-top mechanism alone can be considered a complex work of art. A single person constructs its frame, which is assembled piece by piece on an intricate master jig. Hours more are spent casing the joints, fitting the hardwood elements, tensioning the steel cables. Those cables are sewn into roof fabric to prevent windflap and reduce noise. All that effort pays off in silence inside—a Rolls-Royce trademark. Corniche occupants are not expected to endure the sounds of inclement weather and rapid travel.

The fabric top actually consists of three layers: an outer weatherproof "skin," specially padded filling for insulation and sound absorption, plus an interior headliner of pure wool from the West of England. Each layer is individually tensioned so no wrinkles appear, even after months and years of use. Sitting inside with the top up, you'd hardly know the Corniche was a convertible. Glance up at the roof and you'd swear it's a hardtop.

Inside, you're bathed in sumptuous perfection. Seats, door trim—even the carpet bindings—are finished in choice Connolly hides. The Connolly family firm has operated in Britain for more than a century, turning out what most observers regard as the finest leather in the world.

Much of what isn't covered in leather is made of wood. Fine wood, which betrays its forest origins by highlighting every sweep and swirl of grain. Superbly matched, elegantly polished, crossbanded burled walnut veneers grace the instrument panel and door cappings. Crossbanding, in fact, is a Corniche hallmark. The artful technique involves edging panels and cappings with a narrow band of veneers, each of which shows a pronounced cross-grain.

Veneers are cut by hand and matched by eye, their whorls stained and primed, then dried for 2½ days. Three coats of lacquer are followed by three more days of air-drying.

No two Rolls-Royces are quite identical. Looking at the dashboard alone, you see instantly the difference between a handcrafted Rolls and an assembly-line vehicle. Wooden pieces are handpicked so the right side of each panel serves as a mirror image of the left. If there's a noticeable irregularity on one side (but not the sort that produces rejection of the entire panel), a similar flaw shows up on the opposite end. Production-line vehicles, in contrast, are a little too perfect—but at the same time loaded with imperfections.

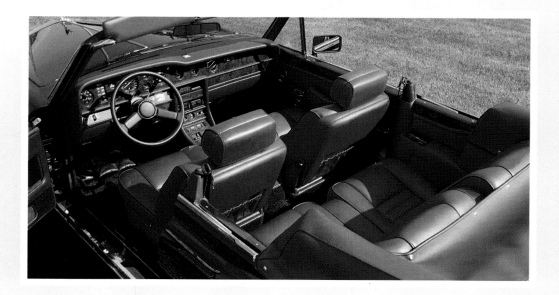

Mulliner Park Ward specialists create a Corniche body largely by hand—only four per week. The power top mechanism alone, framed by a single craftsperson, ranks as a work of art. Silence, a trait for which Rolls has long been noted, is enhanced by the top's snug fit. Upholstery is meticulously sewn in the finest Connolly leather (opposite page), accenting the traditional wood.

"Cocktail requisites" are provided in both doors. In plain talk, that's a set of glassware suitable for beverages of a sophisticated nature. Upon request, folding walnut picnic tables may be fitted to the rear of the front seats.

A center console extends from the instrument panel to the front seats. "Memory" front seats offer a choice of positions. Lumbar support adds to the comfort level for both front occupants. Automatic bi-level air conditioning is standard, of course. All you do is set the control for a temperature between 62 and 91 degrees: one figure for knee level, another for cooling aimed toward the occupants' heads. Set the controls once and think no more about it. No matter what happens outside the car, the interior remains as close as possible to the desired temperature level.

Rolls-Royce spokesmen have traditionally smiled and replied "Enough" when asked the horsepower of their engines. Today's 6750cc overhead-valve, aluminum-alloy V-8 has been estimated to deliver around 260 bhp and a healthy 380 pounds/feet of torque. That much rotational force is needed to push around more than 2½ tons of motorcar. GM's Turbo-Hydramatic 3-speed automatic is the one and only transmission choice. A hydraulic leveling system is so sensitive to load capacity that it even compensates for weight loss as fuel is used up.

Today's Corniche comes equipped with everything from heated door mirrors and central locking to a cellular phone that tucks neatly into a leather-bound, padded center-storage cabinet. Rolls-Royce has traditionally been willing to comply with special requests; some sporty sorts have asked for such extras on their Corniche as a gold-plated Flying Lady, fog lights, or an air dam.

Stealing a Rolls might seem a trifle foolish. But just in case, the door locks have pin tumblers that use hard-to-forge keys. In addition, the transmission automatically locks when the key is removed, requiring that a potential thief tow the car away.

Corniche's electronic odometer is calibrated to 1 million miles. On an ordinary vehicle, that would seem woefully optimistic if not downright presumptuous. On a Rolls it's almost a necessity. Since two-thirds of the Rolls-Royces ever made are said to be running today, a million miles doesn't sound all that far out of line.

Rolls-Royce CEO Robert Schwartz notes that current Rolls-Royce motor cars "have been designed and built to last well into the 21st century. They are the result of a unique tradition of superb individual craftsmanship and painstaking attention to detail." The company's goal is "perfection." Nothing else will do.

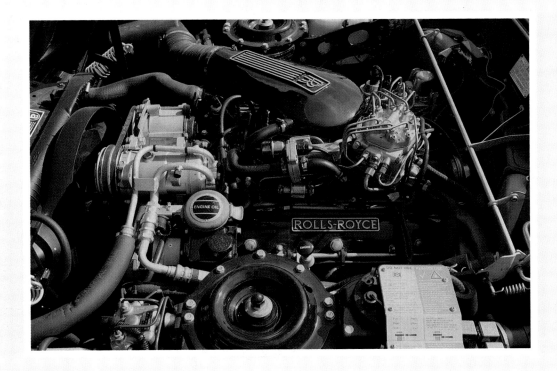

ROLLS-ROYCE CORNICHE II
SPECIFICATIONS

Manufacturer:	Rolls-Royce Motor Cars Ltd., Crewe, England
Body design:	4-passenger, 2-door convertible; steel body on steel frame
Powertrain layout:	front-engine, rear-wheel drive
Wheelbase (in.):	120.5
Overall length (in.):	207.5
Overall width (in.):	77.1
Overall height (in.):	59.8
Track, front (in.):	60.5
Track, rear (in.):	60.5
Weight (lbs.):	5340
Approximate price:	$205,500
Engine type:	ohv V-8
Displacement (liters/cu. in.):	6.8/412
Horsepower @ rpm:	(est.) 260 @ 4000
Torque (lbs./ft.) @ rpm:	(est.) 380 @ 2500
Fuel delivery:	Bosch K-Jetronic fuel injection
Transmission:	GM 3-speed automatic
Suspension, front:	independent; lower wishbones, coil springs, anti-roll bar
Suspension, rear:	independent; semi-trailing arms, coil springs, anti-roll bar, automatic level control
Brakes:	front/rear discs, anti-lock

PERFORMANCE

Top speed (mph):	NA
0-60 mph (seconds):	NA
Quarter-mile (seconds):	NA
mph @ quarter-mile:	NA

No mistaking a Rolls-Royce with its "Spirit of Ecstasy" hood ornament astride the stately and familiar vertical-bar grille (opposite page). Like other R-R components, it's polished by hand. Six tuned silencers help subdue the exhaust noise from the 6.8-liter V-8 engine (above). Though hardly a supercar, the Corniche isn't likely to disappoint its owner on the open road. A hydraulic leveling system keeps the back end on an even keel (left), regardless of load.

ROLLS-ROYCE SILVER SPIRIT AND SILVER SPUR

Tradition counts, particularly when speaking of the finest automobiles in the world. Breeding. Heritage. Elegant words that sound so—well, so British. One upstart after another has tried, throughout this century, to unseat Rolls-Royce from its immodestly claimed title of "The Best There Is." In the eyes of most observers, few, if any, have succeeded. A Rolls remains the standard of comparison in the luxury car league. What other convenyance demonstrates so clearly—and so tastefully—that you've made it?

Stately in appearance as well as demeanor, the twin Rolls sedans are long and wide, silent and civilized. The Silver Spirit is the entry-level Rolls (if such an ill-mannered term may be used in this league), 4 inches shorter than the Spur and some $13,000 cheaper. Some would call the body profiles boxy, showing too much horizontal dominance, not unlike the cars' earliest predecessors. Perhaps, but the cars did develop rounded edges and corners as the aero era approached. The windshields on today's Rolls, too, have a sharper rake than earlier models.

Interior fittings are more reminiscent of fine European furniture than of a mere automobile. Inside and out, you'll find evidence, large and small, of the company's legendary attention to detail; of the painstaking craftsmanship applied by a staff of dedicated experts. Lesser automobiles that pop off the end of an assembly line simply cannot compete.

More than 82,000 separate components go into each Rolls-Royce, many of them created in-house. Each of those components receives lavish and loving attention. The finished cars have traditionally come with a "history book" signed by the craftspeople who did the work with their own hands.

Instrument panels, for example, are expertly assembled from layers of walnut veneer, joined invisibly, and glued atop a hardwood base. Careful staining pulls out each sumptuous detail of the grain and the entire unit is polished to a deep, rich, glass-like sheen. The wood's character is different on every dashboard, but pleasingly symmetrical. The Silver Spur's dash displays a different pattern than that of the more costly Corniche. As a hedge against later damage, the factory even keeps a sample of wood from each individual dashboard.

Eleven carefully matched Connolly hides—no less than the best—make up the Rolls upholstery. Cows that are destined to enter service within a Rolls-Royce interior are never subjected to hide-scratching barbed wire during their lifetimes. Wilton deep-pile lambswool carpeting is of like quality, fleeced from sheep that are bred for hardiness. Other interior accoutrements

"Spirit of Ecstasy" atop each radiator shell (opposite page) makes Rolls-Royce an easy automobile to identify. The stately Silver Spur (above) attracts owners who prefer to be chauffeured.

are no less impressive. Walnut picnic tables fitted to the rear of the front seats carry on an old tradition in luxury automobiles. A more modern convenience, the inevitable cellular phone, doesn't just sit idly on the seat or in the console; it resides within a recess of the armrest.

Steel panels are hand-rolled to a level of smoothness that makes them look as though they emerged from an assembly-line press, but with far more detailing than any mass-production method could deliver. Up to a dozen hand-rubbed coats of paint are followed by deft body striping, applied with a tiny camel's-hair brush.

When it comes to motorcars of character and pedigree, a Silver Spur (both pages) has no true peers. Dedication to detail on the 6.75-liter V-8 engine (opposite page, left) is as painstaking as that of the Mulliner Park Ward body.

Classic, traditional styling begins with the handcrafted radiator shell, topped by its "Spirit of Ecstasy" mascot. Inspect any Rolls model from the past and you'll see an amazingly similar look, especially up front. That squared-off, vertical-bar grille has helped make Rolls-Royce one of the most easily recognizable cars on the road.

Rolls was one of the last automakers to turn from drum to disc brakes, not because the company doubted the discs' efficiency, but because the early ones tended to squeal. Rolls-Royce drivers just wouldn't care for that bit of noise, the firm reasoned. So Rolls waited until the new technology had

reached an acceptable level of sophistication.

Riding comfort is at the level you'd expect from motorcars that cost as much as many homes, carrying on a reputation for quality that reaches almost back to the beginning of the auto industry. All five occupants sit up high, enjoying a superior view of the passing traffic ahead of the long hood. Self-leveling independent suspension compensates for the weight of passengers and luggage.

Performance and power developed by the 6.75-liter aluminum-alloy V-8 are fully adequate, though not exactly hair-raising. You want specific performance figures? Well, Rolls-Royce officials have traditionally declined to discuss such crass matters, which are better left for commoners to estimate.

Rolls has never been big on fads and gadgetry, but each of the Silver models contains all the comforts and conveniences a reasonable person is likely to enjoy.

Standard, of course. Mirrors are electrically heated. A power washer cleans up the headlights. Sophisticated dual-level automatic air conditioning needs to be set only once. After that, it keeps the interior at the chosen temperature regardless of outside conditions, with separate settings for head and toe level. A sensor near the windshield helps compensate for heat generated by the sun. Rolls claims the system delivers the cooling capacity of 30 household-type refrigerators.

A sentry light warns of icy road conditions, signaled by a sensor beneath the front bumper. And you'll never have to worry about facing ashes and matches when you open the ashtray. The Rolls variety empties itself into a concealed receptacle.

Both the outside temperature and time of day appear on a silent electronic display. The speedometer is silently electronic, too. Only a touch is needed to select the range of the 3-speed automatic transmission, which uses an electronic control. And should a tire happen to fail, the Rolls tool kit includes a pair of gloves to keep one's hands tidy during the tire-changing chore.

Buyers who elect to be chauffeured, tend to choose the longer Silver Spur. If you drive yourself, you may be surprised how easily the car handles, considering its size. Its 37-foot turning radius is considerably tighter than that of many smaller vehicles,

even if a Rolls isn't quite ready for hairpin mountain curves at frightful speeds.

The Spirit and Spur were introduced in 1980. Although the pair's appearance has remained largely the same from year to year, nearly every model year has brought a list of mechanical improvements. A new marketing strategy for 1985, in fact, produced a shift to regular, annual model-year revisions, echoing the pattern of other automakers. In 1987, fuel injection replaced carburetion on the V-8 engine, boosting power by more than 20 percent. Anti-lock braking also arrived that year—but only after Rolls engineers were satisfied that the pedal would have a lighter, more pleasing feel than had been true of early ABS systems. Most luxury autos have a seat-position memory nowadays, but Rolls since 1987 has been able to "remember" the requirements for four different people.

More than a mere motorcar, a Rolls serves as a modern-day expression of civility,

carrying the British heritage forward into another century. Roughly two-thirds of the more than 100,000 Rolls-Royce vehicles built since the beginning are thought to remain in running condition today. How many other automakers can come close to making such a statement?

Easy to drive and easy to love. That's how it's been since Frederick Henry Royce teamed up with Charles Steward Rolls in 1906. And that's how it always will be, if the company and its tradition-minded customers have their way.

Each Silver Spirit or Spur takes three to five months to create, at the Mulliner Park Ward coachworks in London and the assembly plant in Crewe. Rolls-Royces are shipped to America in pairs, packed in jumbo containers to minimize the risk of harm. For the family that can afford one, and doesn't care to flaunt its affluence carelessly, there's simply no other reasonable choice.

Silver Spirit (above) is the shorter, "budget-priced" Rolls. Each interior (above right) is a well-bred blend of walnut veneer and Connolly leather. Traditional amenities include walnut picnic tables (right). Both models added computer control to their self-leveling suspensions for 1990, so ride firmness adapts to changing conditions.

ROLLS-ROYCE SILVER SPIRIT AND SILVER SPUR

SPECIFICATIONS

Manufacturer:	Rolls-Royce Motor Cars Ltd., Crewe, England
Body design:	5-passenger, 4-door sedan; steel unibody with aluminum panels
Powertrain layout:	front-engine, rear-wheel drive
Wheelbase (in.):	(Spirit) 120.5, (Spur) 124.5
Overall length (in.):	(Spirit) 207.8, (Spur) 211.8
Overall width (in.):	79.1
Overall height (in.):	58.5
Track, front (in.):	60.5
Track, rear (in.):	60.5
Weight (lbs.):	(Spirit) 5120, (Spur) 5180
Approximate price:	(Spirit) $140,200 (Spur) $154,700
Engine type:	ohv V-8
Displacement (liters/cu. in.):	6.8/412
Horsepower @ rpm:	(est.) 260 @ 4000
Torque (lbs./ft.) @ rpm:	(est.) 380 @ 2500
Fuel delivery:	Bosch K-Jetronic fuel injection
Transmission:	GM 3-speed automatic
Suspension, front:	independent; lower wishbones, coil springs, anti-roll bar
Suspension, rear:	independent; semi-trailing arms, coil springs, anti-roll bar, automatic level control
Brakes:	front/rear discs, anti-lock

PERFORMANCE

Top speed (mph):	118+
0-60 mph (seconds):	approx. 9.4
Quarter-mile (seconds):	NA
mph @ quarter-mile:	NA

VECTOR W2
TWINTURBO

Turning a dream into reality is seldom easy. Or quick. It takes time, hard work, and a little luck. Gerald A. Wiegert's elusive automotive dream first began to take shape in the early 1970s, turned into a full-scale vehicle a decade later, and is only now beginning to bear fruit.

Like Preston Tucker, Malcolm Bricklin, and John DeLorean, three creator/promoters of automobiles with a personal stamp, Wiegert faced tremendous odds from the start. Like many others, he's faced financial obstacles. Although thousands of companies have entered the automobile business over the years, only a tiny handful last long enough to place actual vehicles on the market.

Serving as designer, builder, and marketer of the TwinTurbo, Wiegert received his first order for a car in 1981. By the end of the Eighties, the Vector company held orders for four more, complete with deposits, still based on the original prototype. Automotive journalists wrote some glowing reviews. But year after year managed to slip away, with hope for production growing hazy. Waiting lists are hardly unheard of in the car trade, but those five set a record for tests of patience.

Late in 1988, following a delay as officials evaluated production plans and studied the network of six interrelated companies involved, the Vector Aeromotive Corp. issued a public stock offering. About $6 million was raised. The stock prospectus described a supercar little changed from its initial appearance, either mechanically or aesthetically. First deliveries were scheduled for fall 1989, with a $178,000 price tag. If all goes well, four cars a month might finally emerge from the California firm and appear on American roads.

After training at the Center for Creative Studies in Detroit and the Art Center College of Design in California, Wiegert worked as a design consultant. His goal in creating the Vector W2 was twofold: to produce a dream car that took full advantage of space-age and aeronautical technology, but also to demonstrate America's industrial potential in the wake of rising dependence upon Asian and European products.

Wiegert took on the entire project himself, turning to aerospace engineering techniques from the very beginning. The finished vehicle, he believed, should not only reflect the best uses of technology but be reliable, durable, comfortable, safe—and easy to repair.

Vector's prototype body consisted of a carbon Kevlar fabric composite, bonded and riveted to a semi-monocoque chassis of aluminum honeycomb and structural steel tubing with a chrome molley-tube roll cage. Sounds typical of several top supercars today, but remember, this was around 1981.

Looking nearly airborne even when its four wheels are planted firmly on the pavement, the awesome Vector W2—an amalgation of wicked angles—draws from aerospace and aviation technology.

*Loaded with louvers, carrying the basic wedge
shape to its limit, the Vector W2 (opposite page)
wears a body of carbon Kevlar composite.
Doors tilt upward (above). Undercover lies a
V-8 (right) rated above 700 howling horsepower.*

Space-age materials had not yet made a full transition from race track to road vehicles. In addition to strength and light weight, the composite monocoque construction offered superior corrosion-resistance.

One observer described the Vector prototype as "awesome, even menacing," closer to a fighter plane than an automobile. That writer could think of nothing with which to compare its appearance, with the possible exception of Bertone's 1968 Carabo, a car that contained a like selection of louvers along with pivoting doors.

Comparisons aren't much easier to make today, even though any number of supercars have emerged with a race track pedigree and spacecraft appearance. Vector's dramatically wedge-shaped body, standing only 42.5 inches tall, angles downward to take advantage of the wind's downforce, causing the car to act like an upside-down wing and push itself into the ground as speed gathers. Evidence of the role of aerodynamics can be found almost anywhere, from the dual-element rear wing and the smooth underbody, to flush-mount windows and door handles.

A single line can be traced along the car's silhouette, determining its basic profile. In physics, a vector is a line that implies both direction and magnitude.

Thus, the car's name. With 700-plus horsepower tied to the pedal, a staggering level of magnitude is waiting in whichever direction one chooses to travel.

Styling is sure to be a source of fascination. The first thing the casual observer will notice is the near-horizontal slope of its windshield. Doors lift up and tilt forward, not unlike the Lamborghini Countach (best known of the pivot-door bunch). As in various rival supervehicles, the Vector is most easily entered in backward mode. You ease back toward the seat, drop into position, and only then swing the legs inside. Not so hard at all, once you've tried it.

Spartan is perhaps the best word to describe Vector's roomy but plain interior. Recaro bucket seats are infinitely adjustable for comfort, with aircraft-type 5-point restraints. The seats are also electrically heated, to prevent chilled posteriors on winter mornings. Lack of a center console means you can order an optional seat for a third passenger. Luggage space? Well, don't plan any long trips.

A head-up display for instruments sends images of the speedometer and tachometer into the windshield, visible without the driver having to cast a downward glance. Such a feature has appeared in recent

American cars, but in the early 1980s it was limited to F-16s and other military fighter planes. A ratchet selector for the manual/automatic transmission is flush-mounted in the bulkhead to the driver's left. Other instruments take the form of bar graphs, stacked horizontally so they resemble a complex rack-type home stereo system. Borrowing once again from aircraft techniques, the bar gauges are positioned so when all is normal, their indicators align vertically.

Two Garrett AiResearch turbochargers force air into the all-aluminum 6.0-liter V-8 engine, based on a GM design but obtained from an aftermarket company. It's actually a Donovan engine, developed specially for racing and weighing half as much as an equivalent iron-block design. With 700 horsepower (if not more) at the ready, Vector's claimed 0-60 times of less than 4 seconds, and 0-120 in about 10, are quite believable. An initial top-speed rating of 200 mph seems conservative, if anything. Later estimates reach 240 miles an hour and beyond.

Ever wished for an extra burst of power, if only for a moment? With a W2 underfoot, your wish is its command. A driver's seat control can adjust the wastegates that regulate boost pressure, delivering a brief jolt of added horsepower. Then again, if you're rarely satisfied with a mere 700-plus horsepower, Wiegert has claimed all along that the engine block was capable of twice the initial rating; you might want to talk to him about a 1000-plus-horsepower screamer.

No system of service facilities has been proposed, but that's one advantage of using

VECTOR W2 TWINTURBO
SPECIFICATIONS

Manufacturer:	Vector Aeromotive Corp., Wilmington, CA
Body design:	2-passenger, 2-door coupe; hybrid composite body, semi-monocoque chassis with steel roll cage
Powertrain layout:	mid-engine, rear-wheel drive
Wheelbase (in.):	103.0
Overall length (in.):	172.0
Overall width (in.):	76.0
Overall height (in.):	42.5
Track, front (in.):	63.0
Track, rear (in.):	65.0
Weight (lbs.):	2700
Approximate price:	$178,000
Engine type:	GM-based twin-turbocharged ohv V-8
Displacement (liters/cu. in.):	6.0/366
Horsepower @ rpm:	(est.) 722 @ 5700
Torque (lbs./ft.) @ rpm:	(est.) 700+ @ 4900
Fuel delivery:	electronic fuel injection
Transmission:	3-speed automatic (selectable manually)
Suspension, front:	unequal-length A-arms, concentric coil springs, and adjustable shock absorbers
Suspension, rear:	De Dion tube with upper and lower trailing arms, lateral link, coil springs, and adjustable shock absorbers
Brakes:	front/rear discs

PERFORMANCE

Top speed (mph):	200+
0-60 mph (seconds):	under 4.0
Quarter-mile (seconds):	11.5
mph @ quarter-mile:	128

a GM-based engine. The boys in the service bay down at the nearest Chevrolet dealership might faint away at the sight of a Vector pulling in, but they should have the parts and know-how to handle the bulk of maintenance and repair duties. If not, Wiegert can always fly a mechanic to the car (at your expense, sadly). Either way, the Vector is designed for easy disassembly. Engine, transmission, and differential are mounted on separate, removable modules.

"The ideal is to build a safer superexotic car," Wiegert says. He starts with the full steel roll cage. Three-stage crash protection includes resilient bumpers, energy-absorbing bumper mounts, and finally the chassis itself. It's designed to deform as far as the passenger cage, absorbing the brunt of any brutal shocks. Inside the roll cage is the fuel cell, made of explosion-suppressing foam, again of aircraft origin. Automatic and manual fire-extinguishing systems are provided, just in case. Aircraft-type circuit breakers give both audible and visual warnings of trouble.

Anti-lock braking didn't yet exist as the Eighties began, but the prototype Vector had a sensor to regulate pedal pressure for the ventilated-disc brakes. A dial selects adjustable damping from the suspension— not so startling today, but futuristic when the first Vector took 3-dimensional form.

Automakers have been applying aircraft techniques and designs to their creations for decades, of course. Some were serious. Others, such as the tailfins and bombsight hood ornaments of the Fifties, might be called frivolous. Gerald Wiegert's inspiration is the real thing. But the big question remains whether more than those first few customers will take to the Vector's still-advanced features, and decide they can't survive without 700-plus horsepower at their command. When the old Countach grows boring, maybe it's time to consider one man's appeal to "Buy American."

A full steel roll cage beneath the virile body (opposite page) is part of Vector's three-stage crash protection. Bar graphs serve as monitoring instruments, aircraft style, in the well-equipped cockpit (above), which includes heated Recaro bucket seats. From any perspective, including the rear view (left), the ground-hugging Vector W2 makes a formidable appearance.

ZENDER
FACT 4

Not every aftermarket firm is content with providing parts and accessories for other manufacturers' automobiles. The Zender company of West Germany, widely known for production of spoilers and other add-ons for all sorts of vehicles, turns out a fantastic automobile of its own now and then. Unfortunately, none has led to actual production. Neither will FACT 4, the company's latest and most ambitious effort. Nevertheless, it's a fully operational prototype that mixes race-car styling and sizzling performance. Zender calls it an "uncompromising" design, "undoubtedly one of the fastest roadworthy sports cars in the world."

Shown to the public for the first time at the 1989 International Car Exhibition in Frankfurt, West Germany, the FACT 4 resulted from two years of development work. The radical silhouette was designed by Gunter Zillner, and the car was built solely by the Zender company.

You can't miss this muscular sports car's name with that big "FACT 4" logo on the bodyside, to the rear of the door. Although the deliciously virile, nearly terrifying profile is reminiscent of various racing vehicles, no car built for the road looks quite like the FACT 4. Start with the wildly-angled shape of the forward-opening gullwing doors, which extend far forward of the driver's seat, nearly to the edge of the front wheels. But then, they tilt backward to about a 45-degree angle at the rear, matching the slant of the air-intake slot.

The rather stubby-looking body is only 160.6 inches long (on a 98.4 inch wheelbase). Making it look even stubbier, the car is barely 44 inches tall at the roof. But a broad 78.7 inches of width gives the car a low lean-and-mean look. The driver sits about midway between the wheels. Rear visibility isn't exactly the car's strong point, though it's not quite as limited as it appears at first glance. There's a sharply tapered side window to the rear of the driver, and the slatted rear window looks practically horizontal as it leads into a tiny deck panel below the fin-like, full-width rear spoiler. That whole rear assembly tilts up to reveal the mid-mounted engine. Farther down at the rear, four exhaust outlet pipes burst out of the panel below the license plate.

The Zender's race-style orientation is even more evident at the stubby front end, which gives the car a poised-for-action stance. Not too many cars hug the ground this closely, either.

Though striking in appearance, with

Here's one concept supercar that doesn't go incognito. Hard-to-miss 'FACT 4' logos (above) on front, rear, and bodysides identify the twin-turbo powerplant and the car's West German creator. Fully drivable, ranking high up the supercar scale, it's one-of-a-kind and not intended for production.

design cues borrowed from the race track, power and performance are the FACT 4's hallmarks. A car that looks this fast, after all, should have the performance figures to match. A mid-mounted, twin-turbocharged (intercooled) 32-valve Audi V-8 delivers the necessary power—all 448 horses of it, at a screaming 6500 rpm, along with 390 pounds/feet of torque.

That much strength in a car that weighs only 2447 pounds results in a top speed of at least 186 mph. As for acceleration, the car is ready to blast off from the starting line to 100 kilometers per hour (62 mph) in a blistering 4.3 seconds. Not many speed fans would be disappointed with capabilities in that neighborhood.

Output from a standard Audi V-8 amounts to a mere 250 horsepower. Naturally, that didn't suit the folks at Zender. So an Audi engine specialist—

Lehmann of Liechtenstein, a firm that prepares race engines for Audi's motorsports division—was commissioned to enhance the powerplant. Two KKK exhaust-driven turbochargers have separate intercoolers, and generate a maximum boost of more than 11 psi. A Bosch Motronic system controls the fuel mixture and ignition. A special four-tailpipe exhaust system delivers sound that's typical of a thoroughbred sports car, while boosting performance. A hydraulically-operated, double-plate clutch hooks up to the ZF 5-speed gearbox, which works with a shift gate.

Tremendous amounts of engine power are only half of the FACT 4's performance secret. Light weight is the other. Space-age materials make the difference in producing the impressive power-to-weight ratio (5.45 lbs/hp). Not only the body, but also the interior makes use of modern carbon fiber,

starting with a monocoque design derived from Formula One racing. The carbon-fiber monocoque chassis doesn't use the engine and gearbox as load-bearing elements, in typical race-car fashion. Instead, those units (and the rear suspension) are integrated into a tubular steel lattice subframe that can be detached as a unit for servicing.

Atop the chassis sits a carbon-fiber/aramid fiber-paper sandwich body. The distinctive gullwing doors weigh only 6.6 pounds each (before hardware is added); the big rear lid, only 26.5 pounds. For that matter, the whole unadorned body weighs just 121 pounds. The high-tech carbon-fiber construction, according to Zender, offers "previously unattainable torsional resistance and strength."

To save more weight yet, rear and side windows are made of tinted Plexiglas. The

side windows don't even roll down, but slide forward and back. Fuel is divided between twin 50-liter rubber safety tanks and an additional catch tank. Tanks reside in carbon-fiber honeycomb boxes, which detach by quick-release fasteners.

Girling racing brakes provide the stopping power, with all discs axially drilled and ventilated. Independent suspensions at front and rear use conventional racing-type twin wishbones, with anti-roll bars. The driver can select any of four damper settings for the electro-hydraulic Koni shocks. Ride-height adjustment can raise the car by up to 30mm to overcome road surface irregularities, enter steep garage ramps, or climb over tall curbs.

Hitting the ground are massive Pirelli Zero tires: 245/40ZR17 in front and 335/35ZR17 at the rear, riding three-section Zender star-pattern wheels. The

rack-and-pinion steering with centering control requires only three turns lock-to-lock.

This isn't a car laden with accessories or gadgetry, or with fancy compact-disc sound systems. Not with the symphony of that 448-horsepower V-8 ready to thrill the ears.

No, this is a *driver's* machine. "Everything," according to Zender, "is geared towards driving as an enjoyable experience."

The functional cockpit, too, is designed around the driver. Carbon-fiber/aramid bucket seats weigh less than 10 pounds each. Temperature-equalizing, perforated leather

Racing-car origin is evident in the Zender concept car's stubby nose and crouched-low, aggressive stance (opposite page): tight, poised, eager to display its prowess. Slipping into the cozy cock, it shouldn't be too difficult with the doors tilted up and forward (above). The entire rear assembly tilts upward to reveal the mid-mounted twin-turbo V-8 engine.

covers are made to saddler's standards and carry full-harness seatbelts. Ahead of the driver sits a functional instrument panel with clearly marked dials. The ergonomically-designed leather steering wheel and aluminum pedals (with footrest) stem from motorsport designs.

Like so many concept cars and prototypes, the FACT 4 is meant to serve mainly as a test bed for fresh ideas, not a likely candidate for real-world high-speed motoring. Zender describes it as a "one-off learning tool designed to teach the company and its technicians about carbon-fiber technology." It also gives employees a chance to stretch their skills beyond everyday tasks.

The company "passionately discussed" prospects for a low-production run of cars for sale to the public, but economics intervened. It would simply be too expensive, too great a financial risk. The necessary expansion and staff training might also harm the company's day-to-day operations.

Several years earlier, another team of engineers and designers worked with Gunter Zillner to create Zender's Vision 1. That led to the Vision 3, a luxury sports car shown at the 1987 Frankfurt exhibition. The Vision models were made from fiberglass reinforced plastics (FRP), with conventional tubular frame chassis.

Like its predecessors, the FACT 4 is destined to remain a one-of-a-kind dream beyond the reach even of those able and eager to pay any price for a superpowered supercar. "We learn a great deal by working to these specifications," explains company head Hans-Albert Zender. "By gaining familiarity with new materials ... we are able to turn their qualities into products for our everyday business activities." So even if no FACT 4 lies in anyone's motoring future, the company adds skill in working with contemporary carbon-fiber technology to its expertise with plastics. At the same time, we all get a little taste of what could be, and probably will be, found on sports cars in the 1990s.

Bright yellow seats of carbon-fiber/aramid (above left) beckon the eager driver inside, where a mix of traditional gauges and high-tech switches awaits. A down-to-business lever rises from a shift gate within the massive center console. Outside, the four-tailpipe exhaust system (left) delivers a siren's song to the rear. Passersby can peek at a portion of the engine, or gaze at the graceful rear spoiler (above). Sliding side windows (right) are Plexiglas.

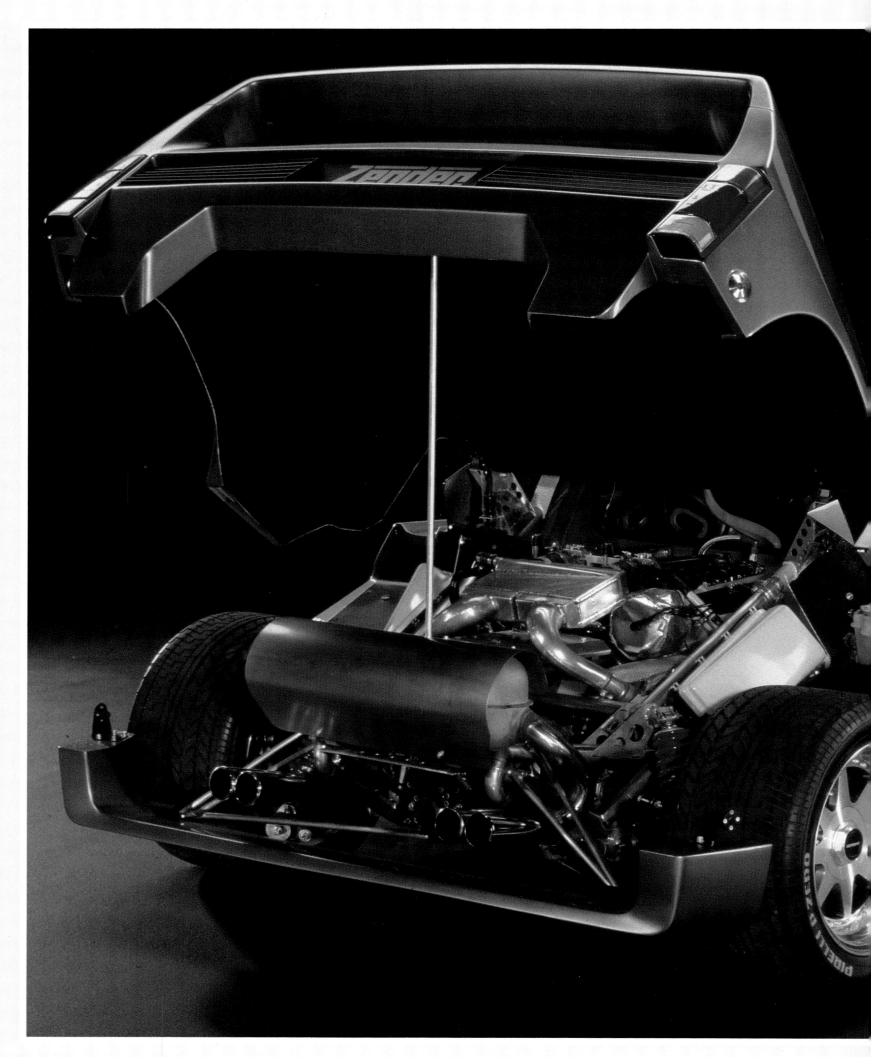

ZENDER FACT 4

SPECIFICATIONS

Manufacturer:	Zender GmbH, Mulheim-Karlich, West Germany
Body design:	2-passenger, 2-door coupe; carbon-fiber/aramid fiber-paper body on carbon-fiber monocoque chassis with tubular steel subframe
Powertrain layout:	mid-engine, rear-wheel drive
Wheelbase (in.):	98.4
Overall length (in.):	160.6
Overall width (in.):	78.7
Overall height (in.):	44.1
Track, front (in.):	63.4
Track, rear (in.):	64.9
Weight (lbs.):	2447
Approximate price:	NA
Engine type:	Audi twin turbocharged, intercooled dohc V-8 (32-valve)
Displacement (liters/cu. in.):	3.6/217
Horsepower @ rpm:	448 @ 6500
Torque (lbs./ft.) @ rpm:	390 @ 4000
Fuel delivery:	Bosch Motronic MP 1.2 ignition/fuel injection
Transmission:	ZF 5-speed manual
Suspension, front:	double wishbones, coil springs, anti-roll bar, adjustable (electro-hydraulic) shock absorbers
Suspension, rear:	double wishbones, coil springs, anti-roll bar, adjustable (electro-hydraulic) shock absorbers
Brakes:	front/rear discs (cross-drilled)

PERFORMANCE

Top speed (mph):	186+
0-60 mph (seconds):	(est.) 4.2
Quarter-mile (seconds):	NA
mph @ quarter-mile:	NA

The hardy heartbeat of the FACT 4, its Audi-based 32-valve V-8 engine, rides just ahead of the back wheels. Twin turbos help to achieve 448 sizzling horsepower—enough to ignite the radical two-seater well past 180 mph. Part of the secret is the lightweight carbon-fiber/aramid body.

317